*Channeled Writing Tips
from 111 Literary Masters*

BOOK #1 IN THE CHANNELED MASTERS SERIES

Channeled Writing Tips from 111 Literary Masters

Julie Bawden-Davis

Copyright © 2018 by Julie Bawden-Davis

Cover by Sabrina Wildermuth
Book Design by Maureen Cutajar (gopublished.com)
Logo Design by Kyle Kane

All rights reserved. No part of this book may be reproduced in any form or by any means, electronic or mechanical, including photocopying, recording or by any information storage and retrieval system, without written permission from the publisher.

ISBN-13: 978-0-9983403-6-4
ISBN-10: 0-9983403-6-7

Distributed by Roses Are Red Publishing
rosesareredpublishing.com

To Writers/Scribes everywhere! May your pen glide on the page, or your fingers "trip the light fantastic" over the keyboard, as your words tumble forth, filling pages and e-readers with words of enlightenment, encouragement, and entertainment.

Acknowledgments

Many thanks to my daughter, Sabrina Wildermuth, for her absolutely perfect cover design. I am also deeply grateful to my niece Monique Vallier for her assistance researching the various writers and their lives. Much gratitude, also, to my sister Mandy Stanley for her keen eye at proofreading. Thanks to fellow scribe Sharon Whatley for her advice and encouragement. And thank you, thank you, thank you to all 111 writers who came through me to express their utterly divine words of wisdom about writing and the writing life. I am truly honored.

Author's Note

Dear Reader,

    I hesitated to call myself the author of this great work, for truly, I am a fellow scribe, simply transcribing. The words of wisdom here—writing tips from the Light—came directly from each author as I heard and wrote them.

    Though I hesitated, all 111 of the writers have asked me to put my name on the book. This does make sense, since I'm the only one "alive" in the bunch. It's certainly a better approach for present day marketing potential. That's why they approached me in the first place—to share their inspirational writing words of wisdom and get them out there.

    No doubt you're wondering how this all came about. I'll tell you.

    I am particularly clairaudient, which means I hear things from the Light, and I have done so since I was a young child. A few years ago, I began channeling messages from the Light. I started with passed on loved ones and angels.

    One day, Lord Byron came to me with a message. I had discovered him back in high school when I read his poem, *She Walks in Beauty*, which I felt compelled to memorize. He told me when I channeled a brief message from him on 1/26/18 that he was available to "help" with my writing and to give me "pearls of wisdom." He also said I was "onto something big" with channeled writing. At that moment, I realized that I would be writing a book of messages from writers in the Light. I just had no idea how and when it would come about.

CHANNELED WRITING TIPS

By the end of March, the scope of the book was revealed to me by Lord Byron. I also learned that it was a project I agreed to shepherd/make a reality in this lifetime. I was told that it'd be a book from Writing Masters in the Light. Then I was told to wait, as more instructions would soon come.

On 4/30/18, I heard from Lord Byron that it was almost time to begin "downloading" messages from Scribes in the Light. On 5/02/18, I was told that "Bill"/William Faulkner was up first, and I was to channel his message the next day. The following morning as I awakened, I heard, *As I Lay Dying*. Is that a poem by Faulkner, I wondered? I looked it up on my cellphone and discovered that it was a book he wrote.

I read no further about the book or Faulkner. Though I'd read him in high school, I couldn't remember much about him. I wanted it that way, so that I wouldn't be influenced by anything I knew about the author when channeling. (I continued that same method for the rest of the authors.) I discovered after finishing Faulkner's selection that when he wrote *As I Lay Dying*, writing the book flowed quite well, and he didn't change a word. Most likely, that book was channeled.

The next name I heard was Shakespeare, as I settled down to sleep the following night. In the morning, I heard Iambic Pentameter when I woke up. I checked and discovered that all but one of Shakespeare's poems were written in Iambic Pentameter! And so the process ensued. I began writing more at one sitting, so I would hear the names as I went. Sometimes it was the author's name, while other times I would hear statements such as, who wrote the play, *Who's Afraid of Virginia Woolf?*

Over the last year, I've also been learning about numerology. This is the reason I was guided by the authors to use numbers, rather than words for those numbers. The authors are all in a certain order, and I was instructed not to change that order. The number assigned to each writer is of significance, as well. Those readers meant to will know the significance of those numbers as they read, I was told. Those numbers that aren't of significance are spelled out.

By 5/26/18, I got the message from Lord Byron that it is a series. So there are many more masters to come in future volumes. These include artists and inventors and photographers, and more. Lord Byron also explained that he is the "project director" for this volume and that the other books will have different directors.

On 6/10/18, I got the message that it would be 111 scribes. Lord Byron confirmed this. He explained that there were many writers wanting to speak. And if you know numerology, you know that 111 is a highly spiritual number that means abundance, enlightenment and spiritual awakening, among other meanings.

As I wrote and accessed various writers, there were many confirmations along the way. Once I finished channeling each writer and discovered more about him or her, I was often astounded at the parallels between their writing lives and works and the messages I'd channeled. James Joyce, for instance, used the same salutation in his message as I saw he'd used in some of his writing during his lifetime. There were also many connections between writers. Some were friends and contemporaries. All of these weren't facts I'd been privy to prior.

Keep in mind that there is a certain "language" coming from the Light. For instance, there are terms that may be repeated amongst the people channeled, though you'll see that each entry has a distinctly different tone, character, and cadence. One of those terms is referring to writers as scribes. At first I thought that they did this when writing from centuries past, but then I noticed more current authors using the term. I came to find that they use scribes, which technically means "to copy," because many of the writers allude to having channeled themselves. Other common terms used in this book include, if you will, and so to speak. While these various terms do mean something in their own right, I've also been told that the terminology allows those in the Light a way to announce themselves and confirm that it's them speaking.

The words put down here in this book are as the authors each requested. This includes punctuation and capitalization. For that reason, many of the salutations, such as Scribes, are capitalized in some places, and not in others. I did as each author asked. When I edited each section, which truly was proofreading, each author guided me.

Although I like to consider myself fairly well read, and I have read some of these writers, there were many I haven't read. Or it's been so long since reading one of their books or poems that I'd be hard-pressed to remember. Some of the writers I'd never heard of, though I'd often heard of what they wrote. Admittedly, that was an advantage in writing this book.

For those of you questioning or doubting if these words are truly coming from these writers, that's most certainly your prerogative. As mentioned by many of these writers, free will, which includes free thinking, is the law of the Universe. Even so, I do hope that these writing words of wisdom will help you with your writing and your writing journey. And that they inspire you overall.

—JULIE BAWDEN-DAVIS

Channeled Writing Tips from 111 Literary Masters

Introduction

HELLO, DEAR READERS, LORD BYRON HERE!

As Julie has mentioned, I am the one who initiated this book on the Earth Plane at this time in history. Yet, the idea and the plan to "hatch" this book, if you will, was born in the Light when Julie and all of us mighty scribes were sitting at a giant table that would look to you all like smoky glass.

At any rate, Julie answered the call. And so here we have this book for you! We are all honored and "ecstatic," as you say on the Earth Plane. We are happy to get the chance to impart our words of wisdom in this way. It is a much less fettered way—unfettered actually—than when we were on the Earth Plane. No more masks that we have to put on or bills that we have to pay—hence no more having to say the "right" things.

As you will see in this book, there is no "right" or even "wrong" way of getting words on to paper or computer screen. Sharing written ideas with the world is a blessed event that involves a birthing by the writer and then a re-birthing, if there are edits involved.

You are all unique, beautiful, inspired creatures of the Earth, and you will all bring forth your own, very dear kernels of wisdom when you are supposed to, in the Divine timing that you have set for yourself. That being said, be patient with yourself, for your soul knows exactly what you came here to do, and the words of wisdom that you came here to share—each and every last one of them—periods, commas, ellipses, and all!

Lord Byron

    Thank you for reading this. My words of wisdom are also shared in the book regarding writing, in particular poetry, as was my gift in my lifetime as Lord Byron. If you would like to read my writing tips, I am number 111!

    Yours Always and Forever,
    Lord Byron

1

⇒ WILLIAM FAULKNER ⇐

Dear Fellow Scribes,
 William Faulkner here, or "Bill," as my writing "cronies" call me here in the Light and did on the Earth. A few tips/words of wisdom, if you will, about the writing life and about writing in general. Thank you for listening to an "old goat." For I know some of you are quite young and wise, and some of you are older in years and equally as wise.

Writing. The writing life. What can I say? Well, plenty, of course. First, sing praises to the Universe for the "affliction" of writing. For in many ways, while it seems like a malady that won't let you go or sleep or even think until you get the words down on paper, or computer nowadays, it is at the same time/at once a delightful occupation/desire. For tapping in to all and writing it down and watching the words form on paper and then reading it back to oneself, how utterly divine and magical, even, I think you would agree?

Here is the thing I want to impart to you, in reference to my former sentence. It is all divine. Those magic sparks that alight on the page to form into words and then tumble off your tongue if you are brave enough to read your own words out loud—they are the stuff of gods, the dreams of angels, the pitter patter of the birds, and the fairies and elves. Truly, all the words that you may utter onto the page were meant to fall onto the page. So when you are editing yourselves, as some of you do again and again and again and again. Sigh. Know that it is divinely inspired. At the same time, you may want to look back at your first writing—so save it. For as you go around in circles again and again and again trying to "fix" your writing, you may just find yourself coming back to your first iteration. And then sometimes you may not, for you may find the better words. The point is not to chide yourself for words put on paper that just aren't "good," for putting any words on paper at all is quite good! It is brilliant, so remind yourself of that. You are writing. And writing is a balm for your soul, and the words become a balm for many other souls.

There is something needling me at this point/something that I feel I must impart to some or all of you at this point. There is no perfection. Throw away that notion. For it is an outdated one—has always been so. And yet there is perfection. Herein lies the quandary many writers find themselves in. Back to the writing and rewriting that we speak of. Many of you may or may not know that my tome, *As I Lay Dying*, consists of all words that I did not change at all from their origination. So if you have a book/poem/short story that people have told you "needs work," but you feel is done, go with your own feelings on the topic. Truly, many cooks in the kitchen/in your writing are generally not a good thing. I fortunately did not have that desire in my lifetime to seek approval for my writing, but I know many of you do this. That's not to say that some good editing when warranted is just what you need, but when you know in your heart that something is done, then close the book and know that you are most certainly right about your writing! Then share that writing with the world—for the world is hungry for all of your droplets of wisdom!

> *That is all for now, Dear Students of Writing. I bid you goodbye for now, but do know that I will be over your shoulders forevermore urging you to speak your truths and to enjoy the process and to know when you are right about your writing, you are simply right!*
> *William Faulkner*

CHANNELED WRITING TIPS

WILLIAM CUTHBERT FAULKNER was born on September 25, 1897 in New Albany, Mississippi. He passed away at the age of 64, due to a heart attack, on July 6, 1962. He was an American author best known for his novels *As I Lay Dying* and *The Sound and the Fury*. He is also a two-time Nobel Prize winner in literature, once in 1949 and a second, posthumously, in 1963, for *The Reivers*. Faulkner also wrote screenplays, short stories, poetry, essays, and even a play.

"All of us failed to match our dreams of perfection. So I rate us on the basis of our splendid failure to do the impossible."
—William Faulkner

2

❖ William Shakespeare ❖

Dear Fellow Scribes,

Shakespeare here! Many greetings to all of you, and much thanks for studying my writing over many years! I am forever grateful and honored. You are true princes, kings, princesses, and queens of the pen! Now for my addition to this masterful work by and from the Literary Masters! I am in quite good company.

Iambic Pentameter. That is the verse I used during my many writings/ramblings they were, to be true, at times, but I am humbled to see over the years that my wide, wide audience, even in many languages, sees the beauty and form in my work, whereas I might not have when I was writing. Were some of my verses, or even all of them, channeled? Perhaps. But I digress. Back to Iambic Pentameter.

Iambic Pentameter gives you a wide latitude to work; to rhyme while not even really rhyming, to gild the lily, so to speak. It is a quite useful cadence, song of song, form of form that you may or may not use, but I beg you, or cajole you, to try using it at times in your writing. For when you do, you will access a fluidity, a form of forms, a way of being and doing and relaying that you will see will quite literally lift the words off the page at times, and then settle them back down, at times, in the most inopportune place that makes you then rewrite. But at other times this use of Iambic Pentameter will settle the words into an area of the page where they are most certainly supposed to be! Then the words will quite literally sing at you, beckon you beyond a doorway of mirth and laughter and sometimes, yes, deep sadness, but beckon you, nonetheless, they will! You will see as you try this method in any type of writing—be it verse, including poetry, or short stories or books, that it is a most useful and beguiling and a quite surprising method.

As mentioned prior, I am so honored to be able to impart my words of "wisdom" regarding writing here, for I have toiled over many lifetimes as have many of you in writing. But as we all so well know, us writers, with our secret pacts and our secret knowing, that to write, to be destined to be a writer, to be anointed with the "gift" of gab on the page, that is the most precious gift of all! And while it may seem at times in the middle of the night or the early morning hours when something must get written that it is a bit of a burden, our souls know—do they not, that it is an honor? An honorable honor, a gift of the flesh and of the mind and of the soul that quite literally sends tingles from the tips of the toes to the fingertips to the mind and back out those fingertips as they write or type, as you do in this day and age! Just know as you do "toil" away wordsmithing that the word angels, us scribes in the Light, truly are looking over your shoulders and wishing you the best and most right and most wonderful gift of written melodies and music on the page!

For now, I leave you with this.

Oh, me, oh my, how glad is the Earth on
this special day; how happy is Mother
Nature as she guides you to play, with the
words on the page and the song in your heart.
This most certainly the art of all arts!

In your humble service and deeply honored always,
Sir William Shakespeare!

William Shakespeare

SIR WILLIAM SHAKESPEARE is believed to have been born on April 23, 1564 in Stratford-upon-Avon, where he died on the same day in April 1616. He is best known for his plays, *Romeo and Juliet*, *Macbeth*, *King Lear*, and *Hamlet*. Shakespeare is considered one of the greatest writers of all time, in-part because he holds the title of best-selling fiction author of all time. His work has sold an estimated four billion copies. Shakespeare is also known for his use of Iambic Pentameter, a rhyme scheme where each line of a sonnet contains 10 syllables. He used Iambic Pentameter in most of his works. In addition to being a writer, poet, playwright, and actor, Shakespeare was also a father to three children.

"Love all, trust a few, do wrong to none."
—William Shakespeare

3

❧ J. D. Salinger ❦

Dear Fellow Scribes,
*   J.D. Salinger here. Author of the famed book, Catcher in the Rye. I am most honored to speak to you today on this marvelous day of days that will be the right day for you when you read my nuggets, tidbits of wisdom. So here we go!*

First-person narrative. How powerful this technique can be. How utterly divine, really. But that is what is happening for me here, now, in the Light from where I speak to you in your place on the Earth Plane, which at times can be most dark, wouldn't you say? But then again, light rays peek in here and there and things can at once be quite light and bright even.

Back to first-person narrative. This is a technique that while you would be wise to use sparingly, at the same time, we, us fellow scribes in the Light, do suggest that you try this method at least once. Write your own letter to yourself, and if things keep moving along, write a book, even. Many pearls of wisdom will come from trying this method. It is quite a good method to use in diary form. So, if you are unsure about how to master this form with a simple book—try this form in diary form.

Some tips for making first-person ring true; ring clear and capture the reader's attention and keep it. For that is truly the intent—that you want more than ever, don't you? To capture and keep the readers' attention; to make him or her not be able to put down your book—even sleep or eat or use the facilities, until that last paragraph on the page is read.

Be your clear and perfect self when you are writing this first-person. Don't let judgments about what is best or what is right or what is decent, even, cloud the creative flow. If you must think of it this way, then do—use stream of consciousness as you write. Let the words flow down as the water flows from a waterfall, without worrying about how the words are falling onto the page, for truly, as the water flows, the words will flow exactly how and where they should. Oftentimes, we in the Light are more than happy to help guide you, but we must first be allowed access in, just as the water is allowed access to those cracks and crevices in the mountainside. So if you let us in—be it a feeling or inkling or kernel of wisdom that you just know is coming from "somewhere else," we will most certainly enter and help you, assist you, with forming those words that are to be flung onto the page at times, while other times they will most certainly flow, out of your pen, or computer keyboard onto the page. If you are thinking here that I am speaking of simply letting your subconscious/unconscious take the lead, then BINGO, you have gotten my "drift" here. No holds barred, as some might say. Just let it flow, flow, flow. You can always edit later. And have no fears or no shame, even, when you write what you write. Know that it is all good in the scheme of things. Whether you choose to share your writing with the world or not—it was meant to come out on the page for one reason or another, or many reasons. I hope that this makes sense to you—this stream of consciousness ramblings from a writer in the Light most eager to help you with your flow of magnificent writing.

Thank you! I am most honored to have been given the opportunity to share my tidbits of writing wisdom here.
    Yours Truly and Forever,
    J.D. Salinger

CHANNELED WRITING TIPS

JEROME DAVID SALINGER was born January 1, 1919 in Manhattan, New York. He died 91 years later on January 27, 2010 in Cornish, New Hampshire. He was an American writer most widely known for his novel *The Catcher in the Rye* and *Nine Stories*, a collection of short stories. Salinger was also famous for not wanting to be famous. His use of first-person narration in *The Catcher in the Rye* is, in part, what made the book so enticing for young readers. Due to the complexity of writing a novel in first-person, *The Catcher in the Rye* took roughly 10 years to write and was later revised to half its original length. J.D Salinger, although being married three times, led a private, quiet life.

"An artist's only concern is to shoot for some kind of perfection, and on his own terms, not anyone else's."
—J.D. Salinger

4

⇒ Leo Tolstoy ⇐

Dear Most Esteemed Fellow Scribes,

Thank you for listening/reading this! I am most honored to be able to come forth in this manner and to share my pearls of wisdom, if you will. And here are those pearls for your perusal. (I am Leo Tolstoy!)

First-person narrative. A most beguiling/intriguing sort of expression, is it not? Here in the Light, we so like to watch you create such precious words and commit them onto the page. Why? In many ways, the first-person narrative is a narrative of the soul. At times gut-wrenching, at times full of wonder and awe—at times light and flavorful, even. But the first-person narrative is one of the most powerful in the Universe. So if you feel yourself tempted/wanting to delve into the first-person, but have been told that it is "too difficult," or not "marketable," or not even valid anymore in this day and age, I urge you to try anyway. If your soul is calling you to this art-form, by all means, please do sink your toe into the water, and you will at once find yourself jumping in and swimming for all of your life and all of your soul!

On to another topic that I wish to impart to you at this time. That is of writing about tragedy. Writing about the depths/dregs of humanity, so to speak. My writing did delve somewhat into this Netherworld of the Earth plane world. This deep, dark passageway of the soul—yet of a soul often fraught with worry and concern and deep longing. If you feel so inclined to delve into this world, then by all means, do! You will find that as you wander amongst the many dark passageways in the tormented soul that there will be flashes of light and longing and awe and wonder here, as well. You will often find a place in your own soul that resonates with these dark places, even though you may not have ever wandered into such dark places here on the Earth Plane—at least in this lifetime. (While these may seem like the wanderings and ramblings of an old fool here, if you re-read this, as I am knowing you will; you will "see" of what I speak.) There is great knowing and wanting and needing and releasing when you write of another's soul wrenching and put it on the page for all to read and assimilate and know and feel.

How much more can you pull from yourself when you pull from yourself of the dark and depth and dank of humanity? You will find out when you try writing tragedy. The tragedy may come in many guises—in the form of Science Fiction—in the form of modern day realities and problems, in the form of age-old problems—as in medieval writings. Whatever you do, know that you will be resonating with your soul and the souls of many.

War and Peace, Peace and War—it could have been named the latter, I often thought after I wrote the former! For we are at once—those scribes who wish to extol humanity while also buoying it up and making it seem fantastical and full of wonder—we souls with pen or computer fingertips—we know what truly matters here on the Earth Plane for you and here for me in the Light. Peace truly is what we seek, yet we must go through war with others and with the self to arrive at that peace. One way to wage war with the soul and seek peace is to write!

Here I am hoping that you may find some nuggets of wisdom. I am most honored, again, to address you, and I bid you a wonderful

day/night filled with much wisdom and insights and peace once you record the war of your soul and that of many on the page.
   Yours Truly,
   Leo Tolstoy

LEO TOLSTOY was a Russian novelist born September 9, 1828. He died from pneumonia at the age of 82 on November 7, 1910. Despite many personal tragedies during his childhood, Tolstoy was able to become one of the greatest writers of all time, writing roughly 15 novels. He is best known for his novels *War and Peace* and *Anna Karenina*. In addition to writing novels, Tolstoy also penned many short stories, including the widely known, *The Death of Ivan Ilyich*. Tolstoy was also a father to 14 children, and he treasured being a parent.

"*Rummaging in our souls, we often dig up something that we ought to have lain there unnoticed.*"
   —Leo Tolstoy

5

❯ JOHN STEINBECK ❮

Dear Fellow Scribes of the Earth Plane, this is John Steinbeck, and I am honored to appear on these pages! Here are a few of my words of wisdom regarding writing and the writing life. I am your humble author in waiting.

Multiple viewpoints. Multiple perspectives. This is most certainly a quite grand way to write, if you can do so! If you wonder and doubt whether you can, I am here to tell you that you most certainly can. If you try, dip your toe in the ink and see what comes out. I assure you that you will be surprised and delighted at what comes forth!

How to do this? Access multiple perspectives. First and foremost, I urge you to let go of any preconceived notions! Just think—put your head inside the head—of each character and write. Write, write, write, write, write! When I was alive on the Earth Plane, I wrote just about every day. I dove onto the page, first in handwritten tomes, and then later on a clicketty, clacketty typewriter that you nowadays would consider antique! My, oh my, that typewriter was my saving grace. It managed to help me write even more! More fluidly, as well. You now have the pleasure and the honor of writing with computer systems. My, how the words flow when you get going, do they not! That is as it should be, and that is what will allow you to write quite a bit. So let the words flow. Don't edit yourself at first; don't stop yourself; don't question yourself—just let it flow!

Now for more words on other matters. Description. Oh, how I loved description when I was writing in my Steinbeck lifetime! I could go on and on and on about a dusty road, could I not, in the *Grapes of Wrath*? While I may have overdone it a bit by today's standards, I do suggest that you look at your descriptions as the setting of a movie. As you set up the background/backdrop, you get to know the characters more deeply and you also get to know how their environment has helped mold them—formed them—even affected their views of the world and their places in it. I know it might seem a bit off-putting to put so much detail on one page at once about something so simple as a wooden bowl and spoon or a cloudless day on the prairie with the brush whistling and rustling in the slight breeze, but it will give you treasures beyond your wildest dreams if you can also give in and let those words of description flow from your fingertips!

Next, (yes, I have a bit to say today—as I always have!), I would like you to think carefully about characterization. Characters. They are the stuff that books and short stories and movies are made of! They are what leads a book; they are what motivates you to turn the page. You need/want/just have to find out what the character does next! Yes, the circumstances—the plot, if you will—is important, but truly, the plot only exists for you to see how the characters react to the situations in which they find themselves! If you think on this a bit, I think you will agree with me. At any rate, the characters—make them rich; make them powerful; make them real; make them human! No robots are allowed on the pages at all! That is why it's so important to see how the situations in which characters find themselves and the surroundings in which they find themselves affects them. And of course, most importantly, how the people they find themselves surrounded by affect them! That is what makes multi-perspective so interesting! When you take your magnifying glass and look in the minds of each and every character on the page—or at least some of them—you are able to weave a fine web-tapestry of the world as the characters see it and their relationships with one another as they relate to that world. And along the way, those who are reading see themselves in at least some, if not all, of the characters—thereby setting up a chain reaction of common wisdom and understanding and pure elation at knowing that the world is full of so many splendid beings—all wanting to interact and understand and even love one another.

Well, I have gone on longer than anyone else yet with my beloved "run-on" sentences! So I will say goodbye for now—but not really, for I will be over your writing shoulder; whispering in your ear about what to write next and next and next, and urging you to listen to the ramblings of those many splendid characters.
Yours forever truly,
John Steinbeck

JOHN STEINBECK was an American author born on February 27, 1902. He died of heart failure at the age of 66 on December 20, 1968. Although he wrote 25 books, Steinbeck is best known for his works, *Of Mice and Men*, *The Grapes of Wrath*, and *East of Eden*. Steinbeck was awarded the Pulitzer Prize for *The Grapes of Wrath* and also won the Nobel Peace Prize in 1962. In addition to being a novelist, he was a war correspondent and college dropout. Until he became a successful writer, he worked as a manual laborer.

"*Ideas are like rabbits. You get a couple and learn how to handle them, and pretty soon you have a dozen.*"
—John Steinbeck

6

✧ Emily Dickinson ✧

Hello, Dear Fellow Scribes,
 I am deeply honored to be able to impart some words of advice here. My time on the Earth Plane as Emily Dickinson was a prolific, yet solitary one. Of the solitude, I wish to comment, that it may lead you to your inner visions and sources of wisdom. That it may lead you to water, so to speak, and that you may drink.

The world in which you currently navigate as writers/scribes is a much different one than when I was on the Earth Plane as Emily D. You are so connected now. While that is of vital importance to the work in many ways—for instance helping you to tap in and to turn on the faucet of knowledge, it is at the same time somewhat of a curse. For as you are tapping away on your Facebook profiles and pages and tweeting and all of that as it is—for we watch you all from here—you are missing some chances and skimming the surface of life, so to speak. That is not to say that all of that "connection" is a bad thing, but there is much wisdom to be gained from disconnecting and truly tapping into the ancient wisdom and knowledge that is within you, so that you may glean from that knowledge and pull it forth and bring it into your modern day challenges that you put onto the pages of your computers.

So my suggestions to you would be to disconnect at times from everything "online" and see how much better you then write. Though my life was quite solitary and bland and austere by many standards, even way back when as Emily, I was able to tap into those ancient, divine pearls of wisdom and to bring those strings up and put them on the page—for I knew somehow—you could now say, that I was a very old soul, and I had what I needed within and in me. And I knew that all I needed to do was pull it forth. And, yes, all of my work—all of my poetry, which seemed to ferret out the darkness and light and the combination of both that comes from the human soul—it all came from me. No one was feeding me information or even feeding me experiences. I didn't need the experiences when I was on the Earth, because I pulled from the experiences that were deep in my soul. I think that you see what I am getting at here. While you may require some input from "outside" of yourself—depending on your nature—it certainly isn't a necessity. So if you are feeling that you truly do have all that you need to tell your story, then listen to that voice and know that that is most certainly true. This is not to discount the value of other's opinions and editing, but at times those things aren't necessary—especially if you feel that is so.

Listen to your own inner scribes, Dear Fellow Scribes of the Earth Plane. For they know much more than you might think. You will, as you listen to them, and record what they tell you, delight in what comes forth. It will be utterly amazing at times—when you unplug completely and simply write. Freehand even. Try that at times. Doing so will promise to pull you to the depths of the human soul and back up again. And you might even try it by candlelight. See what comes forth! I will be over your shoulder as you do. And I will be urging you to call forth all that you know, deep in your soul.

Thank you for listening, Dear Fellow Scribes of the Earth Plane! I so adore you, and I look forward to what you will pull forth from you—your soul. For all of our souls are interconnected in their own ways. Good day or night to you!
Always and Forever,
Emily Dickinson

Emily Dickinson

EMILY DICKINSON was an American poet born on December 10, 1830. She died from Bright's disease at the age of 55 on May 15, 1886. She is best known for her poetry and highly regarded as one of America's greatest poets. Around her hometown, Dickinson was known as the "Myth," due to her self-imposed social seclusion. Even with little to no social interaction, Dickinson was able to write powerful poems that questioned the nature of immortality and death. Her most famous poem is, "Because I could not stop for Death."

"*To make a prairie it takes a clover and one bee, / One clover, and a bee / And reverie. / The reverie alone will do, if bees are few.*"
"*The brain is wider than the sky.*"
—Emily Dickinson

7

❧ Jules Verne ❦

Hello Dear Writers of Late and Writers of Now!
I am quite thrilled to be able to "speak" here. This is Jules Verne. Here are a few "words of wisdom" from me below and above. I do hope they will assist you in your writing journeys and travails, as they may be.

Below. What lies below? I spent much of my writing life on the Earth Plane as Jules Verne contemplating what lies below. Therein was the reason for the many books on the topic. For I was seeking, seeking, fishing, even, for the answers to the Universe. The grand answers and the not so grand answers. Simply answers! Now I know, as I sit here in my Light writing room that the answers were in me, of course, and the answers were and are in the Earth.

On the Earth Plane are hidden the answers that you seek as you strive to pull from yourselves the pearls of wisdom, the strings of pearls of wisdom that are words. Words being the way you communicate on the Earth Plane. Therein lies an interesting topic, does it not? That words are how you communicate there, but how do we communicate here? Well, that will remain a mystery for the most part for now for you, for truly, you are reading this to find out how to make your words sing and resonate so that they tap into the reader's soul and make that person's soul sing.

My advice for doing just that—after my ramblings above—you can see how my mind worked when I was on the Earth Plane. That is the answer, Dear Fellow Scribes, to let your mind wander. If your mind chooses to wander to the depths below, then let your mind wander below. Search the caverns of your soul, if you will, unearth diamonds in the process you will, I promise you that! On the other hand, if you wish to go above. To look down on all that lies below, then please do so! For you will see many diamonds of ideas shining from above as you go!

I do hope I am making some sense! Here I am speaking about perspective. That you may have picked up on by now. Perspective is key in your writing. Think about your perspective before you pick up your pen or go to your computer. Where are you coming from, so to speak? Who are you in the head of as you speak? What is the character's perspective? Is it the perspective you wish to impart? You may, if you choose, not go to the depths or go up high, but stay on the ground. If that is what you wish to do, then that is the perspective you will have as you write. More grounded in reality, if you will, and more able to see things at face value.

> *I am happy to see that my message is coming forth as it is, as I am delighted to share this. I do hope that this helped. I am forever grateful for this chance, and to know so many fellow scribes in the Light and on the Earth Plane!*
>
> *Good day to you always,*
> *Jules Verne*

JULES VERNE was a French novelist, playwright and poet born on February 8, 1828. He died of diabetes at the age of 77 on March 24, 1905. Though his father groomed Verne to take over the family business and become a lawyer, he quit and wrote magazine articles. He is best known for his science fiction novels, *Twenty Thousand Leagues Under the Sea* and *Around the World in Eighty Days*. Both books were truly revolutionary at the time. For that reason, he is considered the father of science-fiction. So captivating and timeless are his books that many have been made into movies. Verne's books gave readers many perspectives into different worlds and laid the groundwork for modern science-fiction.

"On the surface of the ocean, men wage war and destroy each other; But down here, just a few feet beneath the surface, there is a calm and peace, unmolested by man."
—Jules Verne

8

❧ Edgar Allan Poe ☙

Greetings, Dear Fellow Scribes,
   I am most honored to appear here in this book. It is a most glorious honor, I am here to tell you. For I have not graced the Earth Plane since my demise as Edgar Allan Poe. But that is for another story, I may most certainly tell at some point. For now, shall we move on to the matter at hand, which is to give you, Dear Readers, my pearls of wisdom about the writing/creative process.

Meandering…flow…letting the pen or computer keyboard take you where it may. I say, that is a most glorious path. For as you meander and "dilly dally," you will soon find those pearls of wisdom that you seek to put on the page. For Fellow Scribes, you are no different than me or any other "great" writer of today or yesteryear. We are all interconnected, us/we. We are all here to see the beauty of the poetry of life; the beauty of the moon rising as the sun sets; the beauty of a young girl blowing a dandelion gone to seed in the wind. It is images such as this that we long to put on the page—to wrestle to the ground and to make acquiesce for us, so that we may see the splendor in our words—the flow of what we have to say. It is something that we may even pray as we do, or pray to do.

   For me, on the Earth Plane, I struggled with small verse—with verse that I wanted to smash at times—in a way, because it wouldn't surrender to my hand. This may sound rather odd to some, who let the words flow, but to others who struggle, I can see you nodding your heads now. In a way words are like a bushel of wildflowers, are they not? They are so difficult to contain in their exuberance and their glee—especially when they go to seed and wish to spread their fertility around and around.

But if you can think of the words as those flowers—flowers that are willing and happy and able to brighten your days with their loveliness and vivid colors and sweet fragrances, then you will no longer feel the need to contain them or restrain them or get them to do your bidding, for surely, they will do your bidding for you, without you even having to ask or beg or plead or pray.

If you think that I am suggesting that you let the words wander—that you let the sentences meander, that you let your hands go as they wish—a sort of channeling in its own right—then, yes, I am saying just that. I am also suggesting that you give up the struggle. That you just climb into your bubble and let the words come as they may. They may come out in a torrent, like a summer rain, or they may come out one at a time, like a tortoise making his way across a hot summer lawn—whatever way they come, let them. Let them tumble from your soul and pour out on the page, for you can surely work on molding them, as a sculptor molds his or her work, when you have them all on the page.

As you are seeing, suspecting here, when you struggle with the words, when you try to mold them to fit your preconceived notions, they don't all come forth. By doing this, you stifle your soul's calling, and you limit the words—those pearls that you wish to see—from coming forth. So please, as you go about your days, while you do work to let the words flow and let them sing—know that they are all on the right path, as you are. For they will come back to you again and again, those pearls of wisdom that you let flow—and they will quite literally sing from the page. You will know that you have found your muse and calling and the tone that you seek, when you feel those words resound with your soul!

That is all for now. I do hope you can make some sense of my ponderings and musings. It is my hope that you will find some kernels of wisdom here that will help you wrestle your words in a way that they surrender and flow—but in a gentle manner that really isn't anything at all about wrestling.

Good day or night to you all! I do bid you adieu. And I am once again honored to appear here and honored to have your ear.
    Yours forever,
    Edgar Allan Poe

EDGAR ALLAN POE was an American writer born on January 19, 1809. He died on October 7, 1849 at the age of 40. His life and death were shrouded in mystery. He is best known for his short stories and poems, and is said to be the father of modern detective stories. Poe suffered from suspected bipolar disorder and recurrent depression but was still able to accomplish writing tales of mystery. He was also a literary critic.

"*Words have no power to impress the mind without the exquisite horror of their reality.*"
    —Edgar Allan Poe

9

⇝ Louisa May Alcott ⇜

Dear lovely readers, Louisa May Alcott here! I thank you ever so much for reading my little words of wisdom, as they are! It is a high honor here in the Light to be able to come "down" to the Earth Plane for a spell to communicate. To be able to communicate with other writers, how splendid and quite grand!

On to the matter at hand. My message regarding being a writer and living the writing life.

You most likely know me as the author of the "Little Women" series. While that was, of course, by far, my most splendid work, I did have other works not so well-known that were also my "children." And that is what I would like to impart here. Though you may have works that the world at large seems to adore, and most certainly does adore, there will be those "pet" projects, if you will, that others may not notice as much. This happens quite frequently with writers. It most certainly happened with one of my dear friends here in the Light, John Steinbeck (#5). His book, *The Wayward Bus*, which he so adored, didn't get nearly the attention as the *Grapes of Wrath*.

What I would like to tell you is that no writing of yours is less than any other. And if you do adore a certain piece of your writing—or even a certain entire work—more than another, I do understand the hesitancy to admit this. It is something akin to admitting that you like one of your children more. As they say nowadays on the Earth Plane, that is certainly not PC.

At any rate, I digress, which is something I tended to do when I got into the descriptions in my books. I so loved to describe the surroundings and the people and had to corral myself and bring myself back to the task at hand often, which was, where is the plot?

Back again to your little children—all of them. Your writing children. It is certainly okay for you to love one work more than another—to treasure and hold close the work, even. And it is okay to wish that others would notice this little gem or that. But do understand that not always will others see or understand your gems. They could in time—or only a select few could. No matter, however, for your little gem was meant to be born, through your hand, coming from your mind and Spirit and flowing onto the page.

Why do I ramble on and on about this particular nettle in your bonnet, so to speak? Because if it hasn't happened yet with your writing, it will. And when it does—when you write what you consider a masterpiece, something that you hold tightly to your breast and are sure the world will adore, but they don't, you will have one of these three reactions below.

1) You feel quite saddened, and then tell yourself, "Well, it must not be that good, or everyone would adore it as much as me." And then you stuff the little work away—back in the recesses of your drawer or your computer to never be thought of again.

2) You become irate. Why, this is my best masterpiece yet! No one knows what they're talking about. You decide to shout this from the rooftops—push it in the faces of your readers—and then what do you know, you turn those readers off!

3) You become depressed. You think you've lost "it." Perhaps the work you did prior was better? Perhaps you've lost your verve; your "mojo." Perhaps it's time to hang up your writing and just do something else.

Dear me! None of these eventualities is a good one! You can tell that by reading this, can you not? Here is my fourth suggestion, which I think you will quite like should you give it a try.

CHANNELED WRITING TIPS

4) Continue to cleave to your masterpiece. Flip the book open and read various lines from it. Smile when you do and know that you are connecting with your soul when you do. This is your masterpiece. Remember the operative pronoun—your. No one else has to even like it—it really doesn't matter. You've made yourself happy by writing it. Chances are, though, that others will like it. They just might not be that vocal about it. There could very well be a groundswell of people who adore the book. And one day that groundswell will rise and you will know. And even if this doesn't happen, you will know. For writing is about speaking to you. It is about uttering your soul's calling and your soul's words of wisdom, for readers, yes, but ultimately it is about speaking to you and validating you as a person, as you.

That is all for now, Dear Readers. I am so honored, once again, to have spoken here. And I bid you a most splendid day of speaking to your soul. And if readers choose to share that piece of your soul, well, even better!
Yours Truly,
Louisa May Alcott

LOUISA MAY ALCOTT was an American novelist born on November 29, 1832. She died at the age of 56, due to a stroke, on March 6, 1888. Louisa is best known for her novels *Little Women*, *Jo's Boys*, and *Little Men*. She also wrote adult novels, such as *Work* and *A Modern Mephistopheles*, but these books weren't as popular. Louisa was also a Civil War nurse and Women's rights activist, who participated in the Women's Suffrage movement. She became the first woman in Concord, Massachusetts to register to vote.

10

❖ Maeve Binchy ❖

Hello Dear, Precious Readers! Maeve Binchy here!

Oh, my, what a high honor this is to impart "wisdom" from the Light. I was/am one of Julie's favorite authors, so even though I am a bit "new" in terms of the Masters, I am considered one! And what a fabulous honor! I was Irish (and Scottish) in the last lifetime. The Scott in me didn't get much publicity, but there it was. This made for a rather whimsical view of life, mixed in with nitty gritty reality. At any rate, on to the message at hand! I do hope it helps you with your marvelous writing pursuits.

How do you see yourself when you are writing? Truly see yourself? Do you see yourself hunched over your paper or computer keyboard with a scowl on your face, straining to get the words "just right?" Or do you see yourself with a perplexed expression, wondering if you will ever get this writing right? Or do you see yourself in tears, frustrated that it just isn't flowing onto the page?

Well, dear reader, if you see yourself as any of those guises above, I am here to tell you that I was one or more or all of them at once at times! So don't think you are any different in the angst department when it comes to good writing. Do, however, know that those times will pass if you keep at it. Keep plodding away with the words, and they will soon flow from your fingertips—moving from your brainstem somewhere, which is always infused with even a little Light—and down through your heart and solar plexus, and through your fingers onto the page.

The more you can just let things flow, the faster and more quickly (I know redundancy here!) that you will see the results on the page. Better yet, you will leave those above scenarios behind permanently! Will they ever return? Yes, but only for short periods. For once you access the flow—you won't want to turn back to the consternation that you once experienced!

This all sounds rather easy, doesn't it? It sounds as if I'm speaking out of the side of my Light Plane mouth! Well, I am, but not in the same manner you are thinking. For if you give in to the muse, you will ride on the clouds in the Light—though you are actually still on the Earth. That is the "sweet spot," as they say, where you can access the Earth and the Light. For that is when you come up with the pearls for the page. Those pearls that will enlighten your readers and make them smile and laugh and cry and shrug and shake their heads. That is what you want. The emotion from the reader reading your work, rather than your pent-up emotion as you try to write the words that will eventually get to the reader.

Remember, this is not a race. There is infinite time. Just as there is not death (I'm "living" proof!) there is no lack of time, truly. So just let things go. Let the flow overtake you, and you will see that your writing flows so much more easily. Tell yourself, because it's true, that nothing has to be set in stone. You can always, always change what you've written. At the same time, you can always, always simply love what you've written and not change even a comma, and that is okay, too!

So write on, precious, dear readers/writers. Know that the Light Force truly is always at your back. And do call on me if you wish for some Scottish or Irish words of wisdom.

Yours forever and ever in the Light,
Maeve Binchy

MAEVE BINCHY was an Irish novelist born on May 28, 1939. She died at the age of 73, due to a heart attack, on July 30, 2012. She was best known for her novels that portrayed small-town life in Ireland in a humorous and sympathetic way and often ended her novels with surprise endings. Binchy also wrote short stories, travel writing, and even a play. She was dubbed the queen of Irish fiction and rightfully so, as she wrote more than 20 books in her lifetime, all of which turned out to be bestsellers.

"We're nothing if we're not loved. When you meet somebody who is more important to you than yourself, that has to be the most important thing in life, really. And I think we are all striving for it in different ways. I also believe very, very strongly that everybody is the hero/heroine of his/her own life. I try to make my characters kind of ordinary, somebody that anybody could be. Because we've all had loves, perhaps love and loss, people can relate to my characters."
—Maeve Binchy

11

❧ Mark Twain ❦

Dearest Scribes,
Mark Twain here. A pleasure to address you from here. I am quite honored, as we all are, that I was "chosen" to come through. It is a different life here, as you might imagine. Stuff of great fiction comes from here. And comes out of here, through many of you. On to the matter at hand, as I've seen many of us Scribes in the Light say.

Scenes, description, setting, climax, verse, prose, tempo. The verbiage surrounding the art of writing can be quite intimidating all on its own. How do you set up scenes so that they can then convey theme so that they can then lead you eventually to the climax that will then teach the lessons/morals that you aim for your story to tell, but in a subversive fashion that the reader has no idea is occurring?

Dizzying already, is it not? While study is most certainly advised and encouraged when it comes to writing, I urge you not to become overwhelmed by the sheer volume of how to do this, that or the other thing "right" with your writing. For there truly is no right. Other writers here are and will tell you the same thing in their own ways. That is the key here. Their own ways. You have your own unique voice. And if someone tries to tell you that you don't have a voice, I beg to differ. Each and every writer/every soul/ has their own soul stamp—their own soul voice. That cannot help but come out when you write from your heart.

Yet, when you try to copy another—even unconsciously—you don't access your voice. It is then that your writing won't ring true to you or anyone else. So your first order of business, shall we say, is to access your own true voice. Embrace it! Praise it! Shout your voice to the rooftops. For truly, it is unique and like no other amongst the billions and billions of voices throughout the cosmos.

Now to the business at hand regarding some concrete pointers. For myself in the life as Mark Twain did have a practical aspect/flavor to "him," if you will. Just as my soul has that same flavor. So I want to give you some practical tips here that you can use, once you've agreed with yourself to access your own true voice when you proceed.

1) **Scene/setting/description**. Scene and the description in that scene are vital to the set-up of the story, yes, but also to the characters. For characters find themselves in certain surroundings, and those surroundings do define them, in many ways. For instance, if you were to find Huckleberry Finn in a modern laboratory that would define him, would it not? Even if it were to show that those surroundings were alien to him. Those surroundings would surely show his "country bumpkinness" even more clearly. A princess amongst a slum/a vagrant amongst an opulent kingdom. You can see the contrasts, and you can understand the importance of scene/setting/description. Some of you may not like so much the description. You may want to get on to the action. You think that character can pull the story along—and dialogue. While it most certainly can, the reader is left with a "niggle" of something missing. That something missing is sense of place. And that sense of place affects every aspect of the work. Without scene/setting making its way onto the page, there is a lack that may not be verbalized by the reader. And yet it exists.

2) **Dialogue**. Many writers struggle with dialogue. They wrestle with it. They will think how so and so surely wouldn't have said such and such. While that may be the case, and most certainly is on many occasions, there is an easier way with this dialogue. Here is where you

want to let things flow. Put yourself into the "head" of your character. Envision yourself inside of his or her "person" and then let your fingers fly over the keyboard, and you will find that the dialogue comes out effortlessly. Yes, you would be channeling the character, for the most part, but I guarantee you that it works!

3) **Tone and cadence**. While these are most certainly two different aspects, they are interrelated. Tone, of course, is the "mood" which your words impart on the page. It is the "ambiance" of what is occurring within the pages and in the story and even in the minds of the readers. Tone is critical. For instance, if you were to write a Halloween story, you would want an eerie, creepy, or foreboding tone. Another about Christmas would most certainly have a tone of anticipation or of nostalgia. So where does cadence fall in here? Cadence is the clip, so to speak, at which you mete out your words. It can give a sing-song type of effect in some instances—especially rhyme and song—and at other times it can slow down and draw out what may occur—such as a love scene. It is cadence that the reader grabs onto when he or she is reading. It is cadence that moves the words across the page and onto the next. That being said, your tone and cadence need to fit together. They need to be synergistic and work for one another. A Halloween, creepy theme and a long drawn out cadence with an omen-like quality are the perfect partners!

4) **Character**. Yes, character!! We cannot forget the most vital part of the novel/short-story puzzle. Who are your characters? From where do they spring? Where are they going, and truly what makes them "tick, tick, tick?" It is the essence of the characters that keeps the reader reading. He/she wants to see how a character, who is quite faint of heart and feeble physically and purely scared of life might react to a rather harrowing experience. It is character that drives the work—character that makes the reader sympathize and even empathize with the character. It is character that makes a work a work! Without character, you truly have no story.

That is all for now. I can hear the rumblings; for I have used up more words than any other authors prior. And I hear whisperings about setting a precedent for future entries here. But then I was following my muse, as I do hope that you will do!

Always yours truly,
Mark Twain

SAMUEL LANGHORNE CLEMENS, also known as Mark Twain, was an American writer born on November 30, 1835. He died at the age of 74, due to a heart attack, on April 21, 1910. Twain was a jack-of-all-trades. In addition to being a novelist, he was also a comedian, publisher, entrepreneur, and lecturer. He is best known for his novels, *The Adventures of Tom Sawyer* and *Huckleberry Finn*. His stories are well-known for their humor, vivid details, and memorable characters. He was also a huge lover of cats, and once said: "I simply can't resist a cat, particularly a purring one. They are the cleanest, cunningest, and most intelligent things I know, outside of the girl you love, of course."

"When all else fails, write what your heart tells you. You can't depend on your eyes when your imagination is out of focus."
—Mark Twain

12

❧ HERMAN MELVILLE ☙

Dear Fellow Scribes,
Herman Melville here. Yes, the author of Moby Dick! And other works, equally as important to me, but perhaps not to the world. At any rate, let's get on with this, shall we? For I have much to tell you about the writing life and writing!

A groundswell, a volcano, an eruption of sorts. That is what you wish to impart deep in the psyche/soul, if you will, of your readers, correct? But how do you create such a groundswell? How do you elicit emotions that are at times ripped from the essence/deep within the pit/bowels of a person, for lack of a better term? How, how, how do you get your readers to sit on the edge of their seats and then reach for the tissue box at your various climaxes within your works?

While I can't, although that is a word we don't use here in the Light, but while I can't go on and on for pages here, as I would like, I can give you a glimpse, if you will, into my methods on the Earth Plane when I wrote as Herman Melville. So here, my dear fellow scribes, we do go!

Emotionality. Expression. These are the top tips I would give you. For to truly take a deep dive into the psyche of your reader, you must take a deep dive into your own psyche. Specifically into your emotions. If you are writing about "base" emotions, well, then, you must look at your baser emotions, such as jealousy, greed, lust, hate, envy, disgust— you get the picture. If you are thinking that you aren't usually a person who delves into the depths like this, remind yourself that you are human. And, yes, all humans have experienced all of the above emotions in one form or another. Delusion is another base emotion—and it does make for quite a good plot here and there and for the most intriguing characters put onto the page!

So say you can only access a fit of jealousy you had over someone's possessions—that is fine. It doesn't have to be a fit of jealousy over a lover, whom you are just about ready to kill for, as your character is! You are simply accessing the feelings that these emotions bring forth. That way you can bring forth those emotions onto the page. No doubt you've read those books that have a scene about one of these baser emotions—or tragedy—such as grief, despair, longing, yearning, etc. But the scene just doesn't ring true. There is something wrong with it—for the words are there to describe the feeling and emotion seemingly flowing from the character, but you just don't feel it. That is most likely because the writer wasn't feeling it. The writer wasn't "there" for that scene.

So go ahead, wallow in self-pity, if that is what your character is feeling, or lust or greed. Perhaps you don't have the instance to covet your neighbor's big mansion, but you could covet your neighbor's car, or even new paint job on his or her house. You get the picture. To write about emotions, you must feel those emotions, in whatever manner you can. Then things will ring true for you.

The question may be arising in your mind now, did I feel those emotions of being smaller than life and being consumed/inhaled and then exhaled by a larger-than-life source when I wrote *Moby Dick*? As you are suspecting, yes, I did. Did I envision myself in the mouth of the whale, bumping along on the ocean water mixed with digestive juices? I did attempt that, but in the end, I envisioned my finances, which were for many years of my life, in a bit of disarray, and that did the trick. But that is a different story. The point here is that, yes, I did access those emotions that I wished to convey on the page, and so I did. Since the work is a classic, I daresay that those emotions have and are resonating with many generations!

> *I bid you goodbye for now, but I will most certainly be visiting you as you toil away putting emotions onto page—now that you've accessed me and are reading this! Of course, only if you so choose. Many, many thanks for reading. And do have a good day or night, whenever and wherever, you may be reading this.*
>
> *Yours cordially,*
> *Herman Melville*

HERMAN MELVILLE was an American writer born on August 1, 1819 in New York. He died at the age of 72, due to congestive heart failure, on September 28, 1891. Melville is best known for his masterpiece, *Moby Dick,* but also wrote poems and short stories. The author had an exciting life, including spending years at sea on whaling ships and traveling to many faraway locales. Melville had a hard time financially and took many odd jobs to make ends meet. His job on a whaling ship inspired him to write *Moby Dick*. Melville was inspired by real-life experiences, which he poured into his novels, and which made them relatable and bestsellers. Other works that sold well include *Typee* and *Redburn*.

> *"To produce a mighty book, you must choose a mighty theme. No great and enduring volume can ever be written on the flea, though many there be have tried it."*
> —Herman Melville

13

➤ NATHANIEL HAWTHORNE ◆

Hello fellow scribes of the Earth and Light Plane. Nathaniel Hawthorne. For the Light Plane scribes do peer over your Earth Plane shoulders to see what you are reading, and what you are writing! That being said, I am honored, as are all of us included, and do wish to thank you for reading.

On to the words, at hand, if you will. Here are my thoughts on living a writing life and on being a writer. A prolific writer. Let us begin.

Oh, to be young again. To have that fervor and vigor and vim! And then to be "old" in your psyche and your person. For when you are older and wiser, you have so much more to say that tugs at the fabric of humanity, wouldn't you agree? So when you may hit your older years, you might just have the ideas, yet the vim is a bit lacking. No matter. There are ways around that. For one, it is a subject of quality versus quantity. But then again, it is also a matter of saying everything that you came here to say.

For that is what truly tugs at your psyche as you write—that pushes you to finish—that makes you upset when you don't finish or you don't feel as if you are working as fast and as hard as you might. That is your soul's plan tugging on your earth plane reality.

First of all, when this occurs, know that you are most certainly on to something grand! There is something quite wonderful nipping at your mind and trying to break free. And that is a glorious thing! For who wants to have plenty of writing time, yet nothing all that interesting to say? One could beat on the typewriter or keyboard a bunch of nonsense, but that won't get you too far! Or it could get you too far in terms of somewhere you don't want to go—try madness. But that is another story, or could make the beginning of your next story.

For now we start with, or I should say continue with, these words of wisdom. Do not be too impatient with yourself and your writing. While it's critical that you carve out the writing time and space, it is equally critical that you avoid striving to force the writing. Fiction, my dear scribes, simply cannot be forced. While you can try, you will most certainly not be pleased with the results. It will sound forced—like cardboard eggs or Styrofoam French toast. Not viable. Certainly not authentic. And most importantly, not your authentic voice, which you yearn to have spring forth from you onto the page.

Does this mean you should tarry? At times, yes. At times, no. You will know when the time is right when you listen to that inner voice. That inner voice that will whisper in your ear: "It is time." And then you shall sit down at your writing desk, as if moved by spirits, or as if you are a windup robot that must go to where you are being intrinsically led. Once you get to your desk, let the writing pour forth. Let the muse guide you. Let your soul express itself in the most profound way possible—by simply being. And knowing.

You may be thinking, what practical tips would dear Nathaniel give me here in this time and place? That is something I would point out. While it is most certainly intriguing to go to other times and places to write about them, it's not always possible. Look around at your here and now and remind yourself that your here and now will one day be considered quite unique and charming. Write about your here and now, if even only briefly. Encapsulate it. Even if you don't use this here and now writing, it will infuse your writing with a realism that you can't get anywhere else.

That is all for now, Dear Students. I do thank you once again, and wish you a most blessed day or night. As they might say, Amen!
  Nathaniel Hawthorne

NATHANIEL HAWTHORNE was an American novelist born on July 4, 1804. He died 59 years later, due to natural causes, on May 19, 1864. Hawthorne was best known for his dark romance novels and short stories. His most recognizable works are *The Scarlet Letter* and *The House of Seven Gables*. Hawthorne used many elements of realism in his writings, particularly in *The Scarlet Letter*. His writing was greatly influenced by the town in which he grew up—Salem, Massachusetts. His ancestors were involved in the persecution of witches during the witch trials.

"Easy reading is damn hard writing."
  —Nathaniel Hawthorne

14

➤ Hans Christian Anderson ⬅

Hello Dear Scribes on the Earth. Those literary sojourners, who are most certainly seeking the best possible in their writing! I am highly honored to present here. This is Hans Christian Anderson. I do thank you for reading. Here are some "tips," as you now say on the Earth, for writing and following your muse.

First of all, know that you do all—every last one of you reading this—have a muse. In fact, you most likely have many muses. So for those souls who have been told that they haven't yet "found" their muses, I would like to tell you that it is my belief that that is most certainly not the case. Your muse is with you always. Sitting on your shoulder, most likely. You need only access your muse, which is, if you have guessed by now, your writing angel. For I do say angels, actually. Most of you have many. Often you have different muses for different types of writing and different writing purposes.

So now that we have that out of the way. That your muses—most likely plural—do exist, we can move on to creating "color" in your writing. To how you can best make the scenes come alive on the page, so to speak. For that truly is what you want, I do think. To make the scenes come alive so that the reader thinks that he or she is indeed watching the story in 3-D unfold right before his or her eyes!

Color, color, color. Hmmm. How does color come onto the page, do you think? Could it be through the characters? Through the life you infuse in the characters? To the life you let the characters lead right before your eyes? Yes, that is it! It is letting the characters do as they may that leads to the most imaginative stories. And it is those imaginative stories that then make their way onto the page or computer screen and intrigue the reader, and even the writer! For when you as the writer are intrigued, you most certainly stick with the writing. You are enthralled to see what your characters do next!

That scenario is where things should stay. However, being the humans that you are, you begin to think that perhaps if you begin tinkering with the words you've already put down and know are true and the right ones that you will come up with something so much better! So you begin to do so. You begin to tell the characters what they are to do next and next and next. And do you know what? The characters soon turn to cardboard. They become less of themselves than they were when you let them roam the page in a "free-range" style. And you then become bored. Once you start yawning—watch out—for the characters are taking a dip—a downward spiral that may find them in the "round" recycling bin!

So the lesson here? Let the characters roam—run even—all over the page! Let them take over the page, if they wish. Simply let your fingers fly over the keyboard and transcribe what they are doing and saying. For when this occurs, story truly is telling itself. And that story will have more color and imagination and brevity—the latter when necessary—than you have ever seen to this day come from your brain/mind/fingertips!

Character is what we are talking about here. And character just can't be forced. It isn't something that you can figure out by charting all of the characteristics of the character. It isn't something you can make happen, because you want to see a character be humble, for instance, or brave. If the character is neither, the character most certainly won't rise to your challenge. More likely, the character will slink off to be a somewhat subdued character, whom you no longer recognize! Am I suggesting that you don't keep your characters tightly reined in, and that you let them "run amok?" Yes, I am! For when you do, color will burst forth on your pages, and your readers can't help but take notice.

That is all for now, Dear Fellow Scribes on the Earth! I must bid you farewell for now, but most certainly not ever forgotten! Follow your muse, which will take you to your characters, and most certainly to writing Nirvana!
Yours Forever Truly,
Hans Christian Anderson

HANS CHRISTIAN ANDERSON was a Danish author born on April 2, 1805. He died at the age of 70, due to liver cancer, on August 4, 1875. Anderson is a world-renowned author, famous for his fairytale novels and short stories. Some of those stories have been turned into Disney movies, such as *The Little Mermaid* and *Frozen*. His short stories *The Ugly Duckling* and *The Princess and the Pea* are considered classics and have been translated into many languages. Anderson was inspired by many literary works as a child, but his biggest inspiration came from the legends, stories and messages of love in the Bible. His stories use themes and characters that transcend nationality and age.

"*Life itself is the most wonderful fairy tale.*"
—Hans Christian Anderson

15

❧ JAMES MICHENER ❧

Hello, Fellow Scribes of the Earth. James Michener here. I'm very honored to present here. There are many, many, many of us here, so it has not been an easy task to determine who shall speak. While I can't divulge how these decisions were made, I can tell you that those of us who have been asked to step forth and "spill" our words of "wisdom," the Higher Realm has deemed would resonate the most at this time in history. That being said, I do hope that my words fill you with some of your own writing truths. Onward!

As a writer on the Earth Plane this last go round as James Michener, I did write quite a bit of intrigue into my work. And I deeply enjoyed doing that. Does your work always need intrigue? Yes, I believe that it does, as do many of us Scribes of the Light. Does it need to be a plot with many twists and turns and surprises? No, it does not. For as you know, we can't all write the same way. We can't all shock and dismay. We can't all get out of our own ways, either. What am I rambling about, do you think? That of authenticity in your writing. That is what I wish to discuss, though I will also give you some pearls of wisdom regarding how to weave intrigue into absolutely everything you've written and will write.

Authenticity. What on Earth/and Light do I mean? What does this mean to your writing? Authenticity is very important in the scheme of things when you are developing a "make believe" world on the page. It's essential, for instance, if you have a corporate raider raiding a small, unsuspecting company that that corporate raider sounds like a corporate raider would and does those things that a corporate raider would. So, yes, this is authenticity, for your characters! And that is quite important.

But what am I referring to when I say authenticity as yourself—as a writer? I am suggesting that you dig deep into the well of your own soul and draw out your true self. You know who your true self is. You truly do. For your true self is that distinctive part of you that you feel raising its voice—wanting to put words on the page in his/her own time and way. That is your authentic self. Some of you may dig deep for authentic self all of the time and let her/him come to the fore, while others of you may fight with authentic self to stay hidden. While this is most certainly understandable and advisable should you live in a time and place where you could be persecuted for telling your authentic truths, and in particular putting them on paper, this is not something necessary for most of you to do. You most likely live in a time and place when and where you can speak your truths. And if you don't, you can most certainly hide those truths in flowery words that only some will understand.

Enough already, you may be saying! Okay, you agree, I will dig deep for my authentic self and let my authentic self come to the fore in my writing. Well, I hope that you do! If you so choose, for free will does trump all here in the Light—and truly on the Earth Plane, yet it doesn't seem so at times. When you do let your authentic self come to the fore, then you will see the true writing reaches that can be strewn ahead of you for miles and miles and miles. So many miles of good ideas and profound messages that those ideas impart will give you just one problem. How to find the time to get all of those ideas onto the computer screen and into the hands of readers.

Enough said on that, I believe.

On to intrigue. Well, you may be guessing/intuiting right now that intrigue is tied in to showing your authentic self in your writing and letting it come to the fore! For readers want to see authenticity from self—and they find that wildly intriguing! They so want to see the writer in the shadows of the work they are reading. They most certainly aren't interested in author intrusion, but they do so want a peek here and there into the writer's psyche and soul. Human nature at work, most definitely!

So when you are thinking that the intrigue just isn't coming through—let yourself come through in little glimmers here and there—like the ocean wave peaks when they catch the sun, and then the water flows downward once again into the ocean swell. Those glimmers will keep readers turning the page—whether you are showing them a masterful plot or a love scene, or a person simply navigating the challenges that the Earth Plane life is so good at sending your ways!

That is all, Dear Fellow Scribes! I am, once again, honored to have presented here. I do wish you many writing jewels and the rush of pure joy and freedom that comes from stringing word "pearls" in such ways that they make you and your readers' souls and hearts sing!

Yours most ever and ever,
James Michener

JAMES ALBERT MICHENER was an American author born on February 3, 1907. He died at the age of 90, due to kidney failure, on October 16th, 1997. Michener was best known for his novels on historical fiction. He wrote more than 40 novels in his lifetime and many short stories. He won the Pulitzer Prize for Fiction in 1948 for his first and most famous novel, *Tales of the South Pacific*. Authenticity was vital to Michener—so much so that he moved to the areas he wrote about. He was also a teacher, political advisor, naval officer, and philanthropist.

"I love writing. I love the swirl and swing of words as they tangle with human emotions."
　—James Michener

16

➣ Ayn Rand ➢

Hello fellow Scribes! Ayn Rand here! So ever grateful that I am "one of the chosen ones" to speak here. I say that in a bit of jest, but I am also deeply, deeply honored! And I am ever so much grateful that you are reading these Pearls of Wisdom, as James so eloquently said a little bit ago!

Enough ramblings about how I came to appear here! I shall like to begin in order to impart what I can to help you with your writing journey!

Writing is most certainly a journey. It is a journey of spirit, a journey of the heart, a journey of the intellect, and a journey of the soul, first and foremost. You, no doubt, are noticing that theme here and there about in this work! That of the soul's calling. Why? For it is most certainly one of the most profound journeys you can take when you access your soul, and then the words dovetail with your soul's calling and life mission!

Some of you reading this may fear that your work—*your* written pearls—are mere pebbles that come up as if on an abandoned beach filled with bracken and mire! I wish to tell you that your pebbles are most definitely pearls! No matter what you write and how you impart your words on paper or computer, your work is most definitely pearls, for those words are coming from your unique soul! Here in the Light, we don't differentiate between more highbrow "literary" writing and that writing that is done for mass consumption. We simply do not. For we know that all is ordained. Every last kernel of word that comes onto a page is most certainly ordained. Of course, you have your writing systems and your systems for deciding writing that is "better" than another, but we wish for you to know that your writing is like that of the paper/page/art project done by a young child for his/her mother. We see all of your projects from here as simply perfect!

Why do I talk on and on about this? I do this, because one of the major things that stops writers up is the feeling of inadequacy, of not being "good enough" to put words on the page, or to show others those words through publication. (Which we have to say we are so enamored with here in the Light—that of being able to be your own publisher in this day and age!! How grand!) But I digress. Back to the matter at hand, which is that your work is magnificent! You must only believe that, if you wish, so that you can march on to express yourself as you intended when you took this assignment on the Earth Plane.

Will you get better with time and practice and study? Most definitely!! And I am not suggesting that you don't strive to improve. But I am suggesting that you write, no matter how you feel you don't measure up! Even more importantly, that you realize that there are truly no standards! When you write with abandon, knowing that you don't need to be better or even worse than anyone else, you are free to tell your story—your authentic story—stealing a bit from my dear friend, James M. here! But this is the "truth" I wish to impart. You are so good! You are magnificent with your writing! And the only way that you will improve, for that is what you came to the Earth to do, is if you continue to write and to share your writing! Yes, do edit yourself. And do get a good editor or editors to edit you, of course. But then spread your word for all to see!! Or I should say, for all who are supposed to see, to see.

That is all I will say on this subject. Was this a pep talk! Well, yes, you could call this a writing pep talk from the Light! And I do so look forward to seeing what you produce via your writing now that you've read my "humble" words.

Thank you ever so much, Precious Readers and Scribes of the Earth!
I wish you many, many pages of writing joy!
　Forever and Always,
　Ayn Rand

AYN RAND was a Russian-American novelist and philosopher born on February 2, 1905 in Saint Petersburg, Russia. She died at the age of 77, due to cardiovascular disease, on March 6, 1982. Rand was best known for her novels, *The Fountainhead* and *Atlas Shrugged*, both of which were bestsellers. She is also widely renowned as the developer of a philosophical system she coined Objectivism. Rand described Objectivism as "the concept of man as a heroic being, with his own happiness as the moral purpose of his life, with productive achievement as his noblest activity, and reason as his only absolute." Rand was also a playwright and screen writer, and even a Hollywood movie extra.

　"*The question isn't who is going to let me; it's who is going to stop me.*"
　　—Ayn Rand

17

≫ Ralph Waldo Emerson ≪

Hello, Fellow Scribes, Ralph Waldo Emerson at your service. I am humbled by this opportunity, and do wish for you to squeeze out whatever you may from my intended humble words.

Intention. What is your intention when you sit down to write? What is your intention when you put forth your words? Your words? Your words? Your words? That, there, now is what we are concentrating on. For truly, you are thinking of your own words when you read this, and that is well, and as it should be.

Why do I speak in rhyme? In circles? To show off, well no. To sing to your soul? Quite possibly. Where you are going with your work; where you wish to sing; what you wish to sing; where you wish to fling kernels of wisdom and truth and delight. Those are questions that it would be wise for you to ask yourself. For once you know your intention, which could simply be that you have words banging around in your head that just have to come out, then you will more easily glide the words over and onto the page or the computer screen. Then you will be able to say what you want to say in the way that you wish to say it. Intention truly is a glorious thing.

Intention also goes a long way toward keeping you organized with your writing. To keeping you knowing exactly where you need "to go from here," so to speak. As intention will let you know if your message that you wish to impart is better coming through verse or poetry or a short story or a book, or even a saga of a book!

What more besides intention do I wish to leave you with here? Well, it would be good, if you so choose, to look into your own head and extract kernels of wisdom that bang about in there. Do you have recurring thoughts that seem to wish to come forth—sometimes at good times when you can share them with someone in need and at other times when they appear to be nothing more than useless trivia—albeit interesting? Your work is where you can "vomit" out these pieces of wisdom, if you wish. Writing allows you to jiggle every last thought—big or small—odd or even—from the inside of your head so that it can be put down for posterity—even if it is only the posterity of your life and your family members.

As you write, you may even visualize a sort of cleaning out of the pipes. Of putting down that which has followed you around and even tormented you. I have to say that some of that I truly did with my writing in my life as Emerson. I dug out—pulled them out as noxious weeds—some of those thoughts that I didn't want to and couldn't truly live with. That is where pathos and ethos and great understanding and compassion and empathy springs from. That—those little bits and pieces; little nuts and bolts—rolling around in your head—is sometimes where the most inspired and truly out of this world ideas and inventions, and yes, written works—books and poems—come from.

So forge on, dear writers. Write what you hear banging around in your heads. Know that it will stop the banging once you get the words on paper. Also know that a new banging will most certainly start again soon after—as your soul has quite a bit to say—but do know that this is all as it should be in the great scheme of the written word. A form of communication like no other that can't be replicated or duplicated no matter how many technological advances the Earth sees.

Thank you, once again, for listening. I am most honored and know that I am in most esteemed company with those who are imparting here, and you Dear Readers and Fellow Scribes on the Earth Plane.

*Forever and ever to the ends of the Earth and back again,
Ralph Waldo Emerson*

RALPH WALDO EMERSON was an American writer born on May 25, 1803. He died at the age of 78, due to pneumonia, on April 27, 1882. He is best known for being the father of Transcendentalism and for his poetry and essays. One of his most famous essays is, "Self-Reliance." Transcendentalism is the belief "that society and its institutions—particularly organized religion and political parties—corrupt the purity of the individual." The philosophy holds that people are at their best when "truly self-reliant and independent." Emerson was so passionate about individualism that in addition to his poems and essays, he also gave more than 1,500 public lectures on the topic across the US.

"To be yourself in a world that is constantly trying to make you something else is the greatest accomplishment."
—Ralph Waldo Emerson

18

⇾ Gertrude Jeckyll ⇽

Hello, this is Gertrude Jeckyll, here. I am most honored to impart my thoughts here for you Dear Scribes on the Earth Plane. I will get to the matter at hand without further ado.

Writing. Gardening. Living. Breathing. Loving the Earth and loving one's life. That is what I was all about during my life as Gertrude Jeckyll. I have had other lives, but suffice it to say that my life as Gertrude was truly one of my most crowning glories. Why? Because of the written and spoken word. Because I was able to share my love of the Earth, Mother Nature and her handiwork, as well as the love of digging ones hands deep into the Earth and sowing and reaping and harvesting all of the pearls that Mother Nature is so good about bestowing on those who take the time to get to truly know her and her bounty.

It is the same with your words. With the pearls you put on the pages of your notebooks and journals and even spill onto the computer keyboard. You are sharing what you create; what grows in your belly and then flourishes until it fills your heart and flows/spills onto the page. For that you should be, if you so choose, supremely grateful. For all do have the capacity to write, but not all are called to do so.

So how may I be of service to you? How may I "help" you with your writing? First, I would like to say that it is quite grand if you can think of your writing—as that time right before you write—as a jumping off a cliff time. It is when you peer over the cliff into the vast beyond, be it a cavernous canyon like the ones at the Grand Canyon, or a heavily forested one like you might see in the Appalachians. Either way, you are looking out into the vast beyond and what lays beyond and you are about to jump into that abyss of words and to pull out from that abyss the words that most resonate with your soul, so that those words may then strum a sensation in the souls of those who you are speaking to, via voice and via word.

Truly, too, the spoken word would not be as rich without the written word, and the written word would not be so rich without the spoken word. They are in some ways one; and in other ways they ride tandem through the wind, so to speak, to impart glorious messages. You will see how well the spoken word works when you do a reading of your work. You speak your written work and you then impart the message that your written work does impart to those listening.

I do hope this is helping you. I feel that I could say so much more, and indeed I could. But we only have so many pages here at our disposal, each of us scribes! I do suggest that you grab hold of your words, however. That you take them as a butterfly may cling to a bush's slender leaf as it attempts to then put its snout into the flowers on that bush, or as the bird clings with its feet to a branch as it waits to get into the bird feeder while others are feasting. Then you are able to truly resonate with what you've put on the page. And then, when you speak what you have written, the words will reverberate throughout your own soul and mind and heart and that of those who are listening to your words of wisdom.

What am I truly saying here? What am I suggesting? For one, let Mother Nature guide and lead you to your true words. For two, let yourself guide you through the maze of life—perhaps a maze made of tight-clipped shrubs. You know where you are going, Dear Scribes. You know where the road will lead you. Simply follow the road, be it made of dirt, concrete, asphalt, or cobblestones. It will take you exactly where you need to go.

Gertrude Jeckyll

Thank you, Dear Readers and Writers. I feel as if this may be a bit befuddling, these words, at first glance, but once you delve into what has been said here, and let it percolate a bit, and let the seeds planted begin to flourish, you will soon see that the ideas imparted will flourish within you, and you will one day have a forest of good, bright, blessed work to your name.

Yours Always and Forever,
Gertrude Jeckyll

GERTRUDE JECKYLL was a British writer born on November 29, 1843. She died at the age of 89 on December 8, 1932. She is best known for her writing, which included more than 15 books. Her book, *Colour in the Flower Garden*, was her most famous. She wrote more than 1,000 articles for lifestyle and gardening magazines. Jeckyll was also a photographer, craftswoman, artist, and horticulturist and garden designer. She created more than 400 gardens across the United Kingdom, Europe, and the US.

"The lesson I have thoroughly learnt, and wish to pass on to others, is to know the enduring happiness that the love of a garden gives."
—Gertrude Jeckyll

19

⇒ Somerset Maugham ⇐

Hello, there, all of you ripe students of writing! Somerset Maugham here. At your service. I am honored, as we are all here. This is an auspicious project, and we are so, so excited! On to the words of wisdom I am tasked to impart through Julie!

Values. Clarity. Judgment. Honesty. Betrayal. Of what do I speak here? I speak of the various emotions and conditions that are presented to those of you who live on the Earth Plane. Of course, there are many, many more. It is emotions that are so essential in your writing. Emotions of the characters, as you portray them, and resulting emotions of your readers or viewers, should they be watching the results of a script.

Emotions are what pull people into a story. Emotions of hope that the story will resonate. Of yearning that the story may heal. Of fear that the story may peel back layers of a person's soul. Yet, the compelling nature of emotions is such that the readers and viewers just cannot help themselves. They MUST read what you've written. They must uncover the secrets infused in each of your words. They MUST find themselves in your work and the souls of those they've loved and lost and those they hold dear and treasure.

So how do you emote the emotions, so to speak? How does one reveal the inner yearnings of a character so that the soul is bared—laid out for all to see? There are several ways to do this. I will enumerate here for you in a written, list form, as this I find quite helpful.

1) Give in to the emotions swirling on inside of your chest. Those feelings that quite feel like they might erupt at any minute. If you are feeling the urge to cry, then cry with your writing. If you are feeling the urge to sing with pure joy, then do so with your writing. Put your feelings on the page.

2) Betrayal. Injustice. Compassion. Sadness. Glee. What do I speak of here? I ask you to identify the emotions before you put them on paper—or at least during the process. If you are feeling an intense sadness. Is it really sadness? Perhaps it is more accurately described as melancholy? Or regret? There are the nuances of the language—all languages—that must, if you so choose, be addressed and honored, even. So if you are writing about anger, pinpoint exactly what kind of anger. Are you feeling irate? Or are you feeling an anger so intense that it borders on depression? Identifying the emotion will help you then direct the story. For truly you do wish to impart messages as you write.

3) How does this latter sentence that I've written work? I will give you an example, which I'm happy to do. Say, for instance that you are feeling what you think is glee. Yet you feel quite anxious about whatever it is that wants to make its way onto the page. Then you identify that it truly isn't glee. In truth, it is anticipation. This would make a much different story than glee, wouldn't you agree? A character who is gleeful is quite like a honeybee buzzing about a garden when there is much pollen to be had. But a child waiting and anticipating Christmas morning—smiling all the while—portrays a most different kind of happy. These are just two examples. With your creative, genius brains and souls I know you can access many more such instances.

4) Finally, I leave you with this. An assurance of sorts that you have hit the mark with the emotions. If you cry when you get to a particular scene in your book or script. If you feel the tightness in your throat and the knot that makes it difficult to swallow, you can be sure that your readers will, too. At least those readers with whom your work resonates.

That is all for now, Dear Scribes, whom I am so glad to have met and imparted words of writing wisdom to. (Dreadful last sentence, I know, but you get the message!) I do bid you a most wonderful day and night or night and day filled with effervescence and stupendousness that only the writing life can offer!

Always and forever and a day,
Somerset Maugham

SOMERSET MAUGHAM was a British writer born on January 25, 1874. He died at the age of 91 on December 16, 1965. He is best known for his novels *Of Human Bondage* and *Cakes and Ale*. Maugham also wrote plays and short stories. He originally set out to become a physician and successfully worked as one, until the release of his first novel *Liza of Lambeth*. After the rapid success of that first novel, Maugham quit being a physician, so he could focus on his writing fulltime. He was so successful as a writer that he gained notoriety as the most popular and highest paid author of the 1930's.

"Art is a manifestation of emotion, and emotion speaks a language that all may understand."
—Somerset Maugham

20

⇥ Charlotte Brontë ⇤

Well, hello. Thank you most profoundly for reading. Charlotte Brontë here. To offer what I can and may about the writing life and writing.

Wherein lies the truth? Wherein lies the lies? This is something that I most certainly contemplated during my time as Charlotte Brontë on the Earth Plane. For I was most certainly a bit broody at times, as I contemplated the nature of the human existence.

Yet when I wrote, I did manage, as it were, to soar above the clouds at times, to offer a bird's-eye view of the grand forest of life below. That being said, how do you deal with perspective in your writing? How do you handle that eventuality? That you must hone in on the perspective that you wish to portray in your work?

First, what is perspective, exactly? How would one define perspective? (I do ask a lot of questions, do I not?) Perspective is that which helps you to frame the worlds which you are trying to put down in words on page so that your readers may then think those thoughts and then see those pictures that you are so eloquently drawing with your paintbrush, known as a pen or computer keyboard. Perspective is the bird's-eye view. It is where you sit as you frame your photo of words and invite readers to skip down the path of your story.

So where could you sit as you frame perspective? You could be the omniscient author. That view does have its benefits, to be sure. For you can then show everything that is happening and has happened. Which is why they have sometimes referred to this perspective as "Godlike." Again, as everything in life, this does have its drawbacks. For when you are able to display everything, where are the deep, dark secrets to hide?

If you are to embed secrets, then first-person narrative with an untrustworthy narrator is quite the grand master! For you read the person speaking, and though things seem to be quite possible as you are reading them, there are certain discrepancies to let you know, give you a peek, into the fact that there are large secrets here, lingering, waiting to come out. Most likely not through the untrustworthy narrator. Most likely through the people the narrator meets. Or at least seems to meet.

Perhaps you'd like to have the light shine on the secrets and twists and turns in your work, and you don't want things to be too murky and muddy with the potential to be stuck in the mire. Then I would suggest third person. Of course, this is a much used perspective, and for good reason. With third person, you as the author are able to relay what is happening in your story as an "all-knowing" narrator. With this viewpoint, you can bring in great secrets at just the right times.

There is also the second person. Which is a quite literary format, if you are to use it. For the "you" is not an easy perspective to use in fiction. You must know exactly what you are saying, and then you must also know what you wish to impart to your readers, who most likely will think of themselves as the you. It is hard to use this perspective for too much text without being quite bogged down, yet it is a most useful perspective/point of view to use as an effect. For example, if you were to do a multiple viewpoint work, where you were using third person with several characters, there could be a character that speaks with the you. This could express that the character is quite mad, or that the character is the only sane one in the bunch. All for the reader to figure out!

Well, I hope your head isn't spinning too quickly at this point! From my perspective, I see that I've given you much literary food for

thought. That is good, and as it should be! Thank you most kindly for listening. It was a great pleasure and honor to speak to you.
  I bid you good day or night,
  Charlotte Brontë

CHARLOTTE BRONTË was an English writer born on April 21, 1816. She died at the age of 38, due to pneumonia, on March 31, 1855. She is best known for her novels *Jane Eyre* and *Shirley*, as well as her poetry. She is the eldest of the Brontë sisters, all of whom were writers. Charlotte Brontë's novels became classics of English literature, and *Jane Eyre* was translated into an estimated 60 languages. Before Charlotte Brontë became a famous writer, she was a school teacher and governess. *Jane Eyre* was said to have "revolutionized prose fiction in that the focus on Jane's moral and spiritual development is told through an intimate, first-person narrative, where actions and events are coloured by a psychological intensity."

"I'm just going to write because I cannot help it."
  —*Charlotte Brontë*

21

❧ Rudyard Kipling ☙

How marvelous that I am able to speak here to all of you wondrous writing pupils and masters, for we are all pupils and masters simultaneously! Rudyard Kipling here. At your most profound service. I shall begin.

East, west, north, south. Of where do you come? Many think that this is of the utmost importance, and for them, it quite frankly is. But you writers, you know that you come from each direction and even up and down and all around. In my lifetime as Rudyard, I was most definitely of the "East," yet also of the "West." Hence, the work I did, or didn't do, for that matter. But no mind. I am just mentioning this, for I do wish that as you go about your writing days and writing lifetimes and journeys that you do keep in mind, as we know from here, most decidedly, that there are no boundaries, there are no barriers—truly there aren't even any commas between all of us. We are all interconnected and intertwined, and if you can access this idea. This universal truth, if you will, you will find that your writing takes on a color, a tenor, that isn't often found in writing on the Earth Plane at this time in history, or frankly, at any time in history.

So how does one broaden perspective so that one can then get this panoramic view onto the page? It sounds rather overwhelming and difficult, does it not? This grand scheme, it may seem to you. Why, I'll just keep on writing what I've been writing, you think. I really don't have the time or energy to think differently now—to pull up the roots I've planted on the pages, so to speak, and simply change course! I am not suggesting you do so. I am only suggesting that as you look through your telescope and portray what you see through that telescope on the page that you also consider that there are so many other planets and stars in the galaxy. That those planets and stars can most definitely add texture and color and excitement to your writing. You don't necessarily even have to mention those stars and planets specifically. Just knowing in your writing heart of hearts they are there will indeed color your work. And if you decide that you do wish to wander out of your telescopic lens and venture onto the other planets with your words and visions that you paint on the page, well how exciting!

It may seem, at times, as you read our words from "beyond" that we are most certainly talking in circles or rhymes or code of some sort. Truly, we are not. For you are internalizing all of this as you read—and most certainly it will come out on the page.

So, as you go about your days and you view your telescopic scenes that land in your mind's eye and you convey them on the page, you will most certainly have epiphanies that come with the territory, so to speak. It is also those epiphanies that you want to express to others. It is those epiphanies, truly, that are what you are seeking as you look through your telescope, or move it around so that you can see more of the night sky. Those epiphanies not only do you seek, but you seek to express them on the page, so that the reader will have an "Eureka" moment. So that the reader will say to himself or herself or even out loud to those listening, this writer knows of the truths of the soul and of the Earth experience! This writer knows exactly what it is like to be human, to walk around in flesh. This writer is most certainly a gifted writer, and an in tune writer to have pulled these morsels of life, these secrets and these hopes and dreams and put them into this character and infused these thoughts into the plot that the character finds himself or herself dealing with.

How wondrous, truly, is the pen or computer keyboard, is it not? For it has the capacity to delve into the depths of humanity, pull out the most compelling aspects, and spill those aspects onto the page in a way that comes out as pure, unadulterated art that speaks to the soul of all who reads it.

Well, I've been getting a few prods here to sign off—so as not to take too many words! (My trouble as Rudyard at times.) But no matter! I am most deeply moved to have expressed these thoughts here. I do hope that you find them to be comforting and even provide you solace as you plod on further into the writer's journey. For it can be a solo journey at times, but not really, for we are at your back always—our army of Light Plane Scribes!

Here to assist, as always,
Yours Truly,
Rudyard Kipling

RUDYARD KIPLING was an English writer born December 30, 1865 in Mumbai, India. He died at the age of 70, due to a duodenal ulcer, on January 18, 1936 in London. Kipling was best known for his novels *Just So Stories* and *The Jungle Book*. He also wrote short stories, poems, and articles. Kipling drew a lot of inspiration for his novels from his childhood in Mumbai, India. He was awarded The Nobel Prize in Literature in 1907 "in consideration of the power of observation, originality of imagination, virility of ideas and remarkable talent for narration…" Kipling is considered a major innovator of short stories. His children's books are so well loved they're considered classics of children's literature.

"For the strength of the Pack is the Wolf, and the strength of the Wolf is the Pack."
"Words are, of course, the most powerful drug used by mankind."
 —Rudyard Kipling

22

❖ Barbara Cartland ❖

Hello, Fellow Scribes, Barbara Cartland here. I am at your service and deeply honored that I was able to come onto these pages and speak to you. In my days as Barbara, I—I think it is widely known now—channeled the bulk of my work. Suffice it to say that I knew what I was doing, yet I didn't truly know what I was doing, until I stepped back through the veil into the Light. This book is equally exciting! I shall begin.

Romance! Oh, romance! Isn't that what so many of you lovely writers wish to offer your readers? At times it truly is romance. It is a love like no other. A "soul mate" connection (we giggle at this term here, by the way, for we are truly all soul mates—but that is a different topic). But you do wish to confer to your readers the most dazzling of all love affairs. Sometimes with another and sometimes with the self!

So how do you confer romance in all of its guises? How do you get the romance onto the page so that the reader feels in love with love? In love with the very idea of being in love with love?! First, know this. You need only tap into the center of your heart. That really, truly, is all that you must do. Is it a good idea to read other writers (like yours truly)? Of course! Is it a good idea to talk to other writers about how they impart the most perfect love scenes? Of course! But once you've done all of this, know this. You can impart the most fabulous love scene ever, if you simply tap into what lies in your heart.

And what does lie in your heart, do you think? Could it be that you have the kernels of wisdom in your heart for all of this? Could it be that you have stories in your heart that you know nothing about, but that which yearn to spring forth! You most certainly do. Truly, we all do. For lying in "wait," so to speak, in your heart, are fabulous dramas and novellas and love stories that you have lived over many, many lifetimes. That is truly what I speak of here. Will you be "channeling" those lives? Yes, you will, in a sense. Or if you prefer to think of it this way, you are chronicling those lives that come before you. And at times, you are mixing and melding those lives into something even grander and more exciting!

Is this at all possible, I hear you wondering? That *I* could actually do this? You ask yourself. That I could actually access that which has come before for myself and put it on the page and then watch it sing on the page? I am here to tell you yes! It is quite possible! And it is quite grand when it occurs!

You know when this of which I speak occurs. You've seen your fingers fly over the page or over the computer keyboard without your mind engaging at all! And yet, you've felt the stirrings in your heart. The full feeling of pure joy as the words that you just know are perfectly formed and wondrous are spilling onto the page! You know that you have gotten to the "heart" of a matter. That you've managed to spill out the "jewels" onto the page in such a way that it will now communicate what you wish. Even better, it will stir the hearts of all who read your words. So that they may find joy. So that they may truly mate with their own souls!

So dig deep into your heart before you write that great love scene or that great novel about love! When you feel the stirrings, as a flower beginning to bloom, you will know that you've accessed those lives of great joy and love, and yes, even great sorrow from loss of love. Then simply let the words flowing from your heart flow onto the page. Ask your mind to step back and take a rest. Ask your mind to wait until you need to balance the checkbook. You are writing from the heart today and every day. And you will most certainly fill the hearts of those who read your work with pure joy!

That is all for now, dear precious readers and Scribes of the Light and Earth! I am deeply honored to have spoken here. I wish you a lifetime of pearls of wisdom for the page.
   Yours Sincerely,
   Barbara Cartland

DAME MARY BARBARA HAMILTON CARTLAND was an English writer born on July 9, 1901. She died at the age of 98, due to natural causes, on May 21, 2000. Cartland is best known for her 19th-century Victorian-era romance novels. In addition to writing novels, she was a prominent philanthropist and also wrote operettas, plays, music, and magazine articles. Cartland's romance novels were so popular that she is known as the third bestselling fiction author of all time. In her lifetime, she wrote 723 novels, all of which were translated into 38 languages. In 1976, Cartland won the Guinness World Record for most novels published in a year. She was one of London's most prominent and popular society figures and was easily recognizable. She always wore heavy makeup, a blond wig, a plumed hat, and a pink chiffon gown.

   "*A historical romance is the only kind of book where chastity really counts.*"
   —Barbara Cartland

23

⇒ Jacqueline Susann ⇐

Hello, dahling fellow writers! My, oh, my, am I overjoyed to speak here as me! For truly, I have flowed through the fingers of many a writer since my days on the Earth Plane, but, then, that is generally not known. It is quite an honor to appear here as "me," or at least the me that was Jacqueline (Jackie) Susann the last time I traveled the Earth Plane! Enough of my ramblings. I shall begin now!

Sex, love, mystery, suspense, peace with self. How, oh, how do these sentiments connect? They do seem to be rather disjointed, don't they? They do seem to not be words that you would put in the same sentence—well, at least the last words. I shall explain.

The Earth Plane. It is rife with possibilities when it comes to good stories. There is so much that you could write about. Particularly in the area of "sex, love and rock and roll!" But then, is that all there truly is? Yes, and no. Yes, for that is what readers do like to read—at least that is the common wisdom. And, truly, at many times, that is true. Sex, truly does sell. You can look at my book sales and see that is most certainly the case. But is that all there truly is? Is that what one must do in order to have those book sales? Stick in sex scenes here and there willy-nilly? Of course not!

How does one sell a lot of books! How does one get people to look at your writing? I shall tell you. First, it starts with loving your book! With being full of suspense—the idea of suspense, when you write it and when you read it over to see how it "sounds." It is connecting with your words first that will help you connect to your readers. And this does sound like peace with self, does it not?

Okay, okay, you say. I shall love my work. What next? What about all of this marketing and these many tasks that I simply must do in order to sell my books? What did you do, Jacqueline? What did you do to sell so many books?

I can answer that with one word—or actually two.

I believed.

I believed that the books were worthy of publishing, first. I believed that the books were intriguing. I believed that the books had an important message for the world—even with their many sex scenes, and dalliances into the macabre at time with those scenes. I believed that what I had to say indeed would make a difference in some shape or form. Be that to simply entertain or intrigue, or to even change a viewpoint or a life. I simply believed. This is what I suggest that you do, should you so choose. To simply believe in yourself. Believe in your work. Believe that there are readers out there who would indeed love your work. Who would talk about your work. Who would share your work—that is how it all gets going, if you will.

Do you need to know all of the "right" people? (Which here, I must tell you gives us a good chuckle.) No! For you, you, you are the "right" people. Like Dorothy in the *Wizard of Oz*, you truly do have all that you need—and so much more. They speak of the brain only using a segment of its real power. In truth, the heart and soul only uses a smidgeon on the Earth Plane as well, unless you can tap into the power of belief. The power of faith that is tied into that belief.

Of course, do your marketing. But as you go about doing your suggested marketing—do those marketing efforts that resonate with your soul. For when you do, you will come to believe that those marketing efforts will then "work," and then you will see many souls reading your books, loving your books, talking about your books and clamoring for more!

I will end there, so as not to take up too much space here! Although I see that I have taken up less than some! But I say this in jest, for truly, we are all saying exactly what we are supposed to say—as will you with your glorious writing.

    I bid you a blessed day or night, filled with exciting, titillating writing possibilities!

    Yours Truly,
Jacqueline Susann

JACQUELINE SUSANN was an American actress turned writer born on August 20, 1918. She died at the age of 56, due to breast cancer, on September 21, 1974. Before she was an author, Susann was an aspiring actress in Hollywood. After being diagnosed with breast cancer, she turned her focus to writing. She was best known for her three best-selling novels, *Valley of the Dolls*, *The Love Machine*, and *Once is Not Enough*. Her novel *Valley of the Dolls* exposed the sex and drugs related to life in Hollywood, and even won the Guinness World Record in 1970 for being the best-selling novel of all time. With the release of her next two novels, *The Love Machine* and *Once is Not Enough*, Susann became the first author to ever have three consecutive novels earn the No. 1 spot on the New York Times best-seller list.

    "She knew the feeling of love—and she knew it was the whole reason for living."

    —Jacqueline Susann

24

✥ Daphne Du Maurier ✥

Rebecca. By far the book I got "lost" in the most when I wrote. By far the book that I just might call my "masterpiece," should I be speaking to you now as an Earth Plane soul. And, indeed, it was quite a masterpiece. Of Rebecca I shall speak in order to impart words of wisdom to you here. Before I begin, thank you kindly for listening/reading, for us Scribes of the Light are truly, utterly, completely honored to appear here in this work! Let us begin.

Rebecca was one of "those" books. That spring forth from your fingers at the exact right time, in the exact right manner—at a time that resonates with you as a writer, with you and your work. It came at a time when I was in my writing "prime." And yet, I wish to say here and to remind you that you are always in your writing prime!

What was it and is it about *Rebecca* that does truly turn readers' heads? What is intriguing about the book? Well, for one thing, the fact that the main character—the woman-girl for whom you root as she navigates her way through the "wreckage" of the memories of Rebecca—does not have her name mentioned in the book but once. There is much intrigue in that. It is telling, of course, as well. But also quite maddening, too. For why can we not hear her name uttered by him, the "man" of the house? Is he so insular and so full of himself that he doesn't even care! In some ways one might wish to go in and slap him about a bit—but I am digressing. The point here is that the mystery is set by simply not saying anything.

What else? What else was it about Rebecca that worked so perfectly—flawlessly even? Setting to be sure. The house—Manderley. What a glorious setting she found herself walking amongst. Those creepy halls, filled with ghosts—most definitely the grand ghost of Rebecca, whose spirit quite literally took over scenes without her earthly presence. I suggest this to you as you write. Work on your settings. Work on them first before you put your characters into them. For truly, those settings are what your characters will react to. It is of the utmost importance—in my humble opinion—that those settings are somewhat "set in stone," so to speak. That way your characters will be reacting to something solid. At least presumably solid. When you have your settings foundation, you then can let your characters wander where they may—be it through a most intriguing mansion such as Manderley.

What else? Character, of course. We have the character of the dear girl who has found herself in the rather overwhelming shoes of Rebecca. And then we have dear Mrs. Danvers! My, oh, my, what a character she was! As if she embodied Rebecca, and truly became her in a sense. And did she give you the shivers, as she did me? She did react to her surroundings in a much different way than Caroline, the main character—which is what I did call her once in the book, and the name I had in my head as I wrote. She became a part of the surroundings, of Manderley, while Caroline navigated those surroundings, yet remained herself—even though she did seem a mouse, and truly was. She was a mouse who was her own mouse. And then he (Maximilian/Max), in some senses simply tolerated Manderley.

What else? Plot. While plotting can be a topic that can be quite lengthy, I will leave you with this. When you write your plots—when you plan the twists and turns for your characters, think what would be the next most logical step in the plot. While this might seem like it would lack intrigue, truly it does not. For one thing, many readers aren't necessarily looking for the most next logical step. For another, you want the plot to be believable. And for another, the most logical step—for characters with whom you just aren't sure what they'll do next—such as Mrs. Danvers—that next logical step is quite exciting and intriguing! And it will have your readers saying to themselves, of course!

> *It is time for me to sign off. I am honored, as mentioned, to appear here. And I do wish you much luck with your writing endeavors. I only ask that you please finish your works—if you so choose—and share them with as many souls as possible.*
> *Always and forever and ever,*
> *Daphne Du Maurier*

DAPHNE DU MAURIER, Lady Browning, was an English author born on May 13, 1907. She died at the age of 81 on April 19, 1989. She was best known for her novels *Rebecca*, *The Birds*, *The Scapegoat*, and *Jamaica Inn*. Many of her books and short stories were turned into films, due to their popularity. Du Maurier grew up in Cornwall, which is where she drew a lot of inspiration for her works. Once the author started to gain fame, she became more reclusive. Although Du Maurier is classified as a romantic novelist, her novels have hinted at the paranormal and are resonant and moody. Her novel, *Rebecca*, is considered one of the most loved novels of all time.

"*Women want love to be a novel, men a short story.*"
—Daphne Du Maurier

25

⇾ Ernest Hemingway ⇽

Dearest Fellow Scribes. I bid you a wonderful day or evening, as it may be for you. I am most honored to present here. Ernest Hemingway. Indeed, though this project was planned, and we, us Scribes now in the Light agreed to this ordained project, it is always a wonderful thing when the projects planned do indeed come to fruition, for that doesn't always happen. But then that is not this project and certainly material for a whole different matter. On to my message to you Sacred Earthly Scribes!

How does one truly, really, truly express oneself fully on the page? If you've been writing for more than five minutes, you know of what I speak. It is that yearning/that wish/that desire to know that truly, you have put down via the written word that which lies in your soul and itches to come out. At times it is most difficult to know if you've truly shared what smolders/what gestates/what festers, even, deep in your psyche and soul.

So how do you access this? How do you determine that this has occurred? I have a few pointers for you, as it were. A few "tips" to help you determine if you've accomplished your writing mission, so to speak.

1) Do you continue to have a niggling that something has not come forth? That something still festers; still nips at your psyche? Time to return to the "writing board" then.

CHANNELED WRITING TIPS

2) How does the work read? Does it flow; does it sing; does it make your heart go pitter patter, because you know, just know that you have expressed yourself fully? Or do you find yourself stopping as you read, as if there is something amiss or missing?

3) Do you have faith that all has come forth as you intended and as was planned?

4) Are the birds singing? Are the bees frolicking? Are the butterflies dancing? When you've hit the "mother lode" with your writing, those things of the Earth, yet also of the Light plane, do dance around you. Mother Nature's creatures are the most noticeable, but there are other signs and synchronicities that will come to the fore to show you that you have indeed "arrived" with the excerpt or the entire work that you have completed that sits before you.

5) Do you simply just know that all is on the paper or computer screen? That all is just there. You feel no urge to dig deeper; no urge to scour the recesses of your mind for any more glimmers or nuggets of wisdom. You know. And that is all you need do.

What then happens if you determine that 1-5 have not occurred? What do you do to dig out the nuggets of wisdom and enlightenment to then put on the page where they belong? Another list. (I'm particularly fond of them!)

1) Shine a flashlight or torch or lighter into your soul—into its core. What do you see? What do you feel?

2) Tap into your feelings. What is scurrying on around inside of you? What is refusing to show its face? Take the flashlight or torch or lighter and light up the refugee inside of you. Take it apart with your eyes and mind. What is it hiding, do you think? How shall you draw secrets from the secret hoarder?

3) Have faith. There that dreaded word is again! Faith. But, truly, you simply can't write for hours on end and then edit for even many more hours without this most spectacular cornerstone. Faith lies at the

heart of all you do—including writing. Faith will help you access your hidden diamonds so you can use them to sparkle up the page.

4) Write some more—with abandon—even without trying to connect the dots with your current work and what you are spewing onto the page. You will often find once you're done "vomiting" that your new words will dovetail nicely with those words you knew were missing something. Put them together and you will have a beautiful tapestry!

5) Know, just know, that what you've done with the words and what you may even continue to do are absolutely Divinely placed and Divinely curated. Your work just needed a few "tweaks" to become the best it could and can be!

That is all for now, Dear Students of the Light. I am most honored, once again to have appeared, and I do wish for you a most gracious and blessed evening or day, depending on when and where this finds you.

Peace to You Always my Blessed Writing Friends,
Ernest Hemingway

ERNEST HEMINGWAY was an American novelist, short story writer and journalist born on July 21, 1899. He died at the age of 61, due to suicide, on July 2, 1961. He is best known for his novels, *The Sun also Rises, A Farewell to Arms,* and *The Old Man and the Sea. The Old Man and the Sea* won the Pulitzer in 1953. He also won the Nobel Prize in 1954. He developed the theory of omission—known as the Iceberg theory—described in this quote from the author.

"If a writer of prose knows enough about what he is writing about, he may omit things that he knows and the reader, if the writer is writing truly enough, will have a feeling of those things as strongly

as though the writer had stated them. The dignity of movement of an iceberg is due to only one-eighth of it being above water. The writer who omits things because he does not know them only makes hollow places in his writing."

—Ernest Hemingway

26

⇾ Tennessee Williams ⇽

Tennessee Williams here. At your Divine and Earthly service. For truly, during my life as Tennessee (what a name, heh?) I did move in between the Earth and Light—not really knowing I was doing it, of course, really, but I truly did! At any rate, let us begin.

A *Street Car Named Desire. A Cat on a Hot Tin Roof.* My, oh, my, what grand titles, are they not? They do intrigue one. They do have one wondering enough to take a gander at the play. To even look up the script, if you will. Where on Earth (ha ha) did I get such names? Were they truly names from my imagination? Yes, and no. Yes, because they did come from my mind—and at times it was compilation with some of my contemporaries and their input. And did the Light give me fodder with which to work? Most certainly. Of course!

But why am I mentioning this? Of what do I wish to speak? I wish to speak of titles. Of their utmost importance. For they truly are so, so important. Quite frankly, Dear Scribes, a reader or viewer will pass over your work simply because of the title—or should I say, in spite of it. For if the title sings to them, they will most certainly go further to explore your work. Yet if the title bores, well, they may very well march on, unless they know something more about the work, or about you as the writer. So please do take heed with your titles. Know that they do mean a great deal. I shall list below the different manners in which you can access the titles and come up with some "doozies," if you will.

CHANNELED WRITING TIPS

1) Brainstorm. When you brainstorm, your imagination is set off on a course with no seemingly clear direction. Although I can tell you from here, there is a direction. You will hit the "bull's-eye" when you take this approach almost every time. Write out snippets of titles—words even—onto the page, and then connect the dots between the various snippets until you've come up with "the one."

2) Let your mind wander (akin to the brainstorming). Let your mind go here, there, everywhere—hither and yon. For when you do, you will come up with some pearls, so to speak. Even if you only come up with part of the title this way, you can then most certainly add other words to this to come up with your ideal title.

3) Should you explain with your title? Or should you entice and enthrall? Well, quite frankly, you should do both. But how does one "pull this off?" How does one keep the attention of the intended "target" reader? Hmmmm. I shall tell you. It is a most certainly useful tactic to enthrall with the title and then to explain with the subtitle. And most certainly you've seen this occur rather a lot, have you not? Of course, you could simply enthrall and hope to pull people in. That is, of course what I did with my titles. However, in this day and age, when so much is presented to readers and viewers, it is a good thing to "hedge your bets" and give them a little theatrical mixed with some grounded reality. That way they can know that they are certainly embarking on a journey about something of which they find of interest, while also embarking on a journey that is quite artistic and dramatic in its own right.

4) Do let your mind wander so that you may hook together pieces of thoughts that do not seem as if they should go together. This is enticing, yet it is also something that speaks to one's soul. For instance, a hot "tin" roof. How many roofs truly are tin? And then a cat on the roof? Well, yes, cats do climb on roofs, your mind might think. It isn't that far off to think that a cat could climb on a hot tin roof, but then why? Why is that cat on the roof? Well, then you have the reader

enthralled and ready to embark on a journey to find out why. Of course, then your intent is to ensure that the reader—to the best of your ability—comes to those pearls of wisdom for himself or herself that truly don't have anything to do with tin roofs or any type of roof, except maybe for their "roofs" of their souls, or their psyches.

Well, Dear Readers and Marvelous Scribes, I must sign off here. I do thank you for reading, as this is a most honored appointment here—this relaying writing information to you from the Light. I do hope my words have helped and will continue to help you with your writing endeavors.
Yours Sincerely,
Tennessee Williams

THOMAS LANIER "TENNESSEE" WILLIAMS was an American author born on March 26, 1911. He died at the age of 71, due to asphyxiation, on February 25, 1983. He is best known for his award-winning plays, *The Glass Menagerie*, *A Streetcar Named Desire*, and *Cat on a Hot Tin Roof*. His plays were so popular that they earned him the title of being one of the three best playwrights of 20th century American Drama. He also won two Pulitzer Prizes, one in 1948 for *A Streetcar Named Desire*, and one in 1955 for *Cat on a Hot Tin Roof*. His path to fame was not an easy one, as he had to work many odd jobs to get by, such as a factory worker, waiter, and even a caretaker on a chicken ranch.

"Life is all memory, except for the one present moment that goes by you so quickly you hardly catch it going."
—Tennessee Williams

27

✦ Agatha Christie ✦

Hello, Dear Fellow Scribes. Earth Plane Masters! I am so deeply honored to appear here. It is quite enthralling! I shall move on to the matter at hand without further prelude, for I have much to impart to you in the short span which I've been given. However, I am most grateful for this opportunity, to be sure!

Intrigue. Mystery. Travails. Trials. Tribulations. Of what do I speak? I speak of life. Of the mysteries of life. Of the grand mysteries of life, actually. For though here in the Light it is not mysterious at all for us, for we see all and know all, quite frankly—there on the Earth Plane you aren't privy to all that we see. And that is as planned.

There is a puzzle to life on the Earth Plane that you go there to put together, so to speak. At times you look at the pieces of the puzzle of your life and you do wonder where on Earth some of these puzzle pieces will ever fit. Much like a mystery—a good mystery—as those I wrote as Agatha, if I may pat myself on the ephemeral back, as it were. But then suddenly one day, the piece you've been puzzling over, the piece that has caused you much consternation—that piece finally fits, seamlessly, so that you can barely see the seams of the surroundings of that puzzle piece.

That is what I wish to express to you. That you may look at your writing, if you should so choose, as a piece of the puzzle. As a piece of the mystery that is indeed buried in that puzzle piece. Of the piece of the mystery that once it is positioned exactly where it belongs, brings forth the wonders of the universe, of existence, of love, fear, laughter, and even chagrin.

So do infuse intrigue into your work. Intrigue as you see it from your mind's eye. Intrigue that may be quite different from one type of genre to the other. Yet intrigue at any rate. When you do add the intrigue—for readers do so love to wonder and speculate—then you may know that you will most certainly intrigue your readers. That you will most certainly keep your readers turning the pages—page after page after page—until they finish and then sit back as if having eaten a grand feast—satisfied—perhaps burping a bit up, those morsels that still linger in their mind's eyes.

So how does one insert the intrigue? Well, think of the puzzle pieces I have mentioned here. Choose your puzzle pieces wisely, of course, and then look to see where they might fit, yet don't fit them there. Of course, that would ruin the surprise of the plot! Instead, stick those seamless puzzle pieces in odd locations throughout your prose. So that the reader may spot them, yet not be quite sure what to do with them. With this I think you understand what I am getting at.

How not to make those puzzle pieces stand out too brightly, though. For you don't want to appear obvious, of course! Yet, you don't want the readers scratching his or her head and saying, I didn't see that coming at all! And I know that the character didn't either! Because, quite frankly, Dear Author (they would be speaking to you), that was highly unbelievable! Oh, my, no that wouldn't be good, now would it?

Rather, you want the pieces of the puzzle that you sprinkle throughout your work to be as a leaf on a tree that is almost the same shade of green as the other leaves, yet a bit off in color and sheen. So that if an avid, keen reader may look closely, he or she will see that indeed the leaf has no business on that tree. And then, of course, you will also have those horticulturists among your readers—those experts, who will spot the wrong leaf on the tree as soon as it appears! Those would be the master sleuths—those people who, when I was alive as Agatha, and even now, can spot my plot and untwist the turns and tell it back to me. They, however, Dear Readers, are truly few and far between. Instead, you have your astute and interested readers whom you can "fool" with your plot twists—at least part of the time!

Well, that is all from me now, Dear Readers/Scribes. I am at that point in the page (the plot) where I must sign off. Hopefully I've given you much good "info," as they say nowadays, for thought, yet have you a bit intrigued as well!! Soon, as I know you will, being the good sleuths that you are, you will untangle the web I have woven in this prose.
    Most Honored Always,
    Agatha Christie

DAME AGATHA MARY CLARISSA CHRISTIE, LADY MALLOWAN, was an English Author born on September 15, 1890. She died at the age of 85, due to natural causes, on January 12, 1976. Christie is best known for her 66 detective novels. She also wrote 14 short story collections, the most popular being *Hercule Poirot* and *Miss Marple*. Christie also wrote plays, including *The Mouse Trap*, which was the world's longest running play. Many of her novels were turned into television shows and even movies. She was so successful that she earned the title of best-selling novelist of all time, being outsold only by *The Bible* and Shakespeare.

"*The best time to plan a book is while you're doing the dishes.*"
    —Agatha Christie

28

⇸ Bohumil Hrabal ⇷

Dear Fellow Scribes. Such a wonderful thing, shall we say, to address you here. Thank you for reading. I am most honored. Bohumil Hrabal here. At your service.

Oh, the writing life! What a profound life it is! By Earth Plane standards, it is most certainly a crowning glory, so to speak. One of the few—though there are others—professions where you truly can access the Light left and right, so to speak, and it is okay, and actually encouraged, in a way!

That is what I did as Bohumil. I was in quite a state much of my life, that involved being of the Light, yet not truly knowing it was occurring, but truly knowing that I was accessing something "different" than many of those around me, and yet, that was okay and as it should be. I could see that. And I could also write about life and its trials, yet at the same time, its pure joys and triumphs.

So what shall I speak of here? What shall I "talk" about? The first time Julie read anything from me, so to speak, it was as she made her way to the New York City Library. For I am honored to have one of my quotes, as it were, on the stepping stones that have been marked by the "literary elite" that one sees on the way to the library—down the sidewalk. I shall include that quote here, for it does speak to my mention above of being in the Light as one walks along in life, yet also in life feeling those human emotions that you Earth Plane dwellers do.

> *"Because when I read, I don't really read; I pop a beautiful sentence into my mouth and suck it like a fruit drop, or I sip it like a liqueur until the thought dissolves in me like alcohol, infusing brain and heart and coursing on through the veins to the root of each blood vessel."*

Julie was quite enthralled with these words, as I'm sure many on the Earth Plane have been, because it does speak to that magic that occurs when one reads (or writes) those phrases, words, sentences that truly resonate with the soul—to the core of one's being—in such a way that the universe speaks at once, as the bells and whistles and claps and serenades occur in one's head all at once. This speaks of the bliss of the written word, does it not? That place one visits where all things are possible when one is reading or writing, or both simultaneously!

How does one reach this state of bliss when one writes? And is this the cart before the horse or the horse before the cart? Must one reach bliss in order to write bliss? Or must one write bliss in order to reach bliss? Which comes first? Well, I will have to tell you this—not to confuse you—but they do come at the same time. They are simultaneous these two—the bliss and the bliss—so to speak. You are inspired and so you write inspirational words. Yet inspirational words also inspire you to become inspiring.

This does seem a bit confusing, doesn't it? I do apologize for that. My only hope here is that you will just write. Write with abandon. Write when you are inspired by another's writing. Write when you are inspired by your own writing. Write when you feel as if you may not be inspired until you write something inspirational.

Simply write, Dear Readers. For when you do; when you pick up the pen or put the fingers to the computer keyboard, those inspirational sayings and quotes and "knowings," and epiphanies, they will come when and how and where they were preordained to come, so that you may resonate with your soul and the souls of all who came before and all who will follow.

Good reading and writing to you all. I must sign off, as they say. I am quite honored, as I mentioned, to appear here. I do wish you writing riches beyond your wildest dreams!
Yours Truly,
Bohumil Hrabal

BOHUMIL HRABAL was a Czech writer born on March 28, 1914. He died at the age of 82 after falling out of a hospital window while trying to feed the pigeons on February 3, 1997. He is known for being one of the best Czech writers of the 20th century. His most famous books were *Closely Watched Trains*, *I Served the King of England*, and *Too Loud a Solitude*. Before becoming a writer, Hrabal graduated from Prague's Charles University where he received a law degree. He then went on to work manual labor in Kladno ironworks with Vladimír Boudník. As a writer, he was so popular globally that he met the Czech President Václav Havel, the American President Bill Clinton, and the then-US ambassador to the UN, Madeleine Albright. His novels have been translated into 27 languages.

"No book worth its salt is meant to put you to sleep, it's meant to make you jump out of your bed in your underwear and run and beat the author's brains out."
　—Bohumil Hrabal, *Dancing Lessons for the Advanced in Age*

29

≫ EMILY BRONTË ≪

Hello Dearest Fellow Scribes. Emily Brontë here to "speak" to you. I am most profoundly honored. Here I will share my words of wisdom, be they what they may be. We shall begin.

Character. Character. Character. Truly, that is what I did spend a great deal of my writing time "working" on, if you will. What truly is a character made of? What gets a character to do certain things, while other actions the character could take, the character just would never take? These are just some of the questions I might and did ask myself when I wrote as Emily Brontë. In particularly when I wrote my "masterpiece" and only published novel, *Wuthering Heights*.

I do know that others before me here, and no doubt, others after me, will mention character. But that is as it should be, and I know that my words will be different, so do bear with me, if you so choose!

How does one develop a character fully? So fully that the character does indeed come alive on the page—walks about, talks as if he or she is truly alive and engages in activities that are those of the living.

For one thing, the character first becomes alive in the mind of the writer. That is the first vital step that in my humble opinion must be made. For when the character is alive to you—when the character has limbs and a brain and a heart and uses all of those parts of himself or herself to engage in the world around himself or herself—why then, that character truly has become a person!

When you have created a "real" person in your mind's eye, then you can begin to place that real person into eyes' of storms, into rather maudlin circumstances, and then, of course, into joyous circumstances, as well. When you do this, the character truly does spring to life on the page and begin to act as only he or she could act. For, truly, he or she truly is a real person!

If you are scratching your head at this point and wondering how on Earth you might access this place where you can create a real person out of your imagination, I do suggest that you simply believe. Believe that this can most certainly happen, and then it most certainly will! I can hear your wheels turning, and hear you say, why of course, you might say that Emily, for you were a most gifted writer, for one, and for another, now you are in the Light where certainly the imagination can go to any bounds—to any reach—to any realm. Well, I do have to admit that that is most certainly true. However, I was on the Earth Plane as Emily, and I did manage to let my imagination wander to such an extent that the characters did wander onto the pages and come to life in front of me.

I did invite the characters in. I did let my imagination wander long enough to invite them onto the page where they could then go rampant at times, if they so chose, or they could simply sit in a corner and observe. It all, of course, depended on their personalities. I have to say that I did very little molding of my characters. While I did urge them to take this step or that or to try this or that on the page, it was more like a parent with suggestions. For the truth is, Dear Readers, once you let your imagination "birth" your characters, they truly will take on lives of their own.

That is all for now, Dear Readers, for I will stop here. I will leave a little to your vast and vivid "imaginations." For you truly are well-equipped to take it from here! Thank you most kindly for listening. I do wish you a wonderful writing life filled with many "imaginative characters."

Yours Forever Truly and Forever Kindly,
Emily Brontë

EMILY JANE BRONTË was an English writer born on July 30, 1818. She died at the age of 30, due to tuberculosis, on December 19, 1848. She was best known for her one and only novel *Wuthering Heights*, which became a classic of English literature, due to its popularity. Even though *Wuthering Heights* is a novel filled with passion and love, Emily herself never had a romantic love. She was happiest being by herself or spending time with her sister Anne. Emily Brontë was one of four sisters, all of whom were writers. As a child, Emily had difficulty spelling, and had a fear of public speaking, although she was still able to write a novel that is read and adored around the world.

"Love is like the wild rose-briar; Friendship like the holly-tree. The holly is dark when the rose-briar blooms, but which will bloom most constantly?"
—Emily Brontë

30

⇝ James M. Cain ⇜

Hello, Dear Readers and fellow Scribes. Duly honored to be here. I shall begin. Oh, and forgive me for not introducing myself. I am James Cain.

Pigeonholed. That is what may happen to one if one does indeed continue to perfect a certain genre. And that most certainly did happen to me in my life as James Cain. For I was known for hardboiled detective mysteries when I wrote fiction. And then I was also a journalist. And that latter job is a bit of fiction mixed with a bit more fact. But I won't digress and discuss that here. Rather, what I prefer to discuss is my masterpiece. What they called a psychological thriller of sorts—*Mildred Pierce*.

That work, while it swayed much away from my original work—my bread and butter work—was undoubtedly my masterpiece work. For it did resonate with a nation. And it did call forth readers and later viewers, who might not have heard the story had I not written it. But what was I thinking when I wrote the book? What indeed had I accessed when I did so? It was most certainly a thriller in its own right—the story. And yet, it was also steeped in real life with real problems and the real unraveling of a character's psyche.

Some may have wondered if I drew from my own life when I wrote the work. For why would I suddenly veer off of my usual road to produce something so different? Certainly, some wondered, was I pulling from my own family saga—my own family dynamics? While we all pull from our own lives at times, and there may be some similarities in our characters, the truth is that I didn't pull from my own life for Mildred Pierce and her story.

So where did I get the information, you may wonder? Where did I "find" this story, so to speak? How did I come up with something so different? The truth is that the story found me. I wasn't looking for it. Indeed, I had many detective stories left to write—in me waiting to come forth. But then in walked Mildred Pierce. The story that my fingers just itched to tell. The story that had to come out somehow, some way on the Earth Plane. And so it did.

Was one of the reasons that I wrote the book to later talk about how it simply came to me? Perhaps. Like here. It was also a story that was in some ways buried in my psyche. It had to come out so that I could find peace. Though the story didn't follow me around for decades, as I've heard happens to some writers, it did dog me for some months until I sat down and let the words spill onto the page.

Though it might sound like we writers are somewhat stymied or confused or even reticent when it comes to work spilling from our souls onto the page, the fact is that we are often very grateful. For when the work flows—when it shines on the page and flows together and works so well, we know that we have been blessed with what many of us may call the writing muse. That muse that gives us a splendid story that resonates with readers. We also feel ever so grateful when people keep turning the pages. I was grateful. I do admit it. I also wished for many more experiences like *Mildred Pierce*. But truth be told, I only had that one instance of pure, flowing, natural writing that sprang forth with very little effort on my part. Of course, I had to edit the work, but the initial "birthing" of the book—that was much easier than any book before and any book after.

So what am I attempting to relay to you here? Most certainly, if you have the writing muse, if a story sings in your soul and cries to get onto the page, then put it on the page. And don't hesitate if it seems "too easy." For when it comes out with ease, know that it is most certainly possible that you are then telling the story of all stories for you. Don't, I suggest, let such an opportunity go by. For it may be your only chance. Or if you're lucky, it will be one of many chances. Only you will know once you've finished the work and move on to another.

That is all for now. I do hope that you were kept interested reading about Mildred Pierce. While the book and movie aren't a household name now, they once were. And they tell me—and I, of course, see—that it is indeed one of the "classics" today.
Yours Sincerely,
James M. Cain

JAMES M. CAIN was an American author born on July 1, 1892. He died at the age of 85, due to a heart attack, on October 27, 1977. He is best known for his hardboiled American crime fiction novels like *Double Indemnity* and *The Postman Always Rings Twice*. He is also considered to be the creator of roman noir. This literary genre is closely related to hardboiled, but rather than being a detective, the protagonist is a victim, perpetrator, or suspect. Self-destructive protagonists are common in this genre. Many of Cain's novels were turned into movies or inspired them. He was also a journalist and served as a private in France in WW1.

"*I write of the wish that comes true—for some reason, a terrifying concept.*"
—James M. Cain

31

⇾ Orson Welles ⇽

Now how did I, Orson Welles, gain entry here? How did I become a part of this rather stupendous work full of Literary Masters? That, my Dear Readers, is a "Light Trade Secret," but suffice it to say that I am most honored with my appointment here. Thank you much for reading. On to the message for today from me!

Earthbound. Lightbound. From where and from what are you bound? Do you bind yourself perhaps a bit when you insist that your work isn't good enough to be read from a book or by an actor for the most glorious stage? Of course, it is most necessary to refine your work. To look it over until you are sure it is good. But, my Dear Readers and Earthbound Scribes, I would suggest not "over-reading" your own work. For when you do, you become bound by invisible chains, yet chains nonetheless that keep you from finding your true center.

As myself on the Earth—Orson—I most certainly believed and lived by that belief that it was my duty of sorts to share the works that I recorded, so to speak, with the world. And I often chose to do that with cinema—for what a glorious medium it is! But as we all know, it all starts with words. Words put on paper, in my case "way back when" that then made themselves onto paper for scripts that the actors and actresses then interpreted and made their own.

That is what I wish to speak of in this particular instance. Of making your work your own, and then letting your words free to spread themselves amongst the populace and then allow the populace to make the work their own in their individual ways.

If you are thinking of the work as something that takes flight and goes where it must and wishes, that is most accurate. For a matter of fact, it is much like carrier pigeons bringing important words of wisdom and information from one place to another. The writer of those tomes stays put and continues to write while the carrier pigeons spread the word, as instructed.

This does predispose one to know that it is most important not to get "married" to your words, so to speak. It is most important that indeed you do mate with your words and birth them, yet at the same time, you let them go out into the world to grow as necessary and to become what they are to become for all who happen across them.

Why do I speak of this? Why do I go on and on, as it were, about letting your words go out and flutter about and spread themselves thin, even? Because from here, Dear Scribes, we see so many manuscripts and scripts stuck in desk drawers or computer hard-drives, or even in the heads of those writers who wish to let the words spring forth but don't for a variety of reasons.

There is so much good work on the Earth Plane that is not being shared! Not being heard! Not being cherished and reveled upon, even. So do pull out any works you've completed but still need to "work" on. Read them over—make changes here and there—and then get them out so that the Earth can enjoy those words! For truly, there are so many encouraging and enlightening and entertaining works that lie fallow in danger of never being shared during the writers' lifetimes. That we so wish to stop, if you will, so that we may see the pages flutter on the wind, so to speak, as they make their ways to souls ready and eager and waiting for the words imparted on those pages. So that those eager readers and viewers may lap up the words—the intellectual thoughts—the words of wisdom—the words of solace—and the words of great joy. They are ready, Dear Scribes, to become your Dear

Readers, so please do brush off those words and begin or finish, as it were, depending on where you are in the writing journey.

That is all for now. I do feel in a sense that I did give you a "lecture," as they call it nowadays. But it is all free will here and there, Dear Scribes. Do as you choose with your writing. Just know that we see your glorious pearls of wisdom from here—the letters do light themselves up, even! And we assure you that what you have to say, the world most certainly is ready to hear.
Sincerely and Truly,
Orson Welles

ORSON WELLES was an American actor/director/writer/producer born on May 6, 1915. He died at the age of 70, due to a heart attack, on October 10, 1985. He was a man of many talents. At first Welles was a screen actor and then turned to radio, where he did an unforgettable version of H.G. Wells's *War of the Worlds*. Welles was so convincing in his performance of *War of the Worlds* on his radio show that the broadcast caused widespread panic. His listeners thought there was an actual alien invasion occurring. He went on to become a director and producer, with films like *Citizen Kane* and *The Magnificent Ambersons*. *Citizen Kane* ranked as one of the greatest films ever made. Lastly, he was also a writer. His most notable works were, *This is Orson Welles* and *Les Bravades*.

"If you want a happy ending, that depends, of course, on where you stop your story."
—Orson Welles

32

⇝ Joseph Conrad ⇜

Heart of Darkness. Heart of Hearts. Heart of Soul. What a splendid journey I did take during my life as Joseph Conrad when I took the Heart of Darkness book writing journey! Thank you, Dear Readers and Fellow Scribes, for reading. And I do thank the Universal Energies that allowed my entrance here into what is most certainly a grand work! On to the message I would like to impart.

Stupendousness. What a word, heh? A word that sparks joy in some ways, and disbelief in others. At times it is stupendousness that you feel when you get the writing "downloads" and the work pours forth from you as if a vessel of water clunked open—split open to leak forth, spread into every crack and crevice. That was what it was like at times writing *Heart of Darkness*. And at other times, I was plodding along as if through quicksand. When, what, where, who, why, how? Those are questions that writers ask themselves again and again and again while writing, don't they? These are questions that often have to be asked. Or do they?

Okay, I know. I know. I seem to be talking/writing here in circles. In rhymes that I daresay you are thinking may never be answered. In some ways, *Heart of Darkness* never did answer all of the questions that it brought up—at least to some readers. And that is okay, and as it should be. For the universe has its secrets. The universe has its diamonds that it holds close. Like the origins, even, of this book—the truest, deepest of those origins. But I digress.

CHANNELED WRITING TIPS

Heart of Darkness. Heart of Hearts—of Soul of Hearts. You notice here the word heart. I did not, when I came up with the title with some help from the great beyond, put soul in the title. Instead, the book truly is a journey of the soul in many ways.

That being said, does all of your writing need to be a journey of the soul? Yes and no. Of course, you don't always have to dig deep, nor should you. But at times it is most helpful and will lead to some of your absolute best work. At other times, it will lead to work that does resonate with someone. The point being here is that your work will resonate when and where and how and why and with whom and what it's supposed to!

Heart of Darkness. Heart of your Soul. Dig deep into your heart of hearts to discover just what it is you truly want from the writing life. Is it pain? Is it suffering? So that you might then be able to write a gut-wrenching scene? Perhaps yes. And that can be a good tactic. Or do you wish to experience pure, unadulterated joy so that you may impart such joy on the page? The point being here is that you can create the writing life that you wish to live. Just as you can create the worlds that you wish to portray on the page. Do you have control over all—over the dominion of your flocks on the pages? Yes and no. I know. I know. I am appearing as ambivalent here. I appear to be talking in circles (which truth be told is alarming Julie a bit). But truly, I am not talking in circles at all. I am merely relaying what occurs in your own heads before, during and even after you write.

Confusion is okay in the writing life. Not being sure where you are going and how you will get there and when you will arrive and why you are even doing this in the first place is most certainly okay. Grand even! For such questions lead to the pursuit of answers, which leads to words put on paper. And then you arrive to your own Heart of Darkness, to your own soul. To your own ever stupendous soul!

I shall leave you with that. Scratching your head a bit, I know! But that is okay. For such scratching will lead to you wanting to cure the itch with some words on the page or computer screen. And then you will be well on your way!

Yours forever and a day,
Joseph Conrad

JOSEPH CONRAD was a Polish-British writer born on December 3, 1857. He died at the age of 66, due to a heart attack, on August 3, 1924. He is best known for his novels and novellas, *Heart of Darkness*, *Lord Jim*, and *The Secret Agent*. Conrad is considered one of the greatest novelists to write in English, even though he was not fluent in the language until his twenties. He also wrote many notable short stories, including *The Secret Sharer* and *The Lagoon*. Conrad got inspiration for his book *Heart of Darkness* after working as a Congo River Steamboat commander. He wrote many novels and short stories about the sea and jungle-like settings, which gave him a reputation of being a writer of exotic tales, although that was not entirely true. Conrad explained the real reason for his exotic settings, stating: "The problem . . . is not a problem of the sea, it is merely a problem that has risen on board a ship where the conditions of complete isolation from all land entanglements make it stand out with a particular force and colouring." His works often had especially deep underlying meanings. For example, a jungle village wasn't necessarily a jungle village, but rather a representation of his feelings of guilt, insecurity, and responsibility.

"There is something haunting in the light of the moon; it has all the dispassionateness of a disembodied soul, and something of its inconceivable mystery."

—Joseph Conrad

33

⇝ Anaïs Nin ⇜

Voila! Here I am! Anaïs Nin to offer "her" input here. Merci beaucoup! For listening, reading, writing, and discussing literature, both great and "small," over dining! I am so honored to present here, and I will most certainly do my absolute best to impart that which I am to impart! Let us begin.

Erotica. Oh, my! Even the name sounds so, so mysterious? Beguiling even. It nearly gives you permission to throw caution to the proverbial wind, if you will. Why do I mention it here, besides the obvious? While some of you are indeed writing erotica here and there—throwing it into your works, others of you have made this a side business, so to speak. And then there are those of you who might be a mite afraid, shall we say, to put one's toes into such a "naughty" spa-like experience. I say naughty with jest here, Dear Fellow Scribes and Readers, for there truly is no naughty here! But naughty so does get those pages turning, doesn't it? It certainly entrances and causes one to fixate a bit. On what the world—the Earthly World—may offer.

But all in a "good" day's work, as they say! Or is that a "bad" day's work? Ha Ha! We so love to giggle from here at all of the rules and regulations you humans place on yourselves. For example, not using turns of phrases in your writing—those considered overused (cliché), for instance. Which is why we've been using so many of them in this blessed work! To be sure, as you will most readily recognize them. But also because it is so much fun to use them in jest!

And that, Dear Readers, gives me a nice segue, if you will, to what I wish to discuss here. That of "worry" about repeating yourself when you write, or worse, repeating another. Of course, plagiarizing is not a good thing. For, truly, of what value is it not to put your own mark on things on the Earth Plane and even in the Light? Certainly, many of us Scribes of the Light do "help" you a little and perhaps a lot with your work, but truly it is "new" work we are helping you churn out. They are often age-old topics, to be sure, but coming out in a whole new way—a whole new "Light."

But I do encourage you to cast aside any fears you may have about sounding too much like this or that writer. For truly, you will most certainly be sounding like yourself. If you are writing from your heart and from your gut—that cannot help but happen. Have you been influenced by other writers? Most certainly! For that is what happens when you read other writers. And that is most certainly what you are supposed to do. In addition to enjoyment, reading other writers and even emulating them a bit is to be expected. Especially in the beginning of your writing "career." But the more you write, the more you will find that you will begin to emulate yourself. For each word you write builds on the next word and the next and the next, until you begin to build on the words—thousands of words back—that you wrote. You. You. You. Fabulous you write what you write, because of you!

Okay, so I have finished my "shtick" about not worrying about emulating one another. Back to erotica. For that was one of my vast fortes, if you will! Should you write erotica? Well, that is entirely up to you. There is most certainly a market for the "naughty meets nice." Of that there is no doubt! So if you do feel like it, then go for it, as they say in this day! And if you don't feel like having anything like erotica in your books, well, then, don't! That is the most wondrous of revelations to come to on the Earth Plane as a writer. That you are in complete control of each and every word that you write. Each word. Each work. Each book. Each short story. Each sentence and paragraph. You are free, truly, to write and think and feel what you wish. And so it is so.

Merci beaucoup once again for listening! I do wish you many writing riches as you make your way along the Earth Plane with all of its ups and downs and twists and turns and travails and joys!
Until we shall "meet again,"
Anaïs Nin

ANGELA ANAÏS JUANA ANTOLINA ROSA EDELMIRA NIN Y CULMELL (AKA Anaïs Nin) was a French writer born on February 21, 1903. She died at the age of 73, due to cervical cancer, on January 14, 1977. She is best known for her female erotica novels. In fact, she is considered one of the best female erotica writers of all time. She was the first prominent woman to fully explore erotic writing, and the first woman in the modern west to write about it. Her works *Delta of Venus*, *Henry and June*, and *The Diary of Anais Nin* were all wildly popular. She also wrote essays and short stories and was a trained flamenco dancer. In addition to writing, Nin was a women's rights activist. She even spoke out about pro-choice: "The abortion is made a humiliation and a crime. Why should it be? Motherhood is a vocation like any other. It should be freely chosen, not imposed upon woman."

"*We write to taste life twice, in the moment and in retrospect.*"
—Anaïs Nin

34

⇌ Arthur Conan Doyle ⇋

Hello Dear Fellow Scribes! This is a most auspicious project! I am highly honored to participate. Arthur Conan Doyle here. I shall begin.

Where oh, where does one find a good plot? Stuck up in a tree somewhere? Under a rock? In one's head, to be sure! But, truly, where does one get a good plot? One with twists and turns and glorious beginnings and endings and everything so grand in between!

I shall tell you. At least some of the strategies I would suggest you use, including some that I used on the Earth Plane when I appeared as Arthur—creator of *Sherlock Holmes*!

Does one need to stay away from the obvious? Actually, no. For sometimes buried in the obvious are the kernels of truth that you can sprinkle in your story as those points of foreboding—of warnings. Those are the little forewarnings, if you will, that lay the groundwork within your plot in such a way that the reader is not surprised in the sense that the plot makes sense, yet truly in awe that he or she didn't see the signs, if you will.

Okay, what else, you wonder—to make a grand plot? You've set up foreshadowing. Now what else shall you do? For one thing, how does one come up with a good plot in the first place? I mentioned that it can indeed be obvious. By that I meant that it could be believable. For truly, unbelievable plots are, well, unbelievable. Few readers wish to be tricked into reading your prose so that they can be led down a primrose path that leads to pure silliness! They wish to arrive at a shocking revelation, yet that shocking revelation needs to, as you say on the Earth Plane, make sense.

So, considering that fact, how does one come up with a plot that makes sense? Quite easily! Look around at the life before you. The average everyday occurrences that happen to you and those you know—there you will find fodder for your plots. The old saying "truth is stranger than fiction" is most certainly a good axiom to consider. Look around your life. Look around your community. Look around the nearby communities.

Though they are becoming a bit harder to locate and for some passé, I did find that newspapers hold some jewels when it comes to plots and plot points. Peruse your local newspaper with an eye for a gem. Rather than read the articles, let your eye roam over the pages until one word jumps out at you, as if to shout, look at me! Then you will spot the gem you've been looking for. Such a word could be anything, truly. Such as: bandit, or overthrown, or tyrant, or fled, or extortion. You get the picture. Then you will most certainly see and read the little tidbit that you were meant to in order to get to the meat of your plot.

Such small stories stuck in the recesses of the newspaper can give you wonderful plot points and entire plots. You can also do this with the computer. Look about on those pages filled with many side stories. Let one catch your eye—read it, and then let your imagination roam. An antique vase has been stolen from a mansion. The only clue was a green van. Ask yourself what happened next. Visualize the van making a getaway at break-neck speed. See the "thugs" go into their lair to examine the vase, and then contact their sources about the value of the vase. What of the vase? How valuable is it? And is it cursed? Will it bring the bandits bad luck? You see how this can go on and on with one plot point feeding off of another.

There you have it, Fine Readers! A few of my "words of wisdom," if you will, about how to make superb plots that resonate with readers in such a way that they are astounded, yet know that your plot truly makes perfect sense!

I bid you a most humble good day or night! I am truly honored that you have listened, Fellow Scribes.
   Sincerely Always,
   Arthur Conan Doyle

SIR ARTHUR IGNATIUS CONAN DOYLE was a British writer born on May 22, 1859. He died at the age of 71, due to a heart attack, on July 7, 1930. He is best known for his Sherlock Holmes detective fiction novels. His character Sherlock Holmes is widely known as the most famous detective of all time. Growing up, Doyle had a troubled childhood. His family had little money, and his father was erratic. Young Doyle found solace in his mother's storytelling, as he stated: "In my early childhood, as far as I can remember anything at all, the vivid stories she would tell me stand out so clearly that they obscure the real facts of my life." When he turned nine, some of his wealthy family members offered to pay for his boarding school. His writing started there with regular letters to his mother. That is when he discovered he also had a gift for storytelling. He became a physician and practiced as one until 1887 when *A Study in Scarlet*, the first of the Holmes and Watson novels was published. The characters he created in his Sherlock Holmes and Dr. Watson detective novels series became the inspiration for many television shows and movies.

"How often have I said to you that when you have eliminated the impossible, whatever remains, however improbable, must be the truth?"
   —Arthur Conan Doyle

35

❧ George Elliot ☙

Hello Fellow Scribes, Masters of the Pen! George Elliot here, or Anne, if you will, wink-wink. I am highly honored to appear here. Thank you much for listening/reading. We shall proceed.

Pen names! Well, I am a "good" one to talk of them, am I not? For I was in some ways "forced" to use one back in my day. But no matter. My words were able to get to the masses. And for that I was most grateful! I come to you today to speak of your identity in your writing. For that truly is of some import here. For you. For the words you write. For those who come across your work, and you!

When "should" one use a pen name? When is it best? Well, that is most certainly a personal decision, I would say. And yet there are some parameters to consider. For one, in this day and age, you often don't really need a pen name in order to be read. For there isn't much gender-bias with the written word anymore—at least in many of your countries. But there may be reasons why you might want a pen name. For one, to differentiate your works, should they be quite different from one another. Those genres in which you work. For instance, if you are writing erotica and children's books, well, then, you might want to come up with a *nom de plume*, as they say!

But if you are thinking that you require a pen name simply to have one, you might want to rethink that. Do remember, if you choose to, that I do know of what I am speaking here, having been a "George" in writing for so many years, and gaining fame as a George. For if your writing does "hit it big" as they say nowadays, then you *are* that pen name. You become whomever you have taken on—whatever guise with which you've enveloped yourself. For that it will be important to respond to, be in tune with, your pen name. While that does sound rather odd, if you will, it certainly isn't. Just ask all of those actors and actresses who have taken on personas for some time and then in many respects have a hard time untethering themselves from those personas once it is time to move on!

That is not to say that you will necessarily want to move on from your pen name, but then again, you might. However, all will know you by that pen name! And for that, it will be a bit difficult to move on. You will most certainly have to start afresh with a new name and a new tenor and subject matter under your "true" name, if you wish to move on from the pen name. My, oh, my! What decisions here!

If you are thinking that a pen name is of utmost importance for you and your work, then do adopt and use a pen name. I only mention all of this in case you are thinking it might be "fun" to write under a pen name. For you may find, as I mentioned above, that you become "famous," and then you aren't truly you! You may want to shout from the rooftops, but it is I! But, frankly Dear Readers, all will know you by your pen name—all readers that is, and that will most certainly in many ways become "set in stone."

No matter, Dear Readers, if you have already done such a thing! If you have gained fame with one name, you can always start afresh with your true name, and enjoy being both people! On the other hand, if you have had a "sputter-y" sort of beginning with your writing, perhaps it is time to "ditch" the pen name, as they say, and become your true authentic self with the writing! You may just find that that is your key to fame!

Well, I do hope that these words help. I do hope that if you've been thinking about pen names or are in a bit of a quandary about them that this will give you some good "food for thought."
Always Yours, and at Your Service,
George Elliot/AKA Mary Anne Evans

MARY ANNE EVANS (AKA George Elliot) was born on November 22, 1819. She died at the age of 61, due to kidney disease, on December 22, 1880. She was best known as a leading writer of the Victorian era. She penned seven novels, with *Middlemarch* being her most famous and described by many as the greatest novel written in the English language. Her novels were praised for their realism and psychological insight. Evans was also a poet, translator, and journalist. She published her novels under the pen name George Elliot in an attempt to remove bias from her work and shield it from the stereotypes associated with women's writing, which at the time was lighthearted romance. Additionally, she didn't want her reputation as a widely known editor and critic to affect the way people perceived her fiction novels. Rather, she wanted the novels to stand on their own and speak for themselves. Evans was also not fond of the spotlight and used her pen name as a way to protect her private life from the scrutiny of the public eye. This was of importance to avoid scandal and publicity surrounding her relationship with George Henry Lewes, who was married at the time. Evans found herself stuck in an unfathomable position. She fell in love with a man bound by marriage to another woman, a woman he did not love and could not divorce. So, in the end, they accepted what they could not change and loved each other until Lewes's death in 1878. After his passing, Evans founded the George Henry Lewes Studentship in Physiology at Cambridge in his honor.

"Only in the agony of parting do we look into the depths of love."
—Mary Anne Evans

36

⇥ James Joyce ⇤

Good day, Dear Fellow Scribes! I do bid you a most auspicious day and night in which to transcribe your precious words! James Joyce here. I shall go on here, now, to give you what I may in order to help push along your writing, so to speak! I am ever so grateful to be able to present here, and as number 36! How splendid. We shall begin!

The writing life. What a grand life, don't you agree! For you can, quite literally, do and feel and be what you want, in many respects. Of course, there are the "guidelines" that you must adhere to. For one, the words do need to "appear" on the page in some form or another, and they must be readable and understandable. And yet, those words, they can be whatever you choose, in many respects. If they are strung together in coherent sentences and those sentences give the reader coherent thoughts and situations, and the reader wishes to read on to find out more about those coherent thoughts and plots, well, then, your job is complete, right?

Yes, and no. For it is one thing to give the reader something that he/she wishes to read, and quite literally "devours," it is another to also give the reader a message that resonates with said reader. That lets the reader know that you do, truly, understand the meaning of his or her existence, in some way or another. For, truly, Dear Scribe, your readers wish to learn of themselves in your writing.

How is that so, you may ask with a puzzled scratch to the head. For aren't the words being imparted by you, truly you? Truly yours? How can a reader wish to "draw" from your words meanings to help him or her? It is possible, truly, Dear Scribe, to resonate with yourself as you resonate with readers. For truly, as you are most certainly seeing here in this work, and most likely throughout the world as you look about, we are all interconnected in many, many ways.

Oh, my, of what am I trying to impart here to give you some good, useful nuggets? I ask that you suspend yourself a bit when you write. That you instead access some higher knowing as you write. And how does one do that, you question? Simply breathe and be and write. That is all! Simply write without questioning of what you write. Of what you speak. Rather than ask yourself as you are writing, what is my message? Let the universal energies come out. Then you can bring forth the message in whatever they may have to say. Is this channeling? Yes, it is. And, yes, you can do it. For you know those times when you just let your fingers fly, as they say, and you come up with some true pearls? Those pearls, Dear Readers, are indeed inspired.

The writing life. It is quite grand! What other type of life, besides other arts, like painting and inventing and singing and acting, would you be able to access the Divine in such a Divine manner? Do enjoy yourselves, Dear Scribes, on this journey you've chosen to take in this time and space. Do revel in the knowing that you can and do whatever you wish to on the page—within reason, of course! Do know that we are all here to buoy you up, to inspire you, to motivate you—indeed to "come through" you! We are at your service. All you need do is ask. And know that even if you don't consciously ask, we may just come through you, because you've unconsciously asked! We are all one—universal—so your thoughts can and often are also our thoughts—and vice versa, etc., etc.

I am going to close here, lest I confuse you even more! I daresay after reading this passage a few times, you will most certainly extract some kernels of wisdom that will most definitely help you with your writing journey!

Fare thee well, Dear Scribes!
Yours truly,
James Joyce

JAMES AUGUSTINE ALOYSIUS JOYCE was an Irish novelist born on February 2, 1882. He died at the age of 58, due to a perforated ulcer, on January 13, 1941. He is best known for his novel *Ulysses,* widely considered one of the greatest novels ever written. Joyce is also known for using and mastering the stream-of-consciousness writing technique, which launched him into literary celebrity status. The eldest of 10 children, Joyce came from humble beginnings. With a father who aspired to be a musician, but was alcoholic, the family had little money. Joyce's talents and intellect were noticed, however. His family responded by sending him to Clongowes Wood College, Belvedere College, and the University College Dublin. He received a Bachelor of Arts with a focus on Modern Language. Joyce's exploration of language and literary forms gave novelists a fresh approach to writing.

"*Mistakes are the portals of discovery.*"
—James Joyce

37

❧ Virginia Woolf ❧

Wonderful to present here, Dear Fellow Scribes! I am Virginia Woolf. I am most honored. It is with Divine and pure pleasure that I share with you what I may about being a writer, and indeed, about writing "well," which in many ways is akin to dining and living well, in general.

Writing, writing, writing! How utterly delicious is the task when all is flowing, wouldn't you agree? The words come forth like water in a waterfall. Rich and flowing and lush and ever so fresh! But what happens when you get a bit "stuffed up?" When you get a bit of pushback from your writing muse, so it seems? Yes, I am speaking of writer's block here. And I see that I at number 37 am the first to do so!

Writer's block. It did stop me up at times during my life as Virginia Woolf. It did keep me from attaining some of the milestones I wished to attain as a writer, so to speak. Is that to say that I didn't get all written when I was on the Earth Plane, as I had intended? No. For it did come—the words—the pearls of wisdom we all speak of from here in the Light—when it was supposed to. It was all Divinely Timed, as is your writing.

Oh, writer's block. In some ways it is like another type of blockage that occurs with the bowels. I shall go no further with that, as I know that you know of what I speak! And truly, it is a bit "unladylike" for me to even bring it up, but it is a quite accurate analogy. You do get stopped up at times as a writer with your words—some writers more than others. Does that make the writers who are "stopped up" any less than the writers who are not? Of course not! For we are all, as has been mentioned here, interconnected. And we are all most definitely equal in the eyes of the Universe!

So what to do when the writer's block comes to "call?" How to unblock oneself?

First, know that this too shall pass, as they say. This is just a "leg" of your writing journey. A leg you probably want to amputate, but a necessary leg for a necessary reason. Here are some potential reasons why you are experiencing writer's block. This may help you understand it, so then you can get "through" it and move on with fabulous words, words, words on the page, page, page!

1) Fear. Yes, I do hit the hard stuff first! Do you fear that you won't be able to get onto the page what you'd like to get onto the page in the Divine right time and in the Divine right manner, so that it "shines?" Fear will stop you up every time! Just know that you have created this fear for yourself, and so you can "un-create it."

2) Disdain. Hmmm. Of what am I speaking here? Here I am speaking of your disdain for yourself. For your annoyance that the words aren't flowing. This becomes a sort of self-fulfilling prophecy. You become angry with yourself, which breeds disdain, which makes you paralyzed when it comes to the written word.

3) Doubt. Doubt that you are able to get the words down that will sing and "speak" to the world—or the very least to those who choose to consume your words. Doubt that you can do what your soul is crying out for you to do! You can see how this would indeed paralyze your fingers and brain, even! A quick cure for this is to remind yourself of Divine Timing—that no mistakes are made, ever. Truly, you will say what you were meant to say, just as you were meant to say it. You need only begin!

4) You aren't ready. All of the pieces to this particular word puzzle have not settled in your brain. They haven't all come together, so to speak, so that you can impart the message that is niggling your brain. Here you can see the value in doing something else until the pieces come together. That something else most likely is resting your mind,

doing something fun, eating, or resting your physical body!

Now that you've reviewed the various reasons why you may be procrastinating and not writing those ultra-wonderful words on the page, you most likely have identified the reason or reasons that you are stopped up at this time. By doing this, you may find that simply accessing and acknowledging the reason helps you to get unstuck and start writing! Or you may find that a good night's sleep or quick nap is in order. You will know what to do once you access the reason for your writer's block in the first place.

> *I will close for now, Dear Fellow Scribes. I thank you again for reading and listening to the likes of me! Although I do thank you for adoring my writing, as I know many of you do! For that truly is the joy of the writing life. Knowing that there are readers who adore what you write—or at the very least find it absolutely fascinating!*
> *Yours Forever and a Day,*
> *Virginia Woolf*

ADELINE VIRGINIA WOOLF was an English writer born on January 25, 1882. She died at the age of 59, due to suicide, on March 28, 1941. She is best known as a pioneer in using stream-of-consciousness as a narrative tool and is highly regarded as the most important modernist author of the 20th Century. Many of her novels were bestsellers, such as *To the Lighthouse*, *Mrs. Dalloway*, and *A Room of One's Own*. She also wrote essays on an array of subjects, including literary history, artistic theory, and the politics of power. Woolf suffered from lifelong depression, which worsened over time with the loss of many loved ones. She took her own life by filling her pockets with stones and walking into the River Ouse.

"*For most of history, Anonymous was a woman.*"
—Virginia Woolf

38

⇝ CHARLES DICKENS ⇜

Extraordinary to connect with you Dear Scribes of the Earth Plane! I am most honored and eager to begin here, and so I shall. But first! Charles Dickens here. Introductions are always wise, are they not? A quick tidbit further covered in my "bio"—I wrote A Christmas Carol.

Introductions. Predications. Salutations. Mesmerizations. Yes, you are correct! The latter word is not truly a word, and yet, it is the prerogative of writers—those in and out of the Light Plane—to "make up" their own words, as they see fit!

But why did I mention these "things" above? It is most necessary; vital even, that you access that which you want to present. That you encapsulate that which you want to present—prior to imparting on your writing journey. I know, I know. This is in some respects an antithesis to what other writers/scribes have suggested in these pages. For that I must say that my "method" that I will share here isn't always appropriate. But when it is appropriate, it works quite grandly!

So here, Dear Scribes and Readers, is my "method." That worked quite well for me as Charles on the Earth Plane toiling away as I wrote!

What do you wish to say with your work? Call it the theme, if you wish, the lesson, the parable, even. But do come up with a seed of that which you wish to impart. I am not talking specifics here. I am talking broad brushstrokes. But in these large brushstrokes you will find a skeleton of your work of sorts—a pathway for your words to travel.

And when you come full circle—when you "finish" the work—you will have hit all of the pulse points—the plot and lesson points—that you wished to hit.

So how does one go about this? How do you figure out, if you will, what you want to say before you even know much about the story itself? As I mentioned, broad brushstrokes. For instance, here are a few themes that might resonate with you—with what you wish to impart at this time and space on the Earth Plane.

1) Love of self
2) Love of another
3) Love of mankind
4) Patience through perseverance
5) Wisdom
6) To embrace life's many ironies
7) To love unconditionally

Yes, I do mention love quite a bit. It is as it should be—for in many ways, love truly does "make the world go around."

You can see by looking at these potential themes that each would lend a quite different tenor to your work. That each would most certainly teach different lessons—different kernels of wisdom—different ways of being/existing.

Once you have your general theme, you will find that the story comes more freely. For your theme is of a sort, a tour director. It leads the way to the points—those plot/pulse points. It helps you navigate the path of your words while you navigate your readers' lovely journeys reading your words.

That is all for now. For I have run out of "space" here. Wordiness was a strong suit for me as Charles—at the same time it could make me write "off the rails," if you will. But no matter! For I am here now to tell you that you are on the right track! You can, I can see now from here as you read this—you can and are accessing your theme as you read this. I daresay your fingers are itching to start as you access that theme!

I wish you an ever exciting journey following your theme to your foregone conclusions that will present themselves in a most wondrous fashion!

Yours Forever Truly,
Charles Dickens

CHARLES JOHN HUFFAM DICKENS was an English writer born on February 7, 1812. He died at the age of 58, due to a stroke, on June 9, 1870. He is best known for his classic novels, *Oliver Twist*, *A Christmas Carol*, *David Copperfield*, *A Tale of Two Cities*, and *Great Expectations*. His novel, *A Christmas Carol*, is still popular today and has been adapted into movies and plays. Dickens was inspired by the voices of the characters and was known for giving theatrical book readings, even going so far as to use different voices to animate the characters. Dickens was one of eight children, and his father spent time in debtor's prison. He was forced to work in a shoe polish factory and was left to live alone when the rest of his family moved closer to his father's prison. His experiences of hardship and loneliness changed how he viewed the world, and he would later draw on his experiences in a number of his novels. His father got out of prison when he was fifteen, but Dickens still had to work, so he got a job as a reporter and stenographer. Then he did sketches for newspapers and magazines. He compiled the drawings into his first book, *Sketches by Boz*.

"Whatever I have tried to do in life, I have tried with all my heart to do it well; whatever I have devoted myself to, I have devoted myself completely; in great aims and in small I have always thoroughly been in earnest."

—Charles Dickens

39

⇴ Gustave Flaubert ⇷

Hello, I am most honored to present here. Gustave Flaubert at your most humble service. Here to give you a few words of wisdom—be they what they may come to be!

How shall I help you with your writing journey? What can I say that will make the journey even more flavorful and exciting! For truly, it is possible to have a most exciting—even titillating—life as a writer without even leaving your desk, or computer nowadays!

The mind is a wondrous "thing." Actually, the imagination, which makes the mind its home, is the most wonderful thing. When you let your imagination run wild, run crazy, run and roam free—my, oh, my, what treasures you shall find! For as your mind runs, your mind does tip things over here and there as it goes. Some of those items your mind does tip over on its way to the races or the roses, you might just pass by. But I advise you to try, if you are so drawn, to stop at some of the proverbial "apple carts" your mind tips over and examine the contents strewn about on the floor or path.

For in these upsets and spills you will most certainly find gems. Gems that you can then use to begin the what-if game. For truly it is the what-if game that has created some of the most brilliant literature throughout the ages. (However, I must say here and now that your writing/your prose is most magnificent, always!)

Back to the gems you may find lying about after your imagination tears through, as if a cyclone. Treasures unearthed—even when they don't appear to be treasures! For truly, I must say here and now, it was such an unearthing of the more basic aspects of life and letting the leaves blow and fall where they may that allowed me to come up with what is most likely my most magnificent and well-known work as Gustave—*Madame Bovary*. I allowed the chips and pieces of life that get strewn about by an imaginative wind unearth themselves and expose themselves, so to speak, so that I could draw from them the treasures of which I inserted into the book—truly the treasures that drove the book.

So go ahead. Upset your own imagination apple carts. Let your mind go to great lengths—great perilous journeys, even, so that you may then have an upset cart from which to work your way through the pile and find the gems.

Once you have found the gems, use the what-if game to your utmost advantage. For example, say you find that your imagination upset a pile of prose from which you find a few "key" terms, including puppy and lost and found and avarice and glee. What if you put those four terms together? What if someone were to steal the puppy? Someone gleeful. Yet, at the same time, the owner of the puppy is quite powerful. Of course, this is a rather odd scenario. For who wants to steal a puppy? Unless the puppy belongs to a king, perhaps? Or the puppy holds the keys to a cancer cure? Maybe the puppy is an unknowing spy? The possible scenarios do truly boggle the mind, do they not?

The point is to find unusual scenarios—especially for your readers in this time and place. Juxtapose various scenarios against one another so that they may present odd scenarios that you can then play a rather fun and enlightening game of what-if with. I do promise you that you will come up with some rather odd scenarios that won't quite work—but planted amongst such scenarios you will find a true gem that shines brighter and harder than any you've ever seen. Pick it up and begin writing, Dear Fellow Scribes, and you will most certainly find your own *Madame Bovary*!

> *That's it from me, Dear Readers and Scribes. Once again, thank you most kindly and with honor, for listening. I bid you a most blessed life writing, writing, writing, once you've imagined, imagined, imagined.*
>
> *Yours Truly,*
> *Gustave Flaubert*

GUSTAVE FLAUBERT was a French novelist born on December 12, 1821. He died at the age of 58, due to a stroke, on May 8, 1880. He was best known for his debut novel, *Madame Bovary*, which used the technique of literary realism. Flaubert's father was a surgeon and his mother a distinguished magistrate. He started his writing in school, publishing in a review, *Le Colibri*, but it was more of a pastime. It wasn't until Flaubert started law school at Faculty of Law in Paris that he was diagnosed with epilepsy. The diagnosis caused him to give up law and devote his time to his writing.

> "Be regular and orderly in your life, so that you may be violent and original in your work."
> "The art of writing is the art of discovering what you believe."
>   —Gustave Flaubert

40

❧ Honoré de Balzac ☙

Highly honored to present here, Fellow Scribes. Highly honored to give you as much information as possible in this space about how to make your writing shine as brightly as it may! Honoré de Balzac at your most humble service!

Drama and intrigue! Truly, Dear Scribes that is what your readers wish to hear and see. They may not always acknowledge this, but the juicier the better for many! I did find that writing as Balzac. My writing about the *bourgeois* was in fact just that—a bit racy at times! Does that mean that you must put a bit of racy into your novels and writing? No, not necessarily. But I would suggest putting in some intrigue and drama, of one form or another.

Here is what I might propose to you. Look deep in to your own well when you write. Look for those plot points, if you will, that will pluck at your own heartstrings. Here is the order of feelings from that heartstring pulling that I would suggest. It is this string of feelings and perceptions that will intrigue your readers—put a bit of drama into their lives—and then cause them to keep turning the pages.

1) Curiosity

2) Intrigue

3) Blind faith and trust that what comes next will be quite thrilling!

4) A wish for better for the heroine, hero, and sometimes even villain!

5) Knowing that something is amiss, but not able to put one's finger on the niggling feeling.

6) Glimmers of truth, followed by dark corridors of not knowing.

7) A light at the end of the proverbial tunnel that makes the reader flip page after page in order to rush into the clearing of light where all will be revealed.

8) A door which swings open in the tunnel, inviting the reader in. A mysterious, curious door that has an even brighter light shining from within than the one at the end of the tunnel.

9) A warning to the reader that if he or she takes this segue that the light at the end of the tunnel could very well disappear.

10) A rather stunning "reveal," if you will, inside the new doorway, should the reader walk through, which of course, the reader will.

11) A promise that the light at the end of the tunnel is indeed there, should the reader just take a small detour within the new door. A detour filled with more surprises, and treasures of understanding and wonder.

12) The reader finds himself or herself in the clearing that he or she knew was there at the end of the tunnel. All is exactly as it seems it should be, yet the readers is quite entranced and enthralled and surprised by what lies in the clearing.

I do hope that this outline of sorts does help you as you create your splendid plot points designed to intrigue and even ensnare the reader. I do encourage you to plug in drama along the way, as you go. For readers do lap up drama. Your plot—the winding nature of it—will certainly keep them intrigued along the way.

There is, of course, character along the way with all of this. And though I don't have much space left here, I will give a few words of encouragement and advice when it comes to character. First, let characters be themselves. When characters appear, avoid trying to "fix" them to suit the plot. Rather, let characters navigate the plot. That will provide more natural and interesting prose. For what a delight to see how a character may react to your most intriguing, twisting and turning plot!

That is all for now, Dear Readers and Writers! I wish you a most intriguing and dramatic writing life!
  Yours Always Truly,
  Honoré de Balzac

HONORÉ DE BALZAC was a French novelist born on May 20, 1799. He died at the age of 51, due to disease, on August 18, 1850. He was most famous for his novels and short stories, the more popular of them being *La Comédie humaine, Father Goriot, Two Poets,* and *Eugenie Grandet*. It is apparent from his work that Balzac was a supreme observer and chronicler of the contemporary society in France at the time of his writing. His novels are considered unsurpassed for their large casts of interesting, diverse and vital characters and their intricate social relationships, as well as scandal amongst the aristocracy and the *haute bourgeoisie*. Balzac was also an avid lover of coffee, who drank as much as fifty cups a day. He even wrote a short story about coffee titled, *The Pleasures and Pains of Coffee*.

"There is no such thing as a great talent without great will power."
—Honoré de Balzac

41

❧ Edward Albee ❦

Hey, Cool Writing Cats! Edward Albee at your service here! I am so proud and honored to present here, as we all are! But it is quite a "trip," as I used to say on the Earth Plane. And who woulda thought I'd be "back," so to speak? Well, of course, I knew, because we planned this a long time ago, by Earth Plane standards, but that's another story. Let's get to this!

Another story. There's always another story, isn't there? Something else brewing in your head and heart, even, as you go about attempting to finish your current writing project or projects. So how not to go down the proverbial "let's take a look at this new writing project right now, so I can procrastinate on finishing what is just about done?"

That's the thing, right? You know you're soooo close to finishing up something—be it a book, short story, or script. Yet this "new" story starts prodding you. As if to say, put down that "old" idea, I'm here, and I'm new, new, new! And sometimes you can't help but do that. You may even find yourself writing part of the new novel or script, all the while thinking that you really need to finish the other. Especially if you have a deadline!

I'm here to say, that's okay. And actually good. For you want to record the new idea so it's not lost in the deluge of ideas coming at you—because you know it's a "keeper." At the same time, you do want to finish the other work so that you can do what you set out to do, which is spread your work around so that others could experience it and then perhaps find your work as a jumping off point for their work. For truly, we are all co-creating here together, and it can be and is a total blast!

So go ahead. Go ahead and record some notes—write some scenes, even. But when you peter out on the new stuff, as you know you will, turn right back around and get back to the old stuff. Actually, it works quite well, because you can then use the steam from the new—at least the tail end of the steam from the new—to spur you on to finish the "old," which will then get published and distributed and become your new published work!

If you do get the call, so to speak, the urging to just abandon the old and get on with the new, I suggest hanging up on the caller. Of course, this is free will. You can do whatever the heck you want to do!! That's the ultra-cool "thing" about being—simply being. We all have free will, and it's really freeing to use it. But I'm telling you from personal experience that answering that call can, in fact, delay things a bit for you. It's a pretty straightforward process. You will end up having half-done works. And if you keep it up, a pile of half-done manuscripts! Which you know, and I know, aren't ready for anything but being completed!

I get it—actually, a lot of us Scribes in the Light get it. It's hard sometimes when the middle of your book or script starts to drag a bit. You started out with a bang and you know that you've got an explosive ending, but you gotta get through the middle, and make it compelling enough that readers and viewers want to keep turning the page or watching.

It's kinda like when you've cleaned out a closet you've been wanting to clean out for a long time. You're excited to start at first, with visions of the closet when you're finished dancing in your head. But then you've got the contents of the closet surrounding you! You know that all of these pieces need to get tossed, given away, or put back in place where they fit seamlessly. So rather than leaving the mess in the hallway and going on to the living room to make another mess, just get that closet finished, will ya! Then move on.

Okay, so I'm done with my lecture—something else I loved to do on the Earth Plane! I'm going to sign off here. Get to it, Cool Writing Cats! Have a blast as you go!
  Sincerely (truly!),
  Edward Albee

EDWARD ALBEE was an American playwright born on March 12, 1928. He died at the age of 88, due to diabetes, on September 16, 2016. He is best known for his works, *The Zoo Story*, *The Sandbox*, *Who's Afraid of Virginia Woolf*, and *A Delicate Balance*. His play, *The Sandbox*, was written in three weeks. His most iconic play, *Who's Afraid of Virginia Woolf*, won the Tony Award for Best Play and its rendition to film won an Academy Award and was selected by the United States National Film Registry for preservation by the Library of Congress. Two of his plays won the Tony Award for Best Plays, and three of his plays won the Pulitzer Prize for Drama. Albee worked his way to the top. While learning how to write plays, he moved to Greenwich Village in New York and took many odd jobs to support himself. His first two plays debuted in Berlin before becoming big enough to bring to New York.

"Good writers define reality; bad ones merely restate it. A good writer turns fact into truth; a bad writer will, more often than not, accomplish the opposite."
  —Edward Albee

42

➤ Victor Hugo ➤

Hello, Dear Fellow Scribes. Victor Hugo here. I am most honored to present here, as you know many before me have mentioned! How absolutely, positively grand, as you might say in your day today! On to the message just for you!

Of what shall I impart to you today? What can I say that will make your toes tingle, if you will, about the possibilities of the written word? For tingling is most certainly a "good" thing when it comes to writing and imparting the words to the page. In imparting the thoughts that you wish to get into the heads of those who read. Yet, truly, you wish to get those words—the very essence of those words—into the hearts of those who read. Wouldn't you say that is what you are truly trying to do? For without a tugging on the heart. Without a feeling of delight or dread or happiness or glee or....you get the picture. Without a feeling, so to speak, the words are quite like cardboard. They just lay there on the page and do very little.

So how does one make the words come alive? How does one impart the emotions that are so vital to the message? So vital to how your readers will then feel about the message so that the words will then resonate with their souls?

First, I would like to tell you to simply breathe when you start a passage in your work. Rather than become quite fidgety or worried about saying exactly the "right" thing, simply breathe and give yourself time to write what comes from your own heart. That is where all of the magic happens when you are writing. In your heart. For think of this. Isn't it quite sterile in your mind? Literally and figuratively, the mind is a sterile sort of object. While it can have very imaginative thoughts, it is a vessel that truly is relaying the information. The imaginary thoughts that ensue from the mind are most certainly coming; originating from the heart. And the deeper in the heart are those morsels of life wisdom pulled from, the more profound a feeling those morsels will ensue in your readers.

So do pull from your heart when you write. How do I do that? You may wonder. How do I pull from my heart when I'm pretty sure I've been pulling from my mind all of this time? Well, for one, know that you haven't been just pulling from your mind. For I assure you, when you read your own work and others read it and they react with a visceral "gut" reaction, they are reading words that have come from your heart. They may have passed through your mind, but they most certainly started from your heart. Otherwise, they wouldn't have elicited the emotions that they did.

So the answer, you may be suspecting at this point, is to know you are pulling from your heart when the message touches your heart. In fact, you may very well feel a pulling sensation in your heart as you write—like fingers plucking the strings on a string instrument such as a harp or violin. They will be twinges that fill your heart with something that may seem foreign at first, but it is in fact knowledge of the Universe coming from your heart so that you can then share it with your readers.

> *Well, I do wax on, do I not? But then that was one of my fortes as Victor. I do hope that this brings you some measure of understanding about what it means to "write from the heart." How doing so will make your words sing on the page so that they sing their way right into the hearts of all those who read your precious words!*
>
> *Yours until the end of time and back!*
> *Victor Hugo*

VICTOR HUGO was a French writer born on February 26, 1802. He died at the age of 83, of pneumonia, on May 22, 1885. He is best known as the author of *Le Miserables*, which is one of the longest books in history, comprising 1,900 pages in French. *Le Miserables* was and still is very popular. It has been turned in to plays and movies. He also wrote another very famous and notable book, *The Hunchback of Notre-Dame*, which was made into a movie by Disney. Hugo is thought to be one of the best-known and greatest writers from France. He was also a poet, artist, and dramatist of the Romantic Movement. He originally studied law, but his mother's encouragement helped fuel his writing. He started a review, *Le Conservateur Littéraire*, where he published his own articles. Hugo married his childhood friend, publishing his first book of poems the same year. They had five children together.

"*Nothing is more powerful than an idea whose time has come.*"
—Victor Hugo

43

❖ May Sarton ❖

Hello! May Sarton here. I am most honored to present here. Truly, I am humbled by this experience. I shall do my best to impart words of wisdom that will, hopefully, most certainly help you with your writing travails and triumphs! On to the message!

Compunction. Hesitancy. Doubt. Fear. Why do I mention such "downer" types of words? For one, I mention them because they tend to trip us writers up! They tend to make us doubt our words in such a way that we may falter as we write, or we may hesitate to start writing, or even worse, we may not write altogether. In my life as May, I did have a few, if not all, of such struggles. Of course, I wished to learn lessons from those struggles, as you most certainly may be doing yourself! Yet, most likely since you are now reading this, you would like to cast such struggles away—so that you may reach the apex of your understanding in terms of what you wish to write and how you wish to write it. And that you wish to write it in such a way that you have no compunction. That there is no hesitancy. That there is no doubt, and there certainly is no fear!

How to get to this most blessed place of deep insight and no fear to write what you know in your heart is "right" for you to write!

How about this? How about if you write with the idea that no one will see what you are writing? That you are as a child cloistered in her (or his!) bed, writing in your journal. You are squirreling away all of the precious thoughts about yourself and your life and those in your life. And you have no intentions of anyone seeing these pearls!

How does that make you feel when you sit down to write? Do you feel a release, so to speak, when you think this way? Do the words come more quickly and more gaily? Do they spring onto the page in such a way that you know that more will soon spring after them? Like tiny acrobats doing their flips and turns and twists? That is a good thing, wouldn't you say? That means that you have unlatched Pandora's Box in your brain and the words will now flow.

As the words begin to flow, avoid letting go of the image of you writing for an audience of one. For if you do—if you let the "larger audience" sneak in, including critics, you will most certainly see that the acrobatics of the words stop. The little acrobats retreat back inside the words, so to speak, and there is a silence that ensues. And then a sort of mental constipation, if you will.

Am I suggesting that you pretend? Of course, I am. For we both know that once you do get those gems on the page; once you do tell your own story—the story that your heart and soul is stretching and pleading to relate—you will one day let the whole world in on your little "journal" secret writings! And remember this—they will not be little words. They will be quite grand words. You will amaze yourself at what you write when you write with no compunction or doubt or fear or hesitancy. You may even wonder if it was truly you who wrote what you have on paper. But I am here to tell you. It will be you. Glorious you! Singing your own glorious song for all of the world to hear and relish and enjoy and savor.

That is all for now, Dear Readers and Writers. I am honored to have "spoken" here. I do wish you a glorious, glorious writing career!
  Yours Always,
  May Sarton

ELEANORE MAY SARTON was an American poet born on May 3, 1912. She died at the age of 83, due to breast cancer, on July 16, 1995. Sarton was best known for her accomplishments as a memoirist and poet. Her first book of poems was "Encounters in April," and her first novel was *The Single Hound*. In her memoir, *Mrs. Stevens Hears the Mermaids Singing*, released in 1965, she bravely came out as lesbian. Her memoir, *Journal of Solitude*, was about her encounters with a female artist. Sarton originally worked as an actress and even moved to New York City to pursue a career in acting. Her move paid off, because she got an apprenticeship at the Civic Repertory Theatre. After a couple of years, she branched off and opened her own place called the Associated Actors Theatre. When that company went under, she decided to devote all of her time to writing. Sarton was also a frequent traveler and met some fellow authors through her trips, including Virginia Woolf (#37), Elizabeth Bowen, and W.H. Auden.

"We have to dare to be ourselves, however frightening or strange that self may prove to be."
"The more articulate one is, the more dangerous words become."
—Mary Sarton

44

⇾ George Bernard Shaw ⇽

Dearest Fellow Scribes on the Earth Plane. Coming to you directly from the Light! George Bernard Shaw here. At your most humble service. Ever grateful for this most auspicious opportunity. On to my "message," if you will.

Of what would I speak today! Drumrolls. Thunder. Magnificent flashes of lighting. That is truly what you wish for your readers (and viewers, should your work make it onto the "big screen," as they say).

You most certainly want to cause a sort of ruckus with your work, don't you? You want to awe and inspire and make people cry with joy or sorrow. So long as they cry!

How to go about this? How to bring out the absolute best in your work, so that it may be the absolute best in the eyes and ears of your readers and viewers?

Hmmmm. This does seem like a conundrum of sorts, does it not? How does one do this? How does one stay on the straight and narrow, so to speak, and get the job done while at the same time pull from one's heart, and the heart of all readers and viewers, the depths of despair when needed (pathos), and then joy that seeps into ones bones and infuses the core of a person's very being!

Drumroll! You can see, perhaps, what is happening here? It is foreshadowing, yes. It is pacing! Pacing. Pacing. Pacing. Even with these three words, I have created a sort of pace.

Pacing is what you should and may, if you choose, strive for. Pacing that gets the readers to continue to turn page after page after page after page. Or keep watching your play or your movie—until the very bitter or bittersweet or joyous end!

Here I shall enumerate a few of my "tidbits" regarding getting to the heart of the matter and taking a firm grasp of the reigns with your pacing.

1) Breathe. I do know that some before me here have mentioned this. Truly, taking a big breath before you start and remembering to take breaths along the way helps you get down to the "nitty gritty" of pacing. At the same time, it does help you keep a good pace. For if your breathing is shallow, your pace may be too abrupt and quick. And if you are holding your breath as you write, you may lose pacing altogether!

2) Think ahead, but not too far ahead. Consider this. You are marching along, trying to get to a destination. If you think far ahead to your endpoint—to that point when you arrive and sit down, so to speak—you may suddenly in your head stop. Stop and sit down, correct? You don't want to do this when you are creating pacing. When you are creating a buildup with your writing that is going to bring you to the climax with its ear-shattering crescendo! For if you envision a nice cushy seat on which to sit, that pacing will simply fall on deaf ears, so to speak. So keep moving and thinking ahead in tiny steps so that you may keep the pacing!

3) Foreshadowing. Of course, this is a most vital aspect of pacing. It is the very essence of pacing, to be exact. For it will help you keep readers intrigued and get them intrigued if they aren't already. It will help you to unroll your plot as you unroll the secrets along the way. The secrets that beget more secrets and that lead the reader to the ending—to their truth, which they shall find at the ending.

4) That brings up the next point. Think of universal truths as you write your suspenseful plot. Think of how we are all interconnected. While this might not be at the forefront of your mind while you are writing—as it probably shouldn't be—it is good to keep it at the back

of your mind. For this knowing will keep you on the path. The path of pure, blissful, true, every so effective pacing!

5) Know. This is the last and final stage of this divine pacing. Know you are on the exact right path as you clip along, giving your reading and viewing audience what they crave. An understanding of themselves woven together with an understanding of the Universe—most delightfully packaged up into a cocoon of sorts of utter, divine magic and revelation like they think they may never have experienced, and yet their soul truly has experienced! That revelation resonates and satisfies to the very bones!

That is all for now, Dear Fellow Scribes! I do wish you a Divinely Inspired writing life. I do!
Yours Forever Truly,
  George Bernard Shaw

GEORGE BERNARD SHAW was an Irish playwright born on July 26, 1856. He died at the age of 94, due to kidney failure, on November 2, 1950. He is best known as a comic dramatist, social propagandist, and literary critic. His play, *Mrs. Warrens Profession,* was considered provocative at the time, because it portrayed a prostitute, who worked her way up to being a proprietor of brothels. His most widely known play, *Pygmalion*, won an Academy Award and was adapted into the musical, *My Fair Lady*. His plays, *Don Juan in Hell, Man and Superman, Heartbreak House,* and *Saint Joan,* were some of his greatest works.

"Some men see things as they are and ask why. Others dream things that never were and ask why not."
"Life isn't about finding yourself. Life is about creating yourself."
  —George Bernard Shaw

45

❧ Jane Austen ❦

Honored to be here. To present here. Jane Austen at your most humble service. I shall do my absolute best to give you some words of wisdom about writing and the life of a writer. The solitary life of a writer, so that you may know that you are most certainly on the right writing path for you!

Solitude. How does that sound to you when you roll that word around on your tongue, so to speak? Does it make you want to write? Does it make you wish that you were putting words down on the page at that very moment? Does it make you want to sequester yourself so that you can create, create, create? If so, that is most certainly a good omen, so to speak. That is most certainly a good sign. For wishing and wanting to be alone so that you might create with words—that is a most blessed wish.

But what of the writer who feels too much of solitude? Who indeed has some issues, as you now say, about being alone? What of such a writer? Would he or she perhaps have some writer's stoppage, some writer's block from too loud a solitude, as the great writer, Bohumil Hrabal (#28), called one of his most well-known works?

Can solitude indeed be too loud so that you are unable or unwilling to produce as you might if the solitude weren't too hard to bear? If the solitude wasn't bearing down on you in a most cloying effect?

Do I speak here of the loneliness that tends to plague writers—for writing is a most solitary occupation? In a way, yes, but this goes deeper. Indeed, I am referring to when you are hurrying through your days so that you might have some solitude to write, yet when you do finally have that solitude, the empty space, the quiet, seems too loud. So loud, in fact, that you don't know what to write.

Though I had some solitude as Jane Austen, I also had some duties that I needed to attend to in terms of family. After working on those duties, I admit that I would find myself holed up ready to write, yet the silence that I had finally managed to find was deafening.

Why do I ramble on and on about this? Because I wish to first let you know that this is most certainly common. That even the likes of a "famous" writer such as myself has scrambled into solitude with the intent to let the words pour forth, yet nothing comes!

How did I work my way out of the too loud solitude? Well, for one, I hummed. Yes, I would hum a bit under my breath, until I began to not notice the silence and solitude. Until my mind began to fill up with the wonderful hum of words, words, words! Once that occurred, I was, as you say nowadays, off and running!

Truly, it may only take a small move on your part—a small ritual—to get you out of your loud, empty head and onto the page and the marvelous characters and settings and plots and situations that you present on those pages. When this occurs, my Dear Writing Friends, you will most certainly find yourself pouring forth a torrent of writing wisdom.

That is all, Dear Students and Fellow Scribes of the Light. I do wish you a lifetime of words that impress themselves onto the page with very little effort on your part. Once you banish the solitude that is too loud, you can then embrace those quiet moments that allow you to access your messages for the world.

Sincerely and Truly Yours Forever,
Jane Austen

JANE AUSTEN was an English novelist born on December 16, 1775. She died at the age of 41, due to Addison's disease, on July 18, 1817. She is best known for her novels, *Sense and Sensibility*, *Pride and Prejudice*, *Northanger Abbey*, *Mansfield Park*, *Emma*, and *Persuasion*. Many of her novels were so well loved that they are considered classics and are even implemented into the educational system as required reading. Jane Austen was one of seven children, with one sister and five brothers. She grew up in an open learning environment, learning mostly from what her father, Reverend George Austen, and brothers could teach her. She also learned from reading the many books in her father's library. Jane and her sister, Cassandra, attended boarding school, where they learned French, music, and dancing. When they returned from boarding school, Austen, with the full support of her father, started to explore her writing. Her father supplied her with everything she needed, including paper and writing tools, in order to allow her to express her creative side. After many years and the support of her family, Austen wrote *Love and Friendship*, a collection of works that sparked her passion in writing. She went on to write, *First Impressions*, which is now known as *Pride and Prejudice*.

"Give a girl an education and introduce her properly into the world, and ten to one but she has the means of settling well, without further expense to anybody."
—Jane Austen

46

❧ Henry Thoreau ☙

Hello there, Dear Fellow Scribes! Henry Thoreau here. An aside, before I begin imparting all that I will here! When Julie accessed me, she kept hearing Ralph Waldo Emerson, who is number 17 above. She was a bit baffled and concerned that her antennae for this, so to speak, was picking up static. However, she soon discovered that in my life as Henry, I was indeed tied to Ralph. His protégé, to be exact! So another confirmation, of course! On to the topic at hand! Glorious writing and the ever so wonderful writing life!

To follow. To lead. Which way is best, one may wonder, regarding writing? In some sense, it is most certainly a good idea to follow when one is just starting out. Though truly, Dear Fellow Scribes, you have most definitely been doing this for many lifetimes, so you aren't truly starting out in this one! But you do need to get your bearings, so to speak. Start on training wheels and work your way up from there, as they say in this day.

Back to the message, so to speak. Please do forgive the segue! At any rate, how does one know when one is ready for the "big bicycle" without the training wheels or the support of another writer, who might be assisting you? How does one know when one can simply write and edit one's own work and then cast it out into the world?

How about asking yourself a few questions, which I shall enumerate here? They could start as your first step to determining if it is indeed time to spread your wings and fly the coop, so to speak. I know, I know. I am mixing metaphors at random here! Truly, I am doing so, because it's quite fun, and because I can. When you know you can, Dear Fellow Scribes, that sets you up to soar with your writing. Another little tidbit I wished to relate to you here. But back to "the list."

1) How do you feel about the words you've put on the page? Truly feel? Not how you think you *should* feel, but how you *really* feel? Do you feel excitement and joy? Do you think that others would most certainly find some merit in what you've said? Or is there something niggling at you that there is still a bit more work to be done? Would it be a good idea to ask for the advice of another?

2) Do you feel filled up? Do you feel satisfied, as if you've eaten a giant dinner and have filled yourself to the brim, so to speak? Or do you feel as if you still have a thirst or a hunger for something more? That there is one more morsel that will indeed top you off?

3) How do you feel about putting the work out there? Does it give you satisfaction and anticipation? Or does it make you want to retrieve the manuscript to give it a few more tweaks? Not because you think you should, once again, but because you think it needs a bit more.

4) Have you read the piece aloud to yourself and to another and did it sing? Did it resonate? Did the birds break forth in song in reality or in your head? Did the angels sing? If so, it is most certainly "ready to go," as they say. Ready to fly from your fingertips into the Universe for everyone who was meant to, to read and enjoy! If, however, when you read, you falter a bit here and there, look at those areas, Dear Fellow Scribe, make the "nips and tucks" that you find of value, and then let the manuscript contents soar!

5) Do you just know? Do you have faith that all in your work is as it should be? Every last little morsel sings, sings, sings! Then you know that it is most certainly "time" to release your "baby."

That is all for me here and now, Fellow Scribes! I thank you ever so kindly for listening to the ramblings of an Old Soul Scribe! I do! Much joy I wish you during your writing travels. And I urge you to polish up the pearls you have there and let them soar into the Universe, like an Eagle taking great flight!

Yours Forever Truly,
Henry Thoreau

HENRY THOREAU was an American essayist born on July 12, 1817. He died at the age of 44, due to tuberculosis, on May 6, 1862. He is best known for staying on Walden Pond for two years while he wrote his master work, *Walden*. He was also Ralph Waldo Emerson's (#17) protégé. Henry David Thoreau and Ralph Waldo Emerson are widely praised for being the two most influential Transcendentalist writers during their time. Transcendentalism is described as "a philosophy that rejects the idea that knowledge can be fully derived from experience and observation; rather, truth resides in the spiritual world." Thoreau is considered a great essayist and critic, who embraced nature and practiced individualism. With help from his mentor, Ralph Waldo Emerson, Thoreau attacked the political, religious and cultural values of American society and embraced nonconformity.

"It's not what you look at that matters, it's what you see."
—Henry David Thoreau

47

➤ HENRY JAMES ⬅

Greetings, Dear Scribes of the Earth Plane! Henry James here. Much honored, as it were, to be presenting here. I will do my best to impart the best information I may here.

Information. That is what you are expressing when you access what your soul wishes to express and then get that onto your page, do you not? Yet, here I say soul, don't I? This may cause some of you to bristle a bit. For information—facts—they certainly couldn't be housed in the soul, could they? Certainly, one would need to look things up in a book (yes, pun intended!), or on a spreadsheet, as you use nowadays. Those "true" facts could then be put on the page, for they have been verified by centered and logical minds. Then they are most certainly true.

If you think I may be talking with a tongue in cheek bent right now, you would be most right. For as you can imagine, here in the Light, we know that the only "true" answers come from within. That the only true answers are not facts and factoids. Rather, they are feelings and knowings. Hmmmm. How to rectify this with what you've been taught and what wishes to spring forth from your soul? This is quite an extraordinary quandary, is it not?

I say to you now in a way that most likely wouldn't be much different than when I was on the Earth Plane as Henry—hogwash, my dears! Do as you wish with your writing! Say what you wish with your writing! In fact, (haha-pun intended again!) go ahead and "make up" your own facts, for truly those "facts" that come from you are indeed representative of your own truths! That is what we could, if you so choose, look at here—truths. For truths trump facts any day, wouldn't you agree? Truths resonate. Truths uncover pearls of wisdom. Truths reveal that which could not be revealed until the truth appeared. Truths heal; they soothe; they provide a balm like no other!

So go ahead and express your truths as you write. I don't suggest you throw the facts out the window, so to speak, especially if you're doing what they call nonfiction writing! However, I do suggest that you focus on truths, your own truths, first and foremost. When you do this, you will find that your writing flows forth in such a way that you just know you are saying and doing everything you had planned to do when you set forth to come to the Earth Plane.

Do mix in some "facts." Even those "facts" that have been "verified" by ripe, solid, intellectual, "sane," (haha, yes again!) minds. For that will appease many of your readers. At the same time, your truths as they come forth onto the page and resonate with the hearts and souls of your readers—they will be what the readers step forth with as they go out into the world with your words imprinted on their hearts. Those truths they will adjust as they see fit to fit their own molds, their own imprints of their own truths.

They will take your truths and soar with them in a way that melds you and them and the entire Universe into one beautiful package that we can see here from the Light.

I tell you now, for you have seen it before and you will see it again. This magnificent package of knowledge—of truths and their underlings, facts, would blind you on the Earth Plane, yet it is an essential component of the power of the Universe!

I do drone on, do I not? But that is as it should and can be! I am highly honored to have been able to "speak" here and present to you my thoughts on truths and facts. May your days and nights writing keep you soaring on the clouds of your soul!

  Forever Yours,
  Henry James

HENRY JAMES was an American author born on April 15, 1843. He died at the age of 72, due to tuberculosis, on February 28, 1916. He is best known for his novels, *The Portrait of a Lady* and *The Turn of the Screw*. James is widely regarded as one of the greatest novelists of the English language for his influence of transitioning between the use of literary realism and literary modernism. His novel, *The Portrait of a Lady*, was turned into a movie. James also wrote short stories like, *The Beast in the Jungle*, and *The Aspern Papers*. As a child, James was shy. He loved reading books and was happiest observing others, rather than participating. He went to Harvard Law School and even worked as an editor for *The Atlantic Monthly*. He also traveled across Europe and became a British citizen a year before his passing. James never married. He preferred to live in solitude. While he enjoyed being social and observing, he was always careful to not get too involved.

"It's time to start living the life you've imagined."
  —Henry James

48

❖ Beatrix Potter ❖

Darling Fellow Scribes! How divine that I should present here! How grand! How superb! I do love this whole project, I do! Beatrix Potter here. Creator of the darling and dear Peter Rabbit. Who I must say, hopped into my life one day, and then, as you might guess, never left. Here are my thoughts on writing for you to peruse as you wish.

Characters. Creations. Characters that become your most well-known and "famous" creations! How does one go about accessing such characters? Recognizing them? And then harnessing them, so they can become the great characters we scribes all wish to create?

For one thing, there is no force in this. Truly, there is very little "creation" when it comes to such characters, or to be exact, really any characters. For characters present themselves to the writer. Characters tap you on the shoulder. They appear in your dreams. They walk across a wooden floor—a wisp of them—and then disappear. They whisper in your ear. They come through another or another's work. That is how these glorious characters appear. They simply knock on your door one day. Your task is to simply answer the door!

What does one do when one answers the door and there stands the most glorious, or in the case of Peter Rabbit, the most unusual character creature? Well, of course, do what you would do with just about anyone standing on your threshold, invite the character in! Where? Into your writing den. Into your special sphere where you create. Invite

CHANNELED WRITING TIPS

the character to come in and make himself or herself comfortable. In fact, encourage the character to do what he or she pleases. For truly, when you access the characters in this manner—in a way that allows them to do and be and say what they wish—then you will start a magical chain of events that leads to wondrous storytelling and characterization.

This all sounds a bit out of control, you may be thinking. Is there no rhyme or reason to this plan, you are wondering, as you look at your character sketch, which is a bit on the blank side? Yes, this is a little or even a lot "out of control," by Earth Plane standards. However, in the Light it is exactly how and why and as it should be! That, my dear Fellow Scribes is all that you need "worry" yourselves with. For the character will most certainly carve out the life and experiences that the character came here to do!

This may have you scratching your heads, so to speak. What the character came here to do? But isn't the character directly from my imagination? Isn't the character coming out of my "plans" to create a memorable and engaging character that will resound on the page? Yes and no. Yes, the character is most definitely coming from within you. But the difference here, Dear Fellow Scribe, is that you aren't actually creating the character. Rather, the character is born from a seed within you and then that character is either allowed to bloom as your soul intends, or the character is stifled. You will notice when you create a character who becomes stifled that the writing becomes stiff and downright boring. That the character appears more like a caricature and that cardboard becomes the theme!

So please do go ahead and let the characters get birthed in your soul/psyche, and then give them free reign to do as they see fit. Of course, you should and want to guide them along the plot points you've created, although I'd encourage you to make them loose points. At the same time, you want to allow them to scamper into a "forbidden" garden to forage for precious fruits. For it is those forbidden journeys and the revealed precious fruits that will make your writing shine and truly tell the stories you came here to tell!

That is all for now, Dear Fellow Scribes. I do wish you the most glorious of times with your writing and "hanging out" with your characters. Call on me whenever you wish for inspiration. For truly, I am only a hare's breath away!
   Always and Forever,
   Beatrix Potter

HELEN BEATRIX POTTER was an English writer born on July 28, 1866. She died at the age of 77, due to pneumonia, on December 22, 1943. She is best known for her children's books, her most famous being *The Tale of Peter Rabbit*. She also wrote *Jemima Puddle-Duck, Mrs. Tiggy-Winkle,* and *The Tale of Tom Kitten*. She was also an artist/illustrator, conservationist, and natural scientist. Potter was born into a wealthy upper-class family as an only child and heir to a cotton fortune. She was educated at home by governesses, so she was isolated from other children. Her love for animals and watercolor illustration stem from her long vacations in Scotland and the English Lake District. Her first book, *The Tale of Peter Rabbit*, was originally an illustrated letter sent to cheer up a sick child of her former governess. It was so well loved she decided to publish it privately. A year later, it was published commercially with tremendous success. In the next 20 years, she released 22 books. She did the illustrations for all of them using watercolor and even designed the books to be small enough for the smallest child to hold. Potter was also fond of fungi and would illustrate and document her findings. She wrote a paper on spore germination and presented it to the Linnean Society in 1897. She loved her farm and in her later years bred Herdwick Sheep.

"Thank goodness I was never sent to school; it would have rubbed off some of the originality."
—Beatrix Potter

49

❯ Paul Verlaine ❮

Dear Writing Scribes. Splendid to make your "acquaintance!" Although I daresay that we all know one another! But that is another matter. On to my message to you. About the solitary writer's life, as they say. Paul Verlaine at your most humblest of services.

Solitary writer's life. In some ways, this makes me chuckle. For certainly all of you glorious Dear Writing Scribes are far from alone. In fact, we Scribes of the Light hover at every possible turn! We most certainly do! In addition to hovering, we also whisper in your ears, put visions in your eyes and feathery wings on your shoulders so that you can fly throughout your dreams and visit us while we all discuss the writing life and your most splendid writing projects!

For you know when you awake some mornings and the plot has unfolded as you've slept, or a character is no longer putting you into a quandary, that we did all sit at a beautiful clear table that looks like glass, yet most certainly is made of mist, and hashed out your plot or helped you develop a most splendid character!

That is what I would like to impart to you Dear Writing Scribes. That though you may feel as if you are alone, truly you are never, ever alone! Quite frankly, it is impossible to be so. If that makes you feel as if "all eyes are on you," so to speak, then it is quite certainly that way! Of course, there is freewill that comes into play here on the Earth Plane, and you can most certainly tell us all to "take a hike," as you say now in your day. While you may feel as if we've done so, I am here to tell you that we simply scoot ourselves to the periphery of your knowing/your notice/your senses/your intuition. For we shall never, ever leave you, as I said.

How does one deal with this? This knowing that we are there? This knowing that we are only a breath away? Well, you could call on us, most certainly! You could tell us out loud or in your head the quandaries you find yourselves in with your characters. We will, in our own Divine way, find a way to tell you the answer, as we see it. For truly, we will be accessing the answer how your soul sees it, and then sending it back to you in a format that you can grasp and understand.

The writing life. Think of it as a life filled with many friends and acquaintances in the form of writing angels and guides and even the elemental realm. For we truly come forward when asked. And we stay rooted in the shadows when your soul reaches out, but your Earth Plane self keeps us at bay.

For those of you wondering if the fact that you've sent us away on numerous occasions will affect our ability to come forth when you want us to once again come, have no worries or fears. For we, as I mentioned, stay on the periphery of your lives, no matter what. And it only takes one request to send us scurrying/flying/scampering and swimming to be by your side in a heartbeat!

Good day to you, Dear Writing Scribes. I do wish you a lifetime—or should I say, many lifetimes—of wondrous riches writing, writing, writing with the biggest and brightest audience you can ever imagine looking on and beaming at your magnificent prose!

Yours forever truly,
Paul Verlaine

PAUL VERLAINE was a French poet born on March 30, 1844. He died at the age of 51, due to alcoholism, on January 8, 1896. He is best known for being involved with the Decadent Movement and also considered one of the best representatives of *fin de siècle* of turn of the century French and international poetry. The Decadent movement was an ideology characterized by general skepticism, self-disgust, enjoyment of perversion and crude humor. The idea of the movement was that human creativity is superior to the natural world and logic. Verlaine was an only child. He had a father, who was an officer in the military, and an overly doting mother. When he was 14 years old, he sent his first extant poem, "La Mor," to the renowned Victor Hugo (#42). In Verlaine's later years, he worked as a clerk for an insurance company and then for Paris City Hall while honing his craft and writing his poetry. Some of his most notable works are the books *Romances sans paroles* and *Mes Prisons,* and the poem "Sagesse."

"The poet is a madman lost in adventure."
—Paul Verlaine

50

⇥ Maya Angelou ⇤

Hello Dear Writers of the most Magnificent Earth Plane! Maya Angelou here. I am most humbled by this opportunity to come in among such literary masters! I have much to say, which might not surprise you, but I will come up with something here, as they say in this day, that will provide you with wondrous food for thought as a writer in the 21st century.

Universal acceptance and unconditional love. These are precepts with which I spoke quite a bit my last time on the Earth Plane as Maya. For they truly, Dear Writers, are the keys to the kingdom; the keys to the Universe, actually.

So how would and could you weave these two precepts into your work? Of course, it is possible to write of these ideas; these ideals. But many of you are not here at this time and this space to do that. Though some of you are! Rather, I suggest these two precepts to you in order that you can embrace them for your own help; your own buoyancy. You can buoy yourselves up knowing that you are truly magnificent just as you are.

Writers tend to be, I'm sure you won't disagree for the most part, quite low in self-confidence at times—especially about the work. And a feeling of unworthiness may prevail for them. That unworthiness, not feeling as if they can measure up, not surprisingly can harm the writing. It can color the work; prevent the writer from shining brilliantly, or even sadly, silence the writer.

All of these eventualities are most certainly not wanted or needed by the Earth Plane at this time!

Consider this. What if you accepted yourself and loved yourself unconditionally, completely, if only for a day? And then tried your hand at writing during this most glorious time. One thing that will occur when you give yourself permission to be your glorious you without any pretense is that your heart will literally sing with joy. As you are singing and you begin writing, you will find that your writing comes more fluidly and easily, and best of all that you say what you truly want to say. You raise your voice; you sing your song; you praise yourself and all in the Universe when this occurs!

What else do you think may happen during such a day of praising and loving all, including yourself? Do you think, perhaps, that the problems you've been experiencing with any of your writing—the blocks that may have come up—that they simply disappear? That they are gone, and truly you aren't sure *what* they were in the first place even? This can and will happen when you remain in a state of unconditional acceptance and pure love.

Will this mean that your writing will come out as too soft and yielding? Perhaps at first glance. But then you will most certainly see the "wisdom" of the "way" you have put the words on the page. You will see and sense that everything has been divinely timed with your words and their arrangement and the way they sound together. There will be a melodic singsong to your words, yet it won't be intrusive or take one's attention away from the message. In truth, it will all work together in a most glorious way!

And then, Dear Writers, what else do you think will come from your "great experiment?" If you "guessed" more patience and tolerance for yourself and all of humanity, you would be right! For truly, we are all here to buoy ourselves up and to learn that we are all interconnected and that no amount of cutting or cursing can change that! We are one—unconditional love and acceptance always. That being said, the closer you can get to living that way here, the closer you will feel to your soul's calling and life purpose, and the more quickly and more clearly will your prose come!

That is all for now, as I could go on, as mentioned, but there are more mouths to utter wise words of compassion and healing here! Dear Writers, I do wish you a wonderful life full of writing riches! And one of unconditional acceptance for yourself first, and then others!

Yours Sincerely and with Gratitude,
Maya Angelou

MAYA ANGELOU was an American poet born on April 4, 1928. She died at the age of 86 on May 28, 2014. In addition to being a literary icon, Angelou was an actress, singer, screenwriter, and civil rights activist. Her 1969 memoir, *I Know Why the Caged Bird Sings*, made literary history as the first nonfiction bestseller written by an African American woman. Over the course of her 50-year career, she published three books of essays, several books of poetry, seven autobiographies, three cookbooks, and is credited on many plays, TV shows, and movies. In 2005 and 2009, she received NAACP Image Awards for nonfiction. Her collection of poems, *Just Give Me a Cool Drink of Water Fore I Die*, was nominated for a Pulitzer Prize. The poem she wrote for President Bill Clinton's inaugural ceremony, "On the Pulse of Morning," won a Grammy for best spoken word album. So well-loved was Angelou, on the news of her passing even President Barack Obama issued a statement: "…one of the brightest lights of our time—a brilliant writer, a fierce friend, and a truly phenomenal woman."

"I've learned that people will forget what you said, people will forget what you did, but people will never forget how you made them feel."
—Maya Angelou

51

➤ ARTHUR RIMBAUD ⭠

Hello Dear Fellow Scribes! So glad to meet and greet here, as they say! On to the topic at hand. But first, may I introduce myself. Arthur Rimbaud at your Divine service!

Setting. Place. That is what I wish to speak to you about today. Most important to encourage you to set your place. Or place your setting, if you will.

Why is the setting so important? For one, it gives you a sense of place. A sense of place is most important when you are heeding the calls of the Divine and writing what you are hearing or sensing in your head. Yet, again, a sense of place is also a grounding type of thing. It puts the place in the heads of your readers, as well.

You see here I have mentioned two points that are intertwined, and yet not intertwined. One is the sense of place in your head that you are relaying. The other is the sense of place that the reader conjures up once he or she reads your precious words.

What shall we discuss first? The chicken or the egg? Most certainly, I feel at this time and place that it would be good to discuss what you access when you access sense of place. Sense of setting, so to speak.

Where do you get your settings? Sometimes the setting comes with the idea. For instance, Michener's *Hawaii*. Not much work came into conjuring up a place with that one! And yet, dear Michener (#15), a most prolific fellow scribe, still had to conjure up

Hawaii in his own head before he could get the topic onto paper or computer, if you will.

So you have the setting in your head. Now what? Do you simply record what you see, as you might? As a good scribe would? Yes and no.

Yes, you do want to put down words that accurately describe a setting. No, you don't want to describe the setting exactly as you see it. For then there would be something quite important missing. That important ingredient is feeling. How does the setting make you feel? How does the setting then make your characters feel? Of course, the setting may make you feel differently than your characters. So a tweak or two would be in order. But you still need to know how the setting feels to you in order to accurately depict that setting to your readers.

Next, how do your characters (and you) react to said setting? How do you interact with the setting, say in Hawaii, where the sunsets are long and the breeze is balmy and the skies open up with torrents of rain at times? How does one feel in this tropical setting? And then how does the character feel?

I know, I know. I sound as if I'm rambling, but truly I'm not. What I'm trying to impart here, as you may have guessed by now, is that settings are anything but static! They are most certainly as alive as your characters! So that is why it is so important that your settings evoke emotions in your characters, and even create stirrings in your own soul and heart. For when they do—when you access the "aliveness" of a setting, for lack of a better term, the story, the characters, the plot, the everything of the story comes alive!

> *I do hope I've given you some good morsels to chew on here. As you navigate the glorious settings of your works—be they "real," as in Hawaii, or conjured up in your heads—just know that those settings conjured up in your heads are just as real as any other!*

I do wish you a most blessed day and night!
   Yours Truly,
   Arthur Rimbaud

JEAN NICOLAS ARTHUR RIMBAUD was a French poet born on October 20, 1854. He died at the age of 37, due to cancer, on November 10, 1891. He is best known for his influence on the art and modern literature that predated surrealism. Rimbaud was the second child of an army captain father, who was away from home often and eventually abandoned his family altogether. His mother was the daughter of a local farmer. She was strong-willed and bigoted. As a child, he was recognized by his teachers as being brilliant in all subjects and very obedient. He loved to read and discovered he had a talent for Latin verse and even won first place for a poem he wrote, *Concours Academique*. He spent much time obsessing over poetry and tinkering with rhyme. His most notable works are *The Drunken Boat, Illuminations, Voyelles, A Season in Hell,* and *Derniers Vers*.

"Only divine love bestows the keys of knowledge."
   —Arthur Rimbaud

52

❧ LANGSTON HUGHES ☙

Much honored here. Langston Hughes at your most humble service! On to the message, which I am most excited to impart to you regarding your most Divine writings!

Of what shall I discuss that others have not here? Most certainly there is much! So to narrow things down a bit, here we go!

Poetry. Of the soul. Of the heart. Of the Earth and the Light. Poetry resides in all of our souls. It can give us great joy, or even great sorrow. Truly, poetry can even plunge us into despair. Why, would you ask, is poetry so powerful?

I am here to tell you this. Poetry is so powerful, because poetry is quite sparse. Much sparser than books and oration, wouldn't you say? As a matter of fact, poetry is the sparsest of the types of communication—coming in even sparser than music!

Why am I blathering on about poetry and its sparseness? Because I wish to show you, if you will, that poetry is sparse, yet it tells great, big stories! You can say much in this economy of words. Poetry can capture emotions, including love and lust and greed and power-hungriness (for lack of a better term).

Poetry, my Dear Fellow Scribes, can teach you much. That being said, I'd like to encourage you to try your hand, as they say, at your own poetry. Work your own magic with your words into poetry. When you do, you will find that your writing then will take on a more melodic beat, if you will. You will notice a slight sing-song in everything you do that is much like a haunting melody. But haunting, generally speaking, in a good way. For it convinces those reading your work to continue to read your work, and it calls in readers that you might not have had otherwise.

How is this so? You ask? How on Earth or in the Light can your work call in more if it has the undertones of poetry?

I will tell you.

Poetry is much like a siren's song. It is present, yet in some ways, one doesn't even know this. But it does call in all that it seeks. So your poetry will indeed call in your readership!

How, oh, how,
Shall you do,
What your soul
Wishes for you to capture
In your hands
On your tongue
In your mind
Yet deep, deep, deep in your soul?
That is for you, and you alone, to discover,
As you uncover,
The most delicious of those sparks and secrets of the Universe!

Well, Dear Fellow Scribes, I am out of page, as they say. I do wish for you a most poetic journey filled with many miracles! I will wait for your siren's song, and I will most certainly be perched on your shoulders as you work—for I so love to see poetry form on the page and fly out into the ethos to "infect" all with a call to the soul, and a soul to the call! That is all!

Sincerely Yours,
Langston Hughes

LANGSTON HUGHES was an American poet born on February 1, 1901. He died at the age of 66, due to prostate cancer, on May 22, 1967. He is best known for his pivotal role in the Harlem Renaissance, an African American artistic movement of the 1920's. Hughes was considered one of the most important writers and thinkers of this time period. He was also a social activist, novelist, columnist, and playwright. Hughes is considered the inventor of Jazz poetry. This is poetry where the poet writes about or responds to jazz. Jazz poetry is composed of many different rhythms, sounds, and forms. Hughes was in his early teens when he started writing poetry. Upon realizing his talents, his teacher introduced him to the poetry of Walt Whitman (#60) and Carl Sandburg. He later proclaimed both poets as his main influencers. Hughes fought for racial equality and social justice through his works.

"An artist must be free to choose what he does, certainly, but he must also never be afraid to do what he might choose."
—Langston Hughes

53

⇝ Glenn O'Brien ⇜

Why am I here? You might ask? And who am I? I am me, and you are you, and that is as much as you truly need to know. Wouldn't you agree? But for the purposes of this book, I will tell you. Glenn O'Brien here. Ready to give you a little "writing lesson."

Pacing. This has been mentioned by others in this book. Plot. This has been mentioned by others. Character. This has been mentioned by others. Setting. This has been mentioned by others.

I could go on, could I not?

What am I "getting" at here? What am I trying to tell you? If you are suspecting that I am trying to tell you that yes, everything has most certainly been covered before in one way or another, you would be right! At the same time, everything housed in your creative genius has not been covered before, at least not by any other soul in the Universe!

Why do I say this? Why do I even mention this? Because it is important to set a spark under your behind, so to speak. To get you to realize that there truly are no excuses to not utter your most profound words of writing wisdom, if you so choose. Rather than tarry about wondering if you will be repeating another, don't worry about that! For truly, unless you sit down and copy another, you won't be repeating a thing! And yet you will. But that is as it should be! And that is okay!

Your soul. Your calling. Your creative genius. Your most fertile imagination. That is what you came here to share as a writer—in whatever form you have decided to share your writing. You are here to share you with the world. So go ahead and do just that!

Of course, you should and need to be "ready." But examine your idea of ready, if you find yourself a bit stuck or stymied. If your idea of ready is to have something so unique that the world just has never seen the likes of it—then there is a bit of work to do on your noggin in terms of an understanding that that day most certainly won't come. At least not in this particular dimension!

If you aren't ready because of life constraints—well, fine then. You most certainly do need to be settled and ready to work and in a good space in your noggin, so to speak. Do get rid of anything that is constraining or restraining you and do move on with your writing pursuits! For you know, as most writers do "figure out" in time that when you are writing, your soul truly is soaring. No matter what type of writing, even. Writing is writing is writing is writing is writing is writing. I think you get the "picture."

That isn't to say that you won't enjoy more your treasured writing projects. Those you hold close to your breast. Do remember as you cling to them that they are a good indication of what your soul wants to say. You may as you examine these treasures see themes you've seen in other writings. Here is where you don't want to alarm yourself and start wondering if you should make your treasure more "unique." Know that your writing—all of your writing—is quite unique. For it is coming from your most precious and unique soul.

That is all for now, Dear Fellow Scribes. I do thank you for listening to me. I do thank you for accessing my way of thinking, if even for a bit! Tallyho and much success with your truly unique, yet universal writing endeavors!
Most Sincerely,
Glenn O'Brien

GLENN O'BRIEN was an American writer born on March 2, 1947. He died at the age of 70, due to pneumonia, on April 7, 2017. He was best known for his books on art, music, and fashion. O'Brien was "The Style Guy" for *GQ* magazine for many years and even published a book with the same title. His most famous books were, *The Style Guy*, *How to Be a Man*, and *Like Art*. O'Brien lived an interesting life, remaining famous and relevant in many different areas. He was an editor for Andy Warhol's magazine, *Interview*, a music and art columnist, essayist, poet, television show host, standup comedian, screenwriter, creative director at Barneys New York, playwright, book editor, advertising copywriter, and even an underwear model. When asked about his multifaceted career in 2015, O'Brien replied, "I guess I like to be busy."

"Don't be afraid to express all your personalities."
—Glenn O'Brien

54

⇾ E.T.A. Hoffman ⇽

Fellow Scribes! A right good day to you all, or good evening! E.T.A. Hoffman here. Quite a mouthful I know, but you'd be even more tongue-tied with the entire name! At any rate, on to the message at hand. I am eager to get started—or as eager as we become here in the Light!

Meat. The meat of the matter. The heart of the matter. The center/core of the matter. Why do I mention this? And does any of this truly matter?

Most definitely!

For the heart of the matter is that which you are striving to access, wouldn't you agree? The heart. The meat. The theme, if you will. That is what you are striving to portray for your readers.

I shall say this with some gentleness. Sometimes in one's writing, one can forget about the meat and the heart. Sometimes one gets so excited about the plot and the characters and the setting that one forgets what one had meant to say in the first place. These other three items just mentioned, while most certainly important and quite necessary, can sometimes act like shiny baubles that divert the writer's attention.

Okay, so how to access ones meat, one's theme, and then ensure that it makes its way into the story. For truly, the meat cannot be uttered clearly and audibly without ruining the spell of the work. One can't jump into a story, for instance, and say something like, "This is a story of a young man who lost his way and in the meantime he lost his soul and then he found his soul. And this work will show you all of this, so come along and read."

Takes away a bit of the excitement and intrigue, does it not? Unless, of course, the character is one of those unreliable narrators, and then this beginning could become more and more intriguing as you turn the pages.

But if you are trying to impart a "lesson" or "message" within your writing, you most certainly don't wish to come out and state that fact for all of the world to read. All of the world would likely go on to the next book by another writer—unless the reader was one's mother, of course!

At any rate, let's do get back to the meat of the matter, so to speak.

Here I would like to enumerate for you some ways to weave your theme into your work so that readers really don't notice the theme. Instead, they absorb the theme. It becomes a very part of their being, and then they have epiphanies that resonate. This is what a writer truly wants most of anything!

Quickly, for I'm running out of space!

1) Use words that resonate with your theme. Sprinkle them throughout your work—of course as they make sense.

2) Embrace not knowing if you've gotten enough of your theme into your work. For truly, if you take the next indicated steps given to you by us writing "angels" and your own creative genius, you will have just the right amount of theme sprinkled into your work.

3) Read your work in order to see your theme. If you notice areas where your theme seems to be lacking or weak, then work on those particular areas. Ask your characters what you should allow them to say or do to infuse the work with more theme. They will most certainly tell you, and then you will be well on your way to giving your readers meat with their potatoes!

That is all for now, Fellow Scribes. I do wish you a "meaty" writing life filled with good, filling meals of words.
   Yours Sincerely and Truly,
   E.T.A. Hoffman

E.T.A. HOFFMAN was a German author born on January 24, 1776. He died at the age of 46, due to progressive paralysis, on June 25, 1822. He is best known for his Gothic horror and fantasy novels featuring supernatural or sinister characters. He was also a short story writer, caricaturist/painter, composer, music critic, and draftsman. His most famous short story is *The Nutcracker and The Mouse King,* featured in movies and plays at Christmastime. His short story *The Sandman*, became a horror movie. Raised by his uncle, Hoffman studied Law, serving as a Prussian law officer until 1806 when Napoleon defeated Prussia and dissolved the bureaucracy. Hoffman then focused his energy on his other passion, music. He worked as a critic, conductor, and theatrical musical director. He composed the ballet, *Arlequin*, and an opera, *Undine*. He also continued to write short stories, even when elected councilor to the court of appeals in Berlin in 1816. By the time of his passing, he'd written more than 50 short stories.

"Why should not a writer be permitted to make use of the levers of fear, terror and horror because some feeble soul here and there finds it more than it can bear? Shall there be no strong meat at table because there happen to be some guests there whose stomachs are weak, or who have spoiled their own digestions?"
   —E.T.A. Hoffmann

55

➤ F. Scott Fitzgerald ◄

Hello to you all, Fellow Scribes now on the Earth Plane! Much obliged to you for listening. This is your one and only—ha ha ha—F. Scott Fitzgerald! At your most humble service. Here we shall go!

Tarrying. Do you feel at times that you are gadding about, so to speak, with nary a plan to do all that much? Much like my characters in *The Great Gatsby*? Most certainly, many writers feel this way. It is a nagging sensation, truly, that nips at one's mind and one's psyche and pesters. You might even think of it as your writing nemesis. It is a most distressing feeling this. And yet, I am here to tell you that it isn't at all of importance!

Not of importance, you may scoff! Easy for you to say, for you are no longer hampered by the apron strings of the Earth Plane! I must agree that is most certainly true! But do remember, Dear Fellow Scribes, I have come here today to help you Earth Plane Scribes! And so, I shall continue, if I might, and I most certainly will!

What I am alluding to here is the fact that all is Divinely Timed. If you have read the introduction to this book—this writing "wisdom" tome—you will most certainly see the mention of Divine Timing, as well as amongst many of the entries here.

Is this to say that you should purposefully tarry? That you should wait when you feel like going? Of course not! However, it is to encourage you that when things do seem to be delayed a bit, that is most certainly okay, and actually more than okay.

CHANNELED WRITING TIPS

How is this? Let me give you an example. Say you have started your "Great American (or insert any other nationality here) Novel." You are most excited and feel ever so ready, and indeed you are. Until something comes up for you amongst your Earth Plane responsibility reality. Something you must attend to immediately! Oh, my, how exasperating, is it not?

You go on with your day to attend to the Earth Plane matter. In fact, you "take care" of the matter quite well! Furthermore, in so doing, you discover a tidbit or two or three or four that you think would make most delightful additions to the work. Hmmmm. You do see where this is going, do you not? All Divinely timed! And not surprisingly, those "tidbits" turn out to be quite grand. One in particular elevates the work to par excellence and beyond!

Without that experience, be it lowly Earth Plane necessities, you would not have had that utterly delicious addition.

Okay, okay. So where might you go with all of this? How might this help you?

First, just breathe. Know that all is indeed as it should be. That the cloud formation in the sky is exactly as it should be. That the grass pattern after the mower man comes is as it should be. That the way you left your coffee or tea cup in the morning is exactly where it should be! Everything. Every scrap, morsel, etc. It is all Divinely placed. Divinely timed. Divinely existing!

So go ahead and get to your most auspicious writing knowing that it will move along exactly as you had planned for it to move along when you decided to do this project before coming to the Earth Plane. Know that all is so wondrous for you. And indeed, will continue to be wondrous.

That is all for now. I will let you "get back to it." Whatever it may be! Mundane or magnificent—it is all Divinely timed and planned!

Yours Forever and a Century or Two,
F. Scott Fitzgerald

F. Scott Fitzgerald

FRANCIS SCOTT KEY FITZGERALD was an American author born on September 24, 1896. He died at the age of 44, due to a heart attack, on December 21, 1940. He is best known for his short stories and novels that depicted the Jazz Age (Roaring '20s). His most acclaimed novel is *The Great Gatsby*. His other famous novels are *Tender is the Night* and *This Side of Paradise*. He also wrote many notable short stories, including *The Curious Case of Benjamin Button*, which was turned into a film. Fitzgerald was unpopular in school until he reached Princeton, at which point he realized his dream of becoming a novelist and instantly became popular. He fell in love with socialite Ginevra King. After a bad breakup, he flunked out of school. When he returned to Princeton the following semester, he'd lost his popularity and ended up leaving Princeton to join the Army. While stationed in Alabama, he met Zelda Sayre and fell deeply in love and got engaged. The engagement was short-lived, because Fitzgerald moved to New York hoping to achieve success and could only get an advertising job. Zelda broke off the engagement. Determined to prove his worth and marry Zelda, he retreated to St. Paul and rewrote *This Side of Paradise*, which published in 1920. The publication of his novel catapulted him into fame, and he married Zelda. They lived a life of luxury while he continued to write. However, Zelda suffered from two mental breakdowns and never recovered from the last one. In his suffering, Fitzgerald wrote the novel, *Tender is the Night*, his most moving book, and *The Last Tycoon*.

"Show me a hero and I will write you a tragedy."
—F. Scott Fitzgerald

56

❖ Gertrude Stein ❖

Greetings Dear Scribes of the Earth Plane! Most splendid to meet you and to get to know you a bit, if I might. Gertrude Stein here to add my two or three or four cents.

The writing life is quite divine, is it not? Quite breathtaking, really. Like looking out over a cliff onto a most magnificent valley! Like breathing in the sweet scent of rose on a warm summer day, or the intoxicating scent of night-blooming jasmine on a warm spring night. But I wax on.....And that, my Dear Scribes of the Earth Plane is most certainly divine!

Will I continue with my entry to talk about the utter magnificence of the writing life? Yes, I will. However, I will also give you some good hearty morsels—big bites, actually—of writing "wisdom" and "advice." Something for you to sink your great minds into and feel utterly fulfilled when you are done feasting on the words.

Fulfillment. Satisfaction. How does one go about ensuring that these sentiments ensue once a person is finished reading your sentence or paragraph or chapter or entire book?

Let us enumerate, as some Light Scribes here have done. It is a most expedient way to get the points across, if you will.

1) Tell your true story. Relay what you really want to relay. Not what you think you should relay. Not what your editor insists you relay. Not even what your banker or mother want you to relay. Relay what

you wish. What causes you to sing literally and figuratively. For when you do this, you will most certainly strike all kinds of marvelous chords in the psyches and souls of your readers. They will walk away "overfilled" with your words and quite satiated.

2) Embrace confusion. What? Where did this come from? Here I mean to say that you cannot expect to have all of the answers as you write—not even when you're on the last page! For the writing muses come forth at will throughout the writing process. Even with the last word or words! Rather than fret that you don't have all of the pieces of the puzzle in your back pocket ready to put onto the page, simply forge on knowing that it will be as it should be and how you had always planned it to be. Your readers will most certainly be satisfied with all that you write!

3) Have an "attitude of gratitude," as they say nowadays. Thank the Light for your inspiration. Thank yourself—your higher self and soul—for the inspiration and verve and energy to get the writing done. Praise the Universe for helping you. For certainly, many souls are indeed helping you. The more you are thankful, the more you will receive. The more you shall receive, the more you shall convey on the page and the more satisfying it will be for your readers.

4) Believe. That is all. Believe that your readers will walk away satisfied and content. And ready and waiting for your next work!

That is the "end" of my thoughts on this subject for today, Dear Scribes of the Earth Plane. I do wish you many, many, many satisfying travels throughout your written words and projects.
   Very Truly Yours,
   Gertrude Stein

GERTRUDE STEIN was an American novelist, playwright and poet born on February 3, 1874. She died at the age of 72, due to stomach cancer, on July 27, 1946. She was best known for her modernist writings and her literary salons/book reading parties in Paris during the 1920s. Her literary salons were so popular that the likes of Ernest Hemingway (#25), Ezra Pound (#59), Sherwood Anderson (#61), and F. Scott Fitzgerald (#55) attended. Stein wrote many novels, her most famous books being, *The Autobiography of Alice Babette Toklas*, *Tender Buttons*, *The Making of Americans,* and *Three Lives*. Gertrude Stein's partner, Alice Babette Toklas, was also a writer. Gertrude came from a wealthy family and even attended The John Hopkins University School of Medicine before leaving for France to live with her brother and collect art. There she assisted many artists and even had the pleasure of meeting Henri Matisse and Pablo Picasso.

"But the problem is that when I go around and speak on campuses, I still don't get young men standing up and saying, 'How can I combine career and family?'"
—Gertrude Stein

57

❦ JOHN DOS PASSOS ❦

Greetings! John Dos Passos here. I am truly at your service and ever so grateful to be included here. For truly, this is a most magnificent work! If I do say so myself, as they say in your day!

Your most glorious writing!! Well, well, well! Isn't this a most Divine circumstance! I shall go on from here now, and give you some wondrous "food for thought and thought for food," as you also say in your day!

The now. The present. The past. The before. When and how do you set your work? Where is most certainly important, but when is equally, if not more, important. For the when does allude to much, does it not? The when gives you a sense of place in its own right. For it is the place within history in which you are setting your work. Or it could be that you are writing a contemporary work about the "here and now." Or you could be writing about the future!

So I have brought up all of the possibilities here. Now what? At what point in time should you place your story?

Some works just beg for a time, don't they? For instance, often science fiction may do this. However, science fiction could also take you back in time, as well.

Am I talking in circles here? Perhaps. Or perhaps I am trying to show you something here. Perhaps I am trying to show you/illustrate that time is quite relative. That being said, how oh how, do you decide on a time period for your work?

I will do as many Scribes of the Light have done before me here and give you the grand old list!

1) What sort of feeling do you wish to impart in your work? I ask, because when you set a story in a certain time period, you immediately have a feeling that comes with that time period. For instance, the Old Wild West. What immediately comes forward here? Freedom, independence, bravery, courage, and a bit of mayhem, wouldn't you say? On the contrary, Victorian England gives a more staid feeling, yet with undercurrents of mischief and indulgence.

2) How comfortable are you with research? For if you choose a time period that did truly "exist" on the Earth Plane so far, you will want to give that place some authenticity. You will want the reader to feel as if he or she is genuinely at that place in time. If you don't wish to do much research when it comes to place, then I advise "making up" a place in the future, or in the past, that resides in your "imagination."

3) What about your characters? No doubt you've met some characters by now. Where do they want to live in order to relay their story? You could quite literally ask them where they would like to be placed. You may find that their answers surprise you. Of course, only ask one or two of your characters. For if you ask too many, you will have them giving you too many places from which to choose.

4) Where do you want to travel? Where do you want to spend your writing days? For once you start a work, you will be going to the place where it is set, again and again. Do you wish to become immersed in the jungle with its large snakes and bugs and sweaty circumstances, for instance? Or would you prefer a trip to the Antarctic?

That is all for now, Scribes of the Light. I do hope my words, as they say, ring true for you. Do have a grand time writing your characters into their most splendid times in space!
With Humble Gratitude Always,
John Dos Passos

JOHN DOS PASSOS was an American novelist born on January 14, 1896. He died at the age of 74, due to a heart attack, on September 28, 1970. He is best known for his novels, *USA Trilogy*, *Manhattan Transfer*, and *Three Soldiers*. The son of a wealthy lawyer, Dos Passos graduated from Harvard University in 1916. He volunteered as an ambulance driver in WW1. That experience greatly affected him, which became apparent in his anti-war novel, *Three Soldiers*. He traveled extensively in Spain as a newspaper correspondent postwar. His time there resulted in him transitioning from subjectivism to realism, which is apparent in his novel, *Manhattan Transfer*. Dos Passos finished 74 novels by the time of his death.

"If there is a special Hell for writers it would be in the forced contemplation of their own works, with all the misconceptions, the omissions, the failures that any finished work of art implies."
—John Dos Passos

58

➤ WILLIAM WORDSWORTH ⬅

*Greetings! **William Wordsworth** here. (At least that's who I'm representing here, for I've had many lives on the Earth Plane. Another matter, altogether, of course, but worth mentioning for a variety of reasons.) Here we have my "advice" regarding your ever glorious writing!*

How shall I impart what I wish here? How, oh how? Through the written word, most definitely, but is there more? There is, Dear Fellow Scribes. Quite frankly, your words can come into your psyches and spill out onto the page through the wings of writing doves!

This all sounds quite grand, you may think. This all sounds equally impossible. Yes and no. You most likely won't see the actual doves, but do know that the doves are there. For there truly are writing doves! And they are so happy and willing and able and capable of helping you get your words out onto the page in a most glorious pattern and manner.

The doves of writing, they are the most effervescent of them all. They are the most ethereal, truly, and they are the most accurate. I do not wish to say anything amiss about other birds, but truly, doves bring messages for your work under and over their wings.

Of course, in my time as a wordsmith as Wordsworth, I did wax on with much poetry. It was a most glorious life that. Writing poetry as I saw fit and as I was urged by the winged doves! Now in this particular time and space, poetry isn't as revered as it once was. While I could be a bit sad about that turn of events, I am not. For I know that within your work, even if it is called a book or a play or a nonfiction work, you can most certainly infuse your work with melody. And melody is at the heart and soul of poetry!

How does one infuse one's work with melody? How does one go about this most auspicious of acts? Well, for one, you might want to start out your writing sessions reading some poetry. Go ahead and give it a go! Read yours truly, or read someone else. There are many in this book who would do quite well for you! And then there are many others. And then there is you. Do you have poetry tucked away in a drawer or journal or in your head? Pull out your poetry! Give it a read through a few times aloud. Let the melody of your poetry sink into your psyche and soul. Let the words drip throughout your veins until they course through your hands and your fingertips begin to tingle. Then you will know that the poetry has infused what you wish to impart to your readers. Then you will know that it is most certainly time to begin to impart those words.

What else shall I say to you here? What else? What else? What else? There is much that I could impart. There is much that I could let flow through the fingers now mightily typing my words of "wisdom." But I shall just leave you with this.

> Follow your bliss
> Let your fingertips tingle
> Let your mind mingle
> With all that comes forward
> With all that goes backward
> With all that is all that it should and can be
> That is what I wish
> For you
> Dear Fellow Scribes, one day destined to return to the Light
> Who will one day take flight

Like the Doves
The pure, sweet, angelic Doves
From above!

I daresay I couldn't "help" myself. A poem just naturally came forth here. A poem with its melody and message from the soul to the souls—to all of you lovely and loving souls. I bid you a most precious and glorious writing life on the Earth and Light Planes!
Yours Forever,
William Wordsworth

WILLIAM WORDSWORTH was an English poet born on April 23, 1770. He died at the age of 80, due to pleurisy, on April 23, 1850. He is best known for being a romantic poet and Father of the Romantic period. He wrote lyrical ballads with Samuel Taylor Coleridge (#71). The collection contained his ballad, *Tintern Abbey*. He was also an avid nature lover and enjoyed taking long walks. His poem, "I Wandered Lonely as a Cloud," was inspired by being grief stricken as a young child over the loss of his parents and separation from his siblings. He attended Columbia University and married his childhood sweetheart. He enjoyed a quiet life with his family.

"Poetry is the spontaneous overflow of powerful feelings: it takes its origin from emotion recollected in tranquility."
—William Wordsworth

59

➤ Ezra Pound ➤

Ezra Pound here. Totally at your service. Most grateful and honored to be here. And that is what I wish to say in this intro! Let's get to this, as they say.

What can I add that hasn't already been said here about the writing life? Well, a lot, to be sure. But I only have a few lines, as they say, so I'll get right to it, though it seems as if I'm not, doesn't it?

Getting right to it.

Do you get right to it?

Do you plunge in and start writing, or do you stick your big toe into the "writing pool" and test the waters? And then sometimes take your toe out and study your own reflection on the water? As has been said by others here, that truly is all good. That truly is alright. For whatever way you get the words down is most definitely the way you are meant to do so.

So what the heck, as you might say, am I getting at? We Scribes in the Light do tend to speak in riddles, I would agree.

I am telling you/asking you to simply dive in, if you are feeling the urge. Dive into your writing. Let the water of wisdom of words envelope you and soothe you and buoy you up, as they say. Let the water take you over the waterfall, if that is where you intend to go. Take a deep breath at the rush of the water and the might of the waterfall. You will find great wisdom in your words. The wisdom will come forth in your words when you do this.

Or perhaps it is time to simply wade with your big toe, or your foot? Perhaps it's not time to even stick your foot in up to your ankle? That is most certainly a possibility. But I would like to let you know that it would most definitely behoove you if you could simply keep your toe in the water for a while. Rather than pulling it out quickly to further contemplate putting your toe or foot in again, keep your toe in the writing oasis. Let your body get used to that feeling of being enveloped by water, by messages and wisdom that would and could surely surround and envelope you.

Okay, I know, I know. I am not making all that much sense on the surface, but I do think and can see that I am making sense under the surface. For you know, I believe, what I am imparting. That starting anywhere is good with your writing. That staying in the writing for at least a little while is most certainly good. That—and your rational self knows this—without wading into the deep end, so to speak, you won't be able to access the words that you wish to impart here and now for your future audience. The audience that has been waiting for your waterfall of words for quite some time now, though they have no idea in their conscious, rational mind that this is so. At the same time, their souls will know the words when they wash over them. They will embrace your words; suck them until the essence of each word infuses their hearts. They will most certainly love your words as soon as they see them. That being said, what, truly, are you waiting for?

That is all, Dear Fellow Scribes! I will close off for now.
Very Sincerely,
Ezra Pound

EZRA POUND was an American poet born on October 30, 1885. He died at the age of 87, due to bowel obstruction, on November 1, 1972. He was most famous for advancing the Modern Movement in American and English literature. He published many successful books of poetry and was also a literary critic. Pound's biggest contribution to poetry was his development of Imagism, a concept from Japanese and Chinese poetry that stresses clarity, precision and economy of language. His most popular works were, *The Cantos of Ezra Pound*, *Hugh Selwyn Mauberley*, and *Pisan Cantos*. Pound published his first poem when he was 11 years old. He was an eccentric figure, dressing in green pants, a blue shirt and pink coat, accented by a hand-painted tie made by a Japanese friend. On his head sat a giant sombrero. He wore a single, large blue earring, and cut his beard to a point.

"*Good writers are those who keep the language efficient. That is to say, keep it accurate, keep it clear.*"
—Ezra Pound

60

⇻ Walt Whitman ⇺

Hello, there! Walt Whitman here. Much "obliged" that you should invite me onto these pages, so to speak. I am most certainly in awe of all that you are able and willing to do on the Earth Plane as scribes. Here are my words of "wisdom," as they say.

Thank you much, again, for listening. For it is, I/we have to admit, a bit trying at times to watch you Earth Plane scribes struggle, as it were, with your most auspicious writings, when we could so easily help you!

So here, I will strive to help you; as much as I can in these paragraphs I've been given. (But I am not complaining, to be sure!! For to come "back" to Earth to speak is a most honored honor!)

Okay. So how can you not struggle with your words? For as writers, you do know that you struggle mightily at times. And at other times, you do not. Why does this occur? Why? Why? Why?

Perhaps you fancy that you are struggling because you are just not "on," as they say in your day. That you aren't turned on or ready for all of the words to come forth. While that is most certainly possible, I ask you this. What are you thinking on and of? What are you pondering when you feel as if your writing wellspring has shut off? Are you thinking about the fact—very hard—that your writing has shut down? Are you struggling to open up the wellspring knob—to unplug the plug in the dam? Are you trying, trying, trying to get the words to come forth?

If this is how your scenario looks above, I would ask you to do one thing. Stop. Put down the pen or stop moving, or trying to move, the hands across the keyboard. Certainly, walk away from the computer or writing notebook or tablet.

Go out and get some fresh air. Listen to the birds sing. Watch the butterflies flit about. Breathe in the ocean breeze, should you be lucky to be near the ocean. Do anything to distract your mind and infuse your senses with the beauty that Mother Nature provides. If it is night out, look at the night sky. Marvel on the placement of the stars. Admire the moon for his ultra-stunning, glowing beauty. If the weather should be "inclement," thank Mother Nature for her bounty. Catch raindrops in your hand or snowflakes on your tongue. Let the wind thrash your hair about.

This all sounds rather fun, does it not? At the same time it is also therapeutic. Best of all, it will open up the floodgates, if you will, of your words. Those words that have been trapped inside of your head. You will, providing you stay on the coattails of Mother Nature, be able to access all that you wish to impart via written word. Let the smell of jasmine linger in your nose and the beauty of a firefly linger in your mind's eye as you write, write, write! Do let the words flow. Do let the words strum the most magnificent of strumming sensations! Do meet and greet with open arms the words of your most magnificent soul! You will find peace in this, while you also find that you will become quite literate and quite masterful and prolific to the core!

That is all for now, Dear Precious Earth Plane Scribes. I do thank you again for listening to me. And I do wish you all of the writing riches that Mother Nature and the world at large may rain down on you now and forevermore!

Yours Forever Truly,
Walt Whitman

WALTER WHITMAN was an American poet born on May 31, 1819. He died at the age of 72, due to pleurisy, on March 26, 1892. He is best known for his book of poems titled, "Leaves of Grass," which put him on the path to stardom. His other famous works were, "Song of Myself," and "O Captain! My Captain!" Whitman was also an essayist and journalist. A self-proclaimed humanist, he was involved in the transition from Transcendentalism to Realism, with both philosophies being apparent in his works. He is considered one of American's most influential poets and the "Father of Free Verse." His poems often depicted controversial imagery and aspects of sexuality. He was loved by many, because he wrote his poetry in laymen's terms so that everyone could enjoy them.

"Keep your face always toward the sunshine—and shadows will fall behind you."
—Walt Whitman

61

✣ Sherwood Anderson ✣

I am so glad to appear here. I am most humbly at your writing service. Here I am—Sherwood Anderson! We shall begin, as all good soldiers do! In this case, soldiers of the written word.

Battle. Arms. Weapons. Have you thought, Dear Writers of the Earth Plane, how powerful your arms (pens and computer keyboards) and your mind/genius can be? Of course, you might use the written word to tear down and destroy. That is most certainly possible, and most certainly has been done. At the same time, you might also use the written word to buoy yourself up—to pull yourself up by the bootstraps, so to speak. And in the process you would be elevating mankind and indeed, keeping mankind safe from itself.

What am I going on and on about here? Battles and pens and notebook paper? Certainly, Dear Writers of the Earth Plane, you have battled with your own hand as it has written. Certainly, you have been torn about what to write and when to write it and how to write it and….You get the picture.

Why is this of significance? Well, for one, the battle is most certainly unnecessary. For you know, deep in your most blessed soul, exactly what you wish to say. Whether you are writing a work that strives to "convince," which in some circles they refer to as propaganda. Although that is a matter of perspective and opinion, is it not? Or you may be writing a love letter to a significant other, or a child, or a parent. In either case, you may find yourself a bit tormented as you strive to choose the exact right words to fit on the page in the exact right order.

How do you get beyond this, do you think? How do you make it that every time you sit down to write, the words simply flow as they were meant to flow—as a river meanders about a land and ends up draining into a most glorious lake?

Flow. I am speaking of flow here. Battles stop flow, truly. They create a sort of wreckage in their wake. Yet, rivers, oceans, streams, waterfalls—they most certain flow where they are meant to go! Without worrying a bit about being wrong. Without struggle. There is no struggle for the water.

How can you access your water, do you think? How can you jump into the pool/oasis of your soul and simply float/drift to where you want to go?

First, let go of any preconceived ideas. Refuse to give in to stereotypes—for instance that it is a battle that must be won if you have a slight block. Certainly, that slight block could just be the fact that you're hungry, thirsty or tired and need a break from the pen or computer.

Second, believe that all will flow exactly where it will and was planned to go in the exact right time. You needn't set your alarm to wake up for the blessed event, for you will be present and accounted for.

Third, know. Know that all is right with your world. All is military precision right. Your bed is tucked in tightly; your corners are perfect; your weapons—pens, paper, computer keyboard—are ready and standing at attention. All prepared for you to record the voices of your soul and truly the souls who have come before you—both yours and others.

That is all for now Dear Writers of the Earth Plane. I am humbled, as mentioned, and so happy to have presented here to you in this time and space.
  Namaste,
  Sherwood Anderson

Sherwood Anderson

SHERWOOD ANDERSON was an American novelist born on September 13, 1876. He died at the age of 64, due to accidentally swallowing a toothpick that caused peritonitis, on March 8, 1941. He is best known for his novels, *Winesburg, Ohio*, *Death in the Woods*, and *Poor White*. He was also a short story writer, copywriter, and successful business owner in Ohio. Anderson was never formally educated, yet many of his short stories are considered classics today. As a matter of fact, his short story collection is said to have influenced the generation of American writers that he preceded, like William Faulkner (#1), Ernest Hemingway (#25), and F. Scott Fitzgerald (#55). He was also a military veteran, who fought in the Spanish-American War in 1898.

"There is within every human being a deep well of thinking over which a heavy iron lid is kept clamped."
—Sherwood Anderson

62

❧ Guillaume Apollinaire ❦

Hello Dear Scribes. I am Guillaume Apollinaire, and quite honored to present here. I will do my utmost best to bring you some enlightening material that I do hope will assist you with your writing.

I breathe, therefore I am. I cry, therefore I feel. I live, therefore I shall never die. These are precepts, so to speak, that you might live with, if you so choose. Precepts that are most certainly useful and helpful for the scribe.

This seems a little glum, does it not? You could perceive it as such, or you could perceive it in a much different way. That is what I wish to talk to you about today. Perception. And how said perception might color your work—make your work sing, so to speak, or make your work fall a mite flat.

How do you decide on how you would like your work perceived? How does this "work," so to speak?

First, decide how you want the reader to perceive the characters. That is truly the first place to start. While it might seem a good idea to decide how you would like the reader to perceive the story or the setting that is most certainly putting the cart before the horse.

For the characters do "run" your story. The characters do set up your plot and the characters do tear down the plot, if the plot is not to their liking and won't be a good choice for telling their story. Truly, the characters may even flee from the setting you've decided on for them, if they so choose.

So perception of the characters. Hmmm. How does one go about *that*? And truly, what on Earth am I even talking about here?

When you talk to your characters—yes, talk to them—you will have your own perceptions about them. You will soon come to know their hearts' desires and their fears and their plans and their likes and dislikes. You will know soon enough what strums at the heartstrings of their souls. Then you will have your own perception. Is it necessary for you to devise a scheme/a plan/a spreadsheet, even, of the perception of your characters? Not surprisingly, no it is not. For your characters, as I have mentioned, truly are running the show. You need only give them a voice and they will set their own perception.

Okay, so you are perhaps thinking that you just can't talk to your characters. For truly, aren't your characters coming from your imagination, and then you would think of yourself as a bit mad, and anyone who might overhear you would certainly think that! Fine, then. Write down the character traits of your characters. Do a character sketch, as you may have been instructed. Truly, a character sketch is talking to the characters. It is just wrapped up in a pretty, "sane" bow—that is all.

What else can I impart to you regarding perception or anything else that might help you write, write, write to produce your brilliant prose!

I will end with this. The end of the rainbow is most certainly the beginning of the next. Writing begets writing, Dear Scribes. So if you do perceive a work of yours as not totally how you might want to see it, know that the next work will most likely hit your target. And then you may find, as many writers do, when you look back at that first work you were concerned about that it shines just as brightly as the second and so forth.

Thank you once again, Fellow Scribes! I am most honored and grateful to have "spoken" here to such a joyous, rapt audience. Good day or night to you!

Sincerely and Fondly,
Guillaume Apollinaire

GUILLAUME APOLLINAIRE was a French poet born on August 26, 1880. He died at the age of 38, due to the flu, on November 9, 1918. He was also a short story writer, playwright, novelist, and art critic. He is best known as being one of the most prominent poets of his time, which was the early 20th Century. Apollinaire was also a huge defender of Cubism and a forefather of Surrealism. In his early twenties, Apollinaire traveled to Paris and then to Germany, living a bohemian lifestyle. After a failed attempt at love, he was inspired to write his famous oratorio, "Chanson du mal-aimé" (Song of the Poorly Loved). Upon returning to Paris, he became a well-known writer and made many friends, who were painters—most notably Pablo Picasso, who he introduced to Henri Rousseau's art.

"Now and then it's good to pause in our pursuit of happiness and just be happy."
—Guillaume Apollinaire

63

➤ Oscar Wilde ➤

Splendid to connect here, Scribes and Writers Extraordinaire! Oscar Wilde at your most indebted service. I shall give you some "advice" regarding creating prose that truly soars.

Where, oh, where does one go to find one's muse? Indeed, where shall you go, Dear Scribe/Writer? Perhaps the muse is in another? Perhaps the muse is under the table in the form of your best friend, your dog? Or perhaps your muse is in the clouds. Ethereal is your muse, perhaps? Angelic?

Indeed, do you even need a muse to produce quality, substantial work? Truly, is a muse even necessary? You hear writers of yesteryear and writers of today speak of their muses. They wax on about their muses, as if without them they might be mute. Funny, don't you think, how close the words muse and mute are to one another? Only a letter apart in the English alphabet! Is that a coincidence, do you think?

If you've been reading this book for a bit of time, you most likely have seen that there truly are no coincidences, at least not in the traditional sense. For everything in the Universe is most certainly orchestrated, as a violin that shares its melody in the most lilting and beguiling of tones.

Muse. Muse. Muse. Where are you, muse? Should you look for your muse if you're pretty certain that you haven't yet accessed it? Well, that might seem like a good idea, wouldn't it? But where on Earth to look? Perhaps we've hit your problem on the head, so to speak. You most likely won't find your muse on Earth. Unless it's a glorious painting, or a vase filled with luscious flowers, or a person, or animal. But we don't suggest such things—such concrete and alive things. For they may leave you at some point, and then where would you be? Unable to write because your muse has vanished, or Heaven forbid, died?

Forgive the bit of maudlin, but it was used to make a point. Your muse, your inspiration bearer, should come from the Light. For in the Light, nothing dies. Nothing shall run away from you, unless you ask it to.

So discover your muse in the Light. You will most likely recognize it when you see a light shining ever so brightly. It will most certainly beckon to you with a wave or a smile or a whispering in your soul. Acknowledge it when you see it; however you wish, and then do embrace your muse. Fold your arms around your muse, and truly, don't let go! All will most certainly begin to flow when you do this. When you become one with your muse!

What else shall you do to ensure that your writing tinkles with the sound of diamonds on glass? What else shall you do to ensure that your work embraces all—or at the very least many—who venture to read it?

I will tell you. Know in your heart of hearts that you truly have all that you need within you—muse or no muse. For certainly, the muse I have been speaking of here is the very essence of you. You are the muse and the muse is you! You need nothing more to access the splendid prose that will sing as if the angels have broken forth in song!

That's all I have to say on this subject, Dear Scribes and Writers. I do bid you a splendid writing life filled with many, many epiphanies—for you and your readers!
Oscar Wilde

OSCAR FINGAL O'FLAHERTIE WILLS WILDE was an Irish poet born on October 16, 1854. He died at the age of 46, due to meningitis, on November 30, 1900. He is best known as one of the most popular playwrights in London during the early 1890s. Wilde only wrote one novel, *The Picture of Dorian Grey*. His comic plays, *The Importance of Being Earnest* and *Lady Windermere's Fan* are what made him famous. He was a spokesperson for the Aesthetic Movement in the late 19th century. Wilde was also involved in many celebrated criminal and civil suits involving homosexuality, which ultimately resulted in him being incarcerated.

"*Be yourself; everyone else is already taken.*"
—Oscar Wilde

64

❧ Jack London ☙

Hello Writers now on the Earth! I am honored and grateful to appear here to offer up a few tidbits, as they may be. Jack London at your service.

Money. Taking good care of yourself. Ease of life. Those are some of the "buzz" words, as they say today, with which a writer is intrigued. Maybe not familiar with, but certainly intrigued with. Why would that be? Because writers don't tend to "make much money?" By George, that is most certainly right!

So, am I here right now to speak of money? Yes, I am. For, truly, as the old saying goes, money does make the world go 'round. And it pays for the writer's food and shelter so that the writer can continue to do what the writer does best, which is write.

I was quite blessed in my life as Jack London. For I did find the charm in terms of rhythm and what I was conveying at the time. It did resonate and it did result in me gathering and earning and garnering quite a bit of notoriety—all backed up by quite a bit of cash! So what was my secret? How did I get myself so well-known, while other great writers remained obscured—sandwiched somewhere between a tuna sandwich and a bitter sour lemon drink?

I shall give you some tidbits, if you will, of my life as Jack and how I went about living a quite grand life. And not at the expense of others—if you don't count my publishers—and what writer does, ha!

I am here to tell you that any of you can and may and most certainly will, if you choose, be quite lucky with the money—with the pay for the work. How so, you ask, if you've been struggling along for some time getting paid pittances and then occasionally a bit more?

Know. Know that you are creating work that truly can fly on the wings of angels and doves, should you allow it to. For it is necessary to release your work from your breast, so that it may take flight and soar. It is when your writing soars that it will gather great riches in terms of readers and editors, and then the money most certainly will follow.

How to release your work? And by this I don't mean publish the work, although I could mean that. For some of you have your work squirreled away in drawers in the dark recesses of those drawers. What I do mean here is to let the manuscript/book/article/play take flight on its own. Don't try to hold the work up. Don't try to convince the work to come back to your bosom where it will be safe and secure and forgotten about! Rather, let your work go out and reach its audience in its own time and manner. For when you do this—when you let go, you invite in feedback from the Universe about your work. Will all of it be magnificent feedback? No, but much of it will be. Then you will most certainly know that you are on the exact right path at this exact right time.

How do you know if you've released the work? You will feel as if a proud mother or father of a baby bird. You will be overjoyed to see the baby flying and feel a deep sense of pride knowing that the baby bird is flying and doing well, because you decided it shall be so and assisted the bird with its flight.

That is all for now, Dear Writers now on Earth! I do wish to offer you good wishes regarding your writing! And I want you to know that we scribes here in the Light will be waiting to see you let go of your work. For we know when you do that, your work will rush to the Heavens, as if paper doves on a cloud. How glorious it shall be!
Most Humbly,
Jack London

JACK LONDON was an American novelist born on January 12, 1876. He died at the age of 40, due to renal colic, on November 22, 1916. He is best known for his novels, *Martin Eden, The Call of the Wild, The Sea-Wolf, White Fang,* and *The Iron Heel.* Also a social activist and journalist, London was considered a pioneer in commercial magazine fiction. He was one of the first writers to earn an immense fortune from writing and enjoy celebrity status worldwide. His adventure novels, *The Call of the Wild* and *White Fang,* made him one of the most popular American authors of his time.

"*You can't wait for inspiration. You have to go after it with a club.*"
—Jack London

65

❧ Henry Miller ❧

Hello there Writers! Or should I more formally refer to you as Scribes? At any rate, Henry Miller here. At your service, as always. I am most excited to present here. And now I will begin.

The bohemian life. What writer doesn't want to live that life, if even for a week, in order to write about it? How often have you as a writer thought as you go about your life and something odd or untoward happens that it is indeed okay, for you can now "write about the experience?"

If you do this, writers, you are most certainly not alone. In fact, often the more difficult or odd the experience the better, wouldn't you say?

Does that mean you should seek out such experiences in this life so that you have fodder and fuel for your writing?

You most certainly could.

In fact, I did quite a bit of that in my life as Henry Miller.

Or you could simply access your "imagination." For surely, in you somewhere are all of the experiences that you will write about.

Where have those experiences come from? Past lives perhaps? Most certainly. Current life exploration, yet not experiencing, mixed with a bit of voyeurism, if you will. Most certainly, as well.

Truly, I tell you now that you don't absolutely, positively have to experience certain experiences in order to write about them. I say this, because I see now from the Light and I saw on the Earth Plane many writers simply waiting to experience prior to writing. Sitting there as odd, still ducks, waiting, waiting, waiting.

While my solution as Henry on the Earth Plane was to act, my solution now is two-fold—multi-optional. Either act, if you wish and want to experience that which you are choosing to write about. Or simply go into imagination-land—into near dreamland and simply imagine how you think a certain experience might be. Of course, you also have the privilege in this time and space to go onto your computers and to look up experiences and to read about them. Not to say we couldn't do the same thing back in my day. Armchair experiences are also valid!

If you see that the point I am getting to here is that it is most certainly okay to get your experiences where and when you may, you have gotten the idea! The point, my writing friends, is to write. Do what you must to clear the way to write, write, write. Writing comes first always. Let nothing block you from doing so. Certainly not the minor problem that you have not yet experienced what you wish to write!

That's all Writers! Now do go get to your writing, if you wish. Or get to the experience you will write about as soon as you finish with it. Either way, do enjoy your ride in this lifetime on the Earth Plane, for there is nothing quite like "here!"
Yours Truly,
Henry Miller

HENRY MILLER was an American writer born on December 26, 1891. He died at the age of 88, due to circulatory failure, on June 7, 1980. He is best known for developing a new type of literary form of the semi-autobiographical novel. This method combines mysticism, explicit language, sex, surrealist free expression, character study, philosophical reflection, social criticism, and stream-of-consciousness. His best-known works are *The Rosy Crucifixion* trilogy: *Black Springs*, *Tropic of Cancer* and *Sexus*, and the *Tropic of Capricorn*. All were based on experiences he had in Paris and New York. Miller was also an avid watercolor painter and wrote travel memoirs.

"The moment one gives close attention to anything, even a blade of grass, it becomes a mysterious, awesome, indescribably magnificent world in itself."
—Henry Miller

66

⇾ Robert Louis Stevenson ⇽

Hello Fellow Scribes! Thank you much for flipping to this page and reading my "pearls," as many say. I am Robert Louis Stevenson, and I am most grateful to have been chosen here. While we can't say much about the process of who is appearing here, I can tell you that an "application" of sorts was required. Now that I have you intrigued, please do read on!

Intrigue. My, oh, my, how intrigue gets readers interested and causes them to turn page after page! Most certainly, without intrigue many works simply wouldn't work. Others would be as an empty shell—without much merit.

So how does one go about harnessing intrigue? And, of course, first of all accessing intrigue—finding it, even, so that you can weave it into your writing?

I did have a bit of experience in this area as Robert. I did! For I knew the power of intrigue. I knew that intrigue would indeed get readers to continue to read. In fact, intrigue could get readers a bit obsessed. Many a reader failed to cook dinner or go to bed on time or even get work done reading some of my novels, including the *Strange Case of Dr. Jekyll and Mr. Hyde.*

You will see from this title that I began at the beginning with intrigue. And the beginning is the title. For it is the title that people read or hear first. You may admit that the title is quite intriguing. And the use of the word strange. Another intriguing word.

And then there is the beginning of your novel to intrigue readers. The first line, such as from *Dr. Jekyll and Mr. Hyde*: "*Mr. Utterson the lawyer was a man of a rugged countenance, that was never lighted by a smile; cold, scanty and embarrassed in discourse; backward in sentiment; lean, long, dusty, dreary, and yet somehow loveable.*"

Of course, the most intriguing part of this sentence is the last three words. For indeed, how could a man who sounds so dreary be so loveable? The reader simply must know this, and so he or she continues to read, and then becomes ensnared in the story and the intriguing bits and pieces of plot strewn upon the path along the way. Until the reader is in "so deep" that he or she doesn't want to come up for air, but must simply forge on to the end.

Where else can you insert intrigue in your work? Where else will it do the most good? Another good place is in dialogue. Your characters can "not say" certain things that most certainly intrigues the reader, or say things that equally intrigue. Those reacting to the main character in your work can also say intriguing things. Truly, everyone can be quite beguiling and intriguing! So much so that the reader feels as if he or she is truly walking amongst eggshells, or even bombshells, if you will.

How much more can you do and what, to create more intrigue so that your readers are hooked on your prose?

Why not try accessing "the other side" as you write? Perhaps, you may think and it is most certainly true, that we here in the Light may be able to give you intriguing plot points and dialogue and setting. If you do access us, know that you should open up your writing vessel, for we will be happy to fill it with loads of writing tips and wisdom.

That is all for now, Dear Fellow Scribes. I do hope that I've given you some intriguing information on how to create more mystery and surprise in your writing so that your readers can't help but turn and turn and turn your pages!
Very Sincerely Yours,
Robert Louis Stevenson

ROBERT LOUIS STEVENSON was a Scottish novelist born on November 13, 1850. He died at the age of 44, due to a hemorrhagic stroke, on December 3, 1894. He is best known for his novels *Treasure Island, Kidnapped, A Child's Garden of Verses,* and *Strange Case of Dr. Jekyll and Mr. Hyde.* He was also a poet, travel writer, and even a musician. In his early years, Stevenson attended Edinburgh to prepare to take on the family business of lighthouse engineering. After compromising with his father, he studied for the Scottish Bar, instead. He loved writing from an early age, but didn't focus his attention to producing until 1873. *Inland Voyage* was published in 1878. *Treasure Island* was based on a game he played with his step-son Lloyd.

"We are all travelers in the wilderness of this world, and the best we can find in our travels is an honest friend."
—Robert Louis Stevenson

67

❧ Lewis Carroll ☙

Hello, Dear Scribes on Earth! Lewis Carroll here to impart words of wisdom regarding writing, and even the writing life.

Memorable characters. Those that take a skip, hop, jump and leap into the arms and hearts of readers. That is most certainly what writers want! That indeed is what they so crave when they open up a book!

I have to say, as you most certainly are suspecting I will say, that Alice, dear Alice in her most magnificent Wonderland, was and continues to be one of the most loved characters of all time! Of course, her friends along the way were and are also memorable.

How did I come up with Alice, many have asked? While I did have a "model" of sorts for Alice, also named Alice, I did also have to pull Alice from myself—from deep in my imagination, actually.

In order to get to Alice, I had to climb inside of myself. Into my own odd, strange, curious world so that I could access her and then create her and "work on her," so that she could venture out and explore Wonderland.

Fine, you may ask. What else did you do but a bit of introspection? I do know that it has been conjectured that I had a nip or two of a substance that might make one "see" things differently. While I won't deny or confirm that, I do suggest that you do what you must—within reason—to get to a comfortable, creative place in yourself where you can draw out the memorable characters "lying in wait."

For truly, the characters are in you already. So when you "work" on discovering them, know that. Know that it's a matter of accessing, rather than creating or seeking or orchestrating. Allowing would be another splendid word. For that reason, it works to do whatever may get you to a "good, peaceful place" where you can see and access your memorable characters.

As you have seen, I am saying characters here. For truly, there is more than one memorable character "stuck" within your psyche. How many, I cannot say, for we are certainly all different. But I can tell you that there are more waiting to emerge.

That being said, I urge you not to tarry any longer when it comes to accessing and shining a light on your memorable characters. For they will come out in one way or another. Better for you to be prepared and have a potential "home" for them where they can bounce or hop or skip or jump onto the page and begin their merry journey throughout your most illustrious book!

When you do access them and they spring forth, remember that your characters may have big plans for themselves on the page. You may not agree with those plans, or some of them. You may have to hear your characters out and come up with a compromise of some sort. Or you may find that letting them run amok and make their ways down rabbit holes is the best answer!

That is all for now, Dear Scribes on Earth! I do wish you the best life ever writing, writing, writing!
   Sincerely Yours,
   Lewis Carroll

CHARLES LUTWIDGE DODGSON (AKA Lewis Carroll), was an English writer born on January 27, 1832. He died at the age of 65, due to pneumonia, on January 14, 1898. He is best known for his world-famous children's fiction novels, *Alice in Wonderland*, *Through the Looking Glass*, *Jabberwocky*, and *The Hunting of the Snark*. *Alice in Wonderland* was so widely popular that it has been turned into plays and Disney movies. Dodgson had a stutter that he called his "hesitation." He was also a lifelong bachelor, accomplished photographer, and a master logician, who wrote 11 books on mathematics.

"Why, sometimes I've believed as many as six impossible things before breakfast."
—Charles Dodgson

68

❧ Fyodor Dostoyevsky ❦

Writing, writing, writing! How I adored writing on the Earth Plane. I must say, I also enjoy writing here, but we are not speaking of that right now—that is a "later subject." Here I am to talk to you of writing—of making music with words. I am Fyodor Dostoyevsky at your supreme service.

Of what shall you write, first of all? That may give you a bit of a quandary, wouldn't you say? Make you wonder what you have in you that readers would even wish to read about. First, I suggest that you remind yourself that what you have to say is uniquely you. That what you have to say truly is the best for you to say at this time. When you think of it this way, you do realize that you will write what you are meant to write! No doubts about that!

But you do certainly need something to write about, don't you? You do need at least a first line. For if you do have that first line, it will lead to the next and the next and the next.

First lines. They are spoken of quite a bit, are they not? Many worry about their first lines, much like they concern themselves with their dress or their hair or the condition of their house when company is coming to visit. This is not to say that concern over your first line isn't warranted. It most certainly is! For writing your first line is a ceremony of sorts. It is a beginning, and in many ways a middle and an end. It is the first sentence at which some readers may even stop. For without a "good" first sentence, they may understandably surmise, how could the rest of the book be any "good?"

In order to develop a great first line, you must stop and breathe a bit. Put yourself into a sort of meditation. Then you may find that the most magnificent first line pops into your head, and you can then put it on the page! Or you may be going about your business, as they say in this day, and the line will miraculously appear. You can then stop whatever it is you're doing and write it down.

First lines. They can be quite memorable. In fact, a work can be remembered and "go down in history," as they say, just on the merits of that first line! Even if your first line doesn't go down in history, you most certainly want it to intrigue, as has been mentioned here. You want it to make people question the order of things. You want to make your readers agree that it is a most splendid first line!

What else can I tell you about the importance of first lines? Well, they are very telling, in many ways, are they not? And at the same time, they are not telling at all. They may hint at something, to be sure. And that hint is just enough to get the reader to want to keep reading.

First lines can also be musical. They can also be like a song heard over the airwaves. Over the mountains. Like a song that echoes in the canyons. For they are wondrous in their own right, first lines. So wondrous that they could even stand on their own.

You will know a "good" first line when other writers could take that same first line and weave their own most glorious stories from that first line. When they could use that first line as a jumping off point. As much more than a point of reference. When they could use that first line as a way to peek into the window of the world's soul.

I think now you may agree that first lines are indeed quite magical. That first lines do require and deserve your attention. That when you find your "perfect" first line, the rest of your work is most certainly to follow right behind!

Thank you for listening. I am honored that you are and have! Thank you, also, for adding to the great library on the Earth Plane, which most certainly will be added to the great writing of the Light Plane. You can be assured of that. You will most certainly go down in history, you can bank on that!
   Yours,
   Fyodor Dostoyevsky

FYODOR DOSTOYEVSKY was a Russian novelist born on November 11, 1821. He died at the age of 59, due to epilepsy, on February 9, 1881. He is best known for his four especially long novels, *Crime and Punishment, The Possessed, The Idiot*, and *The Brothers Karamazov*, as well as his novella, *Notes from the Underground*. He was also a short story writer, essayist, philosopher, and journalist. Dostoyevsky is considered one of the best novelists of all time, because of his illumination and psychological penetration into the darkest parts of the reader's heart and mind. Many even say that his novel, *Crime and Punishment*, is prophetic, because it accurately predicts the behaviors of the Russian Revolutionaries, if they ever came into power. Dostoyevsky is also considered a "psychologist" of literature and history. His work analyzed the pathological states of mind that lead to murder, insanity, and suicide.

"To live without Hope is to Cease to live."
   —Fyodor Dostoyevsky

69

❧ George Orwell ❦

Greetings. George Orwell here. At your most humble service. Good to "meet and greet," as you do say today on the Earth Plane.

The Earth Plane. What a glorious "assignment" that one. It does truly have you stretching your soul, so to speak, and straining your psyche. For one, if you are of the creative bent, as writers tend to be, you feel an overwhelming urge—from birth—to create. To make your mark, so to speak, with the written word—and ideas. Ideas galore, most certainly!

So how does one narrow down the ideas to come up with the kernel of an idea that can then be used to create a most glorious work? A work that could be dubbed "creative genius." Most certainly, as a writer you would just love to be dubbed a creative genius, wouldn't you?

I daresay that I was dubbed a creative genius at times with the publication of *1984*. That date now has passed, of course, despite the fanfare that the impending date brought up decades ago. But that was as fore-dained. (Yes, I've made up a word here. A reason, of course. There are reasons for everything!)

Reasons. What are your reasons? For writing? For creating? For foretelling, even? For in many works, the writer does foretell and foresee "things" that shall come to pass, or at the very least, things that could likely come to pass.

What, oh my, am I rambling on about here?

If you do have an idea that smacks of another idea that you've heard or experienced, then do, by all means, relay that idea. I am, yes, speaking of mimicking other writers, to a point. Be it their ideas or their style or even their way of being. For when you do this, you shall find your own voice. I bring this up, for one reason, because Julie did write a short story she was inspired to write after reading *1984* while in high school. Did she copy me, as George Orwell? No. But she was inspired by *1984* to find her own voice and to tell her own story.

That being said, if you are feeling inspired after reading a writer, but find that you've tied your own hands, because you fear mimicking, or worse copying, I would suggest untying your hands and simply writing.

We are all interconnected, us beings, even in human form. So when you write, you will find your voice—which is universally tied into all other voices—will ring true as your very own voice. A voice that the world clamors to hear and experience and relate to, and yes, read, so that one can find one's own voice to repeat the cycle. It is a most glorious cycle that truly does "make the world go round."

Therefore, have no fear of this cycle. Have no fear that your foretelling shall lead anyone astray. For truly, you all know, Dear Writers, exactly where you are going and where you will go and where you may never tread. But you know what there is where you won't tread so that you may then write about the experience anyway. There are other writers who have treaded there and are happy to share their experiences.

I do hope this helps, Dear Writers, with your work. I do hope that you can untie your own apron strings—let your hair loose—all of those clichés, and simply write to your "heart's content." For truly, your words will ring true with the entire Universe!
Yours Truly,
George Orwell

George Orwell

ERIC ARTHUR BLAIR (AKA George Orwell) was an English novelist born on June 25, 1903. He died at the age of 46, due to tuberculosis, on January 21, 1950. He is best known for his novels, *Animal Farm*, and *1984*. He was also a journalist, critic, and essayist. His novels and other works contained opposition to totalitarianism, awareness of social injustice, and supported democratic socialism. His views on imperialism, fascism and communism were so well received that people even coined the term Orwellian, meaning "a situation, idea, or societal condition that George Orwell identified as being destructive to the welfare of a free and open society." Both *Animal Farm* and *1984* were wildly successful and even turned in to movies. Blair was raised by his mother and had one older sister. He started writing from a young age, penning his first poem at the age of 4. He published his first poem at the age of 11. In his later years, he explained where his passion for writing came from: "I had the lonely child's habit of making up stories and holding conversations with imaginary persons, and I think from the very start my literary ambitions were mixed up with the feeling of being isolated and undervalued."

"But if thought corrupts language, language can also corrupt thought."
—George Orwell

70

⇸ Edith Wharton ⇷

Hello Dear Writers! Edith Wharton here! Let us begin.

Breadth of perception. Of what am I referring here, do you think? We all know of perception. That which you perceive may be much different than another perceives, or you could be "on the same page."

Perception is a tricky one. It may stop you up a bit, even, with your writing. For how do you relay your perceptions in a way that others with different perceptions may then understand what you are trying to convey in your writing?

I dig deep here, don't I? That thought may strain your mind a little. May pull at the edges of your consciousness and nearly begs for an explanation. So here I shall explain to the best of my Light Plane ability to you Earthlings!

Perception is the end all and be all of your work. It truly is. For how readers perceive your work influences how they then go about talking about your work and telling others. It also affects what they do with the messages and information you impart. And it truly affects if your readers shall have epiphanies and glorious experiences reading your works, or if they are a bit stumped and stunted from your messages. Or—and this is a big one—they may run from your work. For the perception that they pick up as they begin to read quite literally scares the bejeezus, as you say, out of them!

Their perception, these runners, of your perception may not even be jiving, but there is something they perceive in your work; your message, that makes them cringe or protest or freeze in fear.

Why am I mentioning this, Dear Fellow Scribes? I mention this to let you know something that probably won't surprise you. There will be readers who don't "get" your perception—who won't perceive as you do. Who may perceive quite differently than you do! They could, in fact, if you were to talk to them, relay their perceptions in such a way that you wonder if they even read your work.

What are you to do with this? These other perceptions that don't jive with yours—that have readers scratching their heads?

You may have been guessing I might say this, and maybe you have not—it all depends on perception. At any rate, I say to you, do nothing. Yes, nothing.

For you most likely know that perception is a most delicate balance and that you can't change another's perception any easier than you might change their eye color without adding colored contact lenses! There truly is not changing perception.

Instead, concentrate on your own magnificent perception. Hone your perception, stroke your perception, encourage your perception, until your perception shines so brightly that anyone reading your work, who is supposed to be reading your work, will become one with your perception. So that it resonates deeply with them, as both of your souls intended.

Yes, we are meant to read what we are meant to read, just as we are meant to write what we are meant to write. Nothing—no perception—can change that.

So, write with abandon. You will reach writing riches in no time!

Thank you, Dear Fellow Scribes. I am most grateful and honored to have presented here.
    Yours Truly,
    Edith Wharton

CHANNELED WRITING TIPS

EDITH WHARTON was an American novelist born on January 24, 1862. She died at the age of 75, due to a stroke, on August 11, 1937. She is best known for being the first woman to win the Pulitzer Prize in Literature for her novel, *The Age of Innocence*, in 1921. She was also awarded the American Academy of the Arts and Letters Gold Medal in Fiction. Her other notable works are *The House of Mirth* and *Ethan Frome*. All three of her novels, including *The Age of Innocence*, were turned in to movies. After she married a wealthy banker by the name of Edward Wharton in 1885, Wharton began writing stories about New York society during the turn of the century. She was able to realistically portray the morals and lives of the upper class in the Gilded Age, because she drew inspiration and knowledge from her own insider experiences of New York upper class aristocracy.

"True originality consists not in a new manner but in a new vision."
"There are two ways of spreading light: to be the candle or the mirror that reflects it."
—Edith Wharton

71

❧ Samuel Taylor Coleridge ❦

Hello Fellow Scribes! Most pleased to meet and address you here in this most auspicious work! I am Samuel Taylor Coleridge. And I will do my best to give you some good, "meaty" advice for your writing!

Here I would like to give you my top ten pointers for being successful as a writer!

1. Think. Ensure that you think throughout the day. Rather than engage in pursuits that cause your mind to wander aimlessly, take a good three-quarters of your day and think. For when you think, you shall come up with creative ideas. And those ideas are the seeds of your great work.

2. Know. Know that you are most certainly on a writer's journey. A journey that will take you quite far! A journey that will feed your very soul! A journey that will also, in kind, feed the souls of your readers!

3. Thank the heavens. What a glorious life is this as a Scribe! To be able to share your "imaginings" with the world! To be able to sink into the deep, inner knowing and sense of peace that overtakes the soul when one begins and continues to write.

4. Practice. Yes, good old practicing. Am I speaking of practicing writing? Of course. I am also speaking of practicing the "art of allowing." Allow the words to come to you, rather than running out to find them. For when you do this, you invite in the most glorious ideas, and

CHANNELED WRITING TIPS

those ideas soon turn into words, and the words string together as a chain of pearls into most glorious thoughts and those thoughts create paragraphs. You get the picture!

5. Envision. Envision your characters going about their days. Envision the book being written and finished and published. Envision readers enjoying the book, and you enjoying big, fat royalty checks!

6. Have faith. Alluding to #5 here, have faith that you will reach the "finish line" with your work and that it will indeed "go the distance." It will find its way into the hands and minds of all who are meant to experience it.

7. Pray. Yes, some good old-fashioned praying never hurt anyone or anything! Pray to whomever you think of as your Higher Leader, or however you wish to look at it. Pray to the Universe, even, for the Universe will most certainly answer. As you pray, pray for guidance, so that you may heed the calls to express as you wish to express so that readers will flock to your words.

8. Take care of yourself. This may sound like a "no-brainer," as you say today on the Earth Plane, and yet writers who have found themselves hunched over the computer keyboard for hours on end know of what I speak. Stop when you hear the voice that says to walk away and eat or stretch, and heed the voice's guidance.

9. Prepare. Prepare your life for the work. As you begin, prepare your schedule so that you may write as much as possible. In the middle, continue to prepare your schedule so that you may continue and finish the work. In the "end" (although there truly is no end!), prepare for the clamoring of success!! Prepare for the riches that spring forth to rain upon you for words well put.

10. Internalize. Internalize your greatness as a most wondrous Earth Plane Scribe. And know that you are equally as brilliant on the Light Plane Side of things. You are a writer, my dear Fellow Scribe, and you will most certainly be one forever!

Samuel Taylor Coleridge

I bid you a good day or night, Dear Fellow Scribes! I am most honored to have presented here, and I do thank you always for listening!
   Sincerely and Reverently,
   Samuel Taylor Coleridge

SAMUEL TAYLOR COLERIDGE was an English poet born on October 21, 1772. He died at the age of 61, due to congestive heart failure, on July 25, 1834. He was best known for his involvement in the English Romantic Movement and for his poems, "The Rime of the Ancient Mariner" and "Kubla Khan." Rumor has it that "Kubla Khan" was written while he was taking opium. In addition to being a great poet, Coleridge was also a philosopher, literary critic, member of the esteemed Lake Poets, and a theologian. With the help of his friend, William Wordsworth (#58), Coleridge co-founded the Romantic Movement in England. The lyrical ballads he composed with William Wordsworth, the most significant being, *Biographia Literaria*, are praised for their literary criticism. As a child, Coleridge was an avid reader. It wasn't until adulthood during the French Revolution that he started writing.

"Advice is like snow; the softer it falls, the longer it dwells upon, and the deeper it sinks into the mind."
"Poetry: the best words in the best order."
   —Samuel Taylor Coleridge

72

❧ William Blake ☙

Greetings! William Blake here. At your service. And here to "help" you with your writing journey, though certainly, you are well on your way, as they say!

Help. Do you need help with your writing, truly? Of course, we could all use a little help, right? At least those on the Earth Plane—for truly "up here" in the Light, we do have all that we require. But I am dallying a bit here, in getting to the message. After all, I only have so much space.

So then, I will jump right in to what I wish to say!

You do, truly, have all you need to write. I say this now to you, in this time and space, because it is most critical that you realize, I am being told by the Universe, that you truly are ready to ascend, so to speak, with your writing. As you are reading this, and should you continue reading this, I know you know what I mean. And yet, and yet.... You hesitate, don't you?

Hesitation can be your friend, and hesitation can be your most formidable of opponents. For it is hesitation that can stop one from running into a burning building, so to speak, and then it is hesitation that can stop one from publishing his or her version of the great American novel. Hesitation can most certainly become a bane, so to speak, of one's very existence.

But no matter! For you can learn to use hesitation as your friend! You most certainly can!

I shall enumerate, as they say, here, as to how to use hesitation as your writing life friend.

1) Know that hesitation may protect you. It may protect you from jumping into the deep end, as they say, without flippers or even before you know how to swim!

2) At the same time, hesitation may also soothe you. For when you hesitate, you are led to review all that you are concerned about. As you do that, you in a way, self-soothe and come to realize that all is quite well. Or if need be, you are guided to the minor or major tweaks you must make before proceeding.

3) Enthusiasm. Hesitation may allow you to build up enthusiasm around your writing and your upcoming success.

4) Anticipation. Hesitation does build up the anticipation, wouldn't you agree? It does make one anxious to get started already!

5) Readiness. When you hesitate and anticipate and build up enthusiasm, you are more likely to be readier than you've ever been once you do indeed begin.

6) Gratitude. When you hesitate and then realize you are finally ready and enthusiastic, you become quite grateful with the hesitation that started this whole splendid writing trajectory in the first place. It is good for you, Dear Writers, to know that gratitude is what makes the world continue to orbit. It is what makes you able to further access more writing wisdom and splendid ideas that will catapult you to writing Nirvana. Truly. You shall go far!

That is all for now, Dear Writers. I am most honored to have shared here. Please do hesitate when necessary, and then when no longer necessary, do take the plunge, as they say. Tally ho!

Yours,
William Blake

WILLIAM BLAKE was an English poet born on November 28, 1757. He died at the age of 69, due to liver failure, on August 12, 1827. He was a poet, songwriter, painter, and engraver. Blake is best known for his books of poems, which he also illustrated. His most famous works are *Songs of Innocence and Experience*, *The Tyger*, and *London*. Blake is considered a huge influencer during the Romantic Age in poetry and visual arts, even though his work was not widely appreciated during his time. His lyric, *Jerusalem*, is considered to be a second national anthem for Britain. He was a happily married man, who with the help of his devoted wife, Catherine, was able to sell his works. Growing up, Blake was one of six children in a modest income household. He never received a formal education, but instead learned everything from his mother, whom he adored. He would later state: "Thank God I never was sent to school/ To be Flogd into following the Style of a Fool."

"To see the world in a grain of sand, and to see heaven in a wildflower, hold infinity in the palm of your hands, and eternity in an hour."
—William Blake

73

⇝ Percy Bysshe Shelley ⇜

Hello, Dear Scribes of the Earth Plane, and those of the Light, as well! Percy Bysshe Shelley here. At your most humble service.

How shall I help you, Fellow Scribes? How may I? Well, first I would like you to shout to the heavens a thank you for being a writer/scribe/journalist/storyteller/journaler/copywriter—a writer in whatever manner you have come here to portray the written word for the Universe. For truly, truly, truly, the writing life/being a writer is a most wondrous gift. I think you would agree, most of the time!

Being a writer has so many gifts tied into it. Being a writer truly is as if you become a winged creature coming from the Light. It is as if a blessed kiss from the Universe. It is like a unicorn—magical. Yet at the same time the gift of being a writer grounds you; ties you to the Earth, like a big rock attached to the side of a cliff.

I do rattle on, I know. But I am most driven, at this point and time, to assure you that being a writer is a grand, grand, grand gift! You most likely have accessed this pure knowing about the grandness of your soul's calling, yet you may not realize it as you go about your Earth Plane lives taking care of all of those duties that you must take care of. But I am here to tell you right here, right now that you are on a spiritual journey of the soul when you write. You know, you can feel the pure Divineness, for lack of a better term, that comes from the Light when you write as a scribe! You can most certainly feel it!

CHANNELED WRITING TIPS

Okay, so shall I get to a "message," here, you may be wondering at this point, if you're still with me? Yes, I shall. I shall number as my dear pal, William, did prior. I shall enumerate the many ways that the writing life is a true gift from Heaven/the Light. As if dropped down all packaged up in white with a golden bow!

1. The writing life gets you to climb mountains—literally and figuratively! You climb, climb, climb, the Divine, Divine, Divine, and come out on top—a true winner!

2. You get out of the mundane of life's many "little" things. Like the dishwasher that won't work and the car that needs new tires and the job that is driving you a bit buggy.

3. You learn. When you write, it is a daily and even hour-by-hour, minute-by-minute adventure of learning new things; soaking up knowledge.

4. You soar. Quite literally. You know this. You find yourself soaring through the cosmos with your writing—even if your writing is not a sci-fi type of thing, as you say today. Just the act of tapping in and turning on and typing the words that spring forth puts you into the soaring realm. You can't help but ascend when you write.

5. You know. You know deep in your soul that you are on your exact, right path with your exact right words pouring forth. You know that all is well with your world and always will be.

6. You feel a connection like no other. A connection to other scribes, of course, and a connection to the Universe. Best of all, you experience a connection with your soul and your soul's calling. This latter connection is the most precious connection of all!

I will "sign off" here for now. I do know that others wish to speak, and so I shall open the door for them. Before I do, I urge you to embrace your inner and outer writer. Let him or her know how much you adore him or her. Let your writer know that the keys to life's innumerable castles are on a ring attached to your wrist. You need only take out any key you want and unlock the door. When you do, writing riches—a treasure trove of them—will reign down on you indefinitely!

Yours Truly,
Percy Bysshe Shelley

PERCY BYSSHE SHELLEY was an English poet born on August 4, 1792. He died at the age of 29, due to drowning, on July 8, 1822. He was best known as a renowned English Romantic poet during the 19th century and is highly regarded for his lyrical and philosophical poems. Shelley is considered by many as one of the best and most influential poets in the English Language. His most popular works are his classic anthology verse works, *The Masque of Anarchy* and *Ode to the West Wind*. He is also known for his long-form poetry, *Queen Mab* and *Alastor; or, The Spirit of Solitude*. Shelley was an adventurer and loved nature, spending much of his youth fishing and hunting in the meadows near his home. The eldest of 7 siblings, he was a child prodigy, enrolling in Eaton College at the age of 12. Due to his young age, Shelley was severely bullied, so he retreated into his imagination and was able to write the novel, *St. Irvyne*, and the book of poems, *Posthumous Fragments of Margaret Nicholson*, within a year's time. He loved to travel and went on many excursions with his wife, Mary Shelley (#81), the author of *Frankenstein*. He met his demise while sailing in Italy during a sudden storm.

"Poets are the unacknowledged legislators of the world."
—Percy Bysshe Shelley

74

⇒ John Keats ⇐

Hello, Fellow Scribes! Greetings and good day (or night). I am John Keats, and I am here to speak to you in this most auspicious way! On to the message at hand.

The writing life. It is quite a glorious life, isn't it? Full of fancy and whimsy and most certainly surprises along the way! What could I talk to you of right now that would most certainly help you in your writing life? What could I tell you that would make your prose sing!

This I can tell you. Make your heart sing, and your prose will most certainly follow.

That is a rather odd sentiment, is it not? Not that your prose will sing if your heart will sing, but the fact that I suggest that you "get happy" before your prose will jump off the page and into the waiting arms of your readers. Firstly, you may ask why such a suggestion. And secondly, you may ask how on Earth (pun intended!) that would make a difference for your prose. How would that improve your prose?

Let me relay the answer to this as we do see this from the Light.

When your heart sings
Then your prose can
Most certainly sprout wings
Then your eyes will see
And your manner will be quite free

John Keats

For you will know
Down deep in your soul
That you have hit the right string
On the harp of your life
There will be strife
Of this you can be sure
But you will be able
If you so choose
To create a most glorious song of the heart
This I promise you
Until your days shall shorten
And your nights lengthen
And you find yourself back taking flight
Into the Light

This is a rather "quick and dirty," as you say nowadays, little verse. But I do think it gets the point across. Many thanks again for listening and this opportunity.
   Yours Most Sincerely,
   John Keats

JOHN KEATS was an English poet born on October 31, 1795. He died at the age of 25, due to tuberculosis, on February 23, 1821. He is best known for his status as one of the main figures in English Romantic poetry during the second generation, along with Lord Byron (#111) and Percy Bysshe Shelley (#73). He worked to perfect his poetry using vivid imagery, sensuous appeal and expression of philosophy through classical legends. His works were only in publication for 4 years prior to his early passing. As a young child, he and his sister and two brothers bounced amongst relatives, which resulted in them not getting much of a formal education. Eventually, his guardian, Richard Abby, forced Keats into a surgeon apprenticeship at Edmonton, which he later abandoned to live in London. While in London, Keats worked as a junior house surgeon at hospitals, until he quit and devoted his time to writing poetry.

"The poetry of the earth is never dead."
—John Keats

75

❧ Robert Southey ☙

Robert Southey at your service. Glad to "visit" here for a spell. I do hope this time finds you well. On to the message at hand!

How on Earth does one come up with a splendid plot? One that makes the reader and even the writer turn the page, so to speak? How does one come up with the necessary twists and turns for a wonderful, wonderful book!

If you might be thinking that I might say that it is most certainly easy, should you tap into the Light, I'm not going to say that. Not that it wouldn't be very easy, if you chose to do so. Rather, you came here to the Earth Plane to have a bit of struggle. Perhaps part of the struggle is to figure out your own plots—or at least some of them!

So if tapping into the Light Plane's wisdom isn't on the table, so to speak, what shall you do?

I shall enumerate, as they say!

1) Make a plot map. Put all points of interest on a big piece of paper. In different colors for different interest points. These points of interest should be scenes/instances/occurrences that you wish to include in the work, and that have presented themselves to you.

2) Then use a marker of the same color to draw lines between these particular points. Where it seems that these points do intersect, even peripherally. You may have some points where the lines are coming in from many other instances; whereas some points may only

have one line, or even none. Don't concern yourself with the numbers, etcetera!

3) Then stare at the points for a time. See what "pops" into your head. Avoid, if you can, questioning from where the ideas pop up. That will stop this flow we are creating for you!

4) Jot down the ideas that pop into your head on the same page to the side, or on another paper—whatever works and feels best.

5) Stare at the new ideas, yet at the same time, read them over and over.

6) Take those "new" thoughts and see where they may fit within the different interest points you have initially recorded.

7) Believe. Believe this shall work. Rather than questioning this, just try this! When you question and as a result decide why something won't work, it certainly won't.

8) Take a break. Walk away from the plotting. Put it out of your head. Do something to distract yourself—such as take a walk, talk to a friend, or even watch the good old telly for a spelly.

9) Go back when your mind is clear. Take a look at the new points put into the interest points that you had already had. Do you see synchronicities? Parallels? New points of interest even grander than the first? You most certainly will! Now use a different color pen to connect them.

10) Start the same procedure again. Repeat this until you have the plot well-formed and filled out. Until you feel you have the "meat" of the plot and can now start the cooking of said plot.

If you are wondering if a bit of "magic" comes into play during the process, you can, if you choose. Or you don't have to. For truly, the key is to get the plot down, isn't it? To have a plot that rings true while it also intrigues and keeps one interested. However you might come about this plotting—short of doing harm to another—is really not the point, now is it?

Robert Southey

I do wish you a wondrous, exciting journey to your plot and then sharing that plot with your characters and, in turn, readers! Splendid day to you chaps! And ladies, of course.
  I shall bid you a good day and adieu,
  Robert Southey

ROBERT SOUTHEY was an English poet and storyteller born on August 12, 1774. He died at the age of 68 on March 21, 1843. He is best known for his fairytale, *Goldilocks and the Three Bears*, as well as the poems, "Thalaba the Destroyer," "Curse of Kehama," and "Madoc." Southey was one of the Lake Poets and one of England's Poet Laureates. The author was closely associated with Samuel Taylor Coleridge (#71) and William Wordsworth (#58). His story *Goldilocks and the Three Bears* is considered a classic children's book in many countries. Although Southey attended Westminster School and Balliol College, he left without a degree, yet went on to become quite well-known in the literary realm.

"No distance of place or lapse of time can lessen the friendship of those who are thoroughly persuaded of each other's worth."
  —Robert Southey

76

➤ William Butler (W.B.) Yeats ⭠

Hello, Splendid Writer Pupils!!!! William Butler Yeats at your most humble service. I am so excited, as it were, and profoundly grateful to present in this most auspicious work! We shall, as they say, begin!

Lemon butter sky
Pink purple moon
What a grand weight
Has been lifted
From my psyche
When I look to the beauty
Of the moon
And the stars
And afar
As I stare
Into the night's sky
I am reminded
Of the breathtaking beauty
Of the grand old Light
And the Dark
Yet the Light shall forever shine
In my most blessed mind
And soul
Forevermore

William Butler Yeats

Oh, I just couldn't "help" myself, as they say. Poetry, for sure, is most intertwined in my very soul! It is something that I can't escape, this urge to write short prose, no matter where I may find myself—the Light or the Earth Plane or another dimension!

Is this you, Dear Splendid Writing Pupil? Do you find yourself needing, wanting, *having* to write, no matter what? Do your fingers itch and your mind twitch, if you aren't creating? Do you feel in a bit of a funk or a lot of a funk when you aren't able to create? Does the thought of not writing for the rest of your days make you feel quite bleak?

If so, I am most honored and excited to tell you that you have the writing bug—yet it is quite grander and bigger than any bug you might "catch" while on the Earth Plane. For writing, as others have mentioned in this most magnificent work, is something that feeds your soul, while at the same time is a deep and utter part of your soul. It is something that you most certainly cannot "divorce" yourself from ever. Hence, the feelings of un-wellness or discord or dissatisfaction when you aren't creating/writing.

> *I shall sign off for now, as I feel/know that you most certainly see, feel and hear what I am saying here. Do pick up your pen or go to your computer screen and create when the urge comes—when the unrest comes—when the dissatisfaction comes—and even when the joy comes. For you, my Splendid Writing Pupils, are most certainly writers through and through!*
>
> *Good Day to You!*
> *William Butler Yeats*

WILLIAM BUTLER (W.B.) YEATS was an Irish poet born on June 13, 1865. He died at the age of 73, due to congestive heart failure, on January 28, 1939. He is best known as the leading Western poet during the 20th century. He was a pillar of the British and Irish literary communities and establishments, even going so far as to aid in founding the Abbey Theater. He also served for the Irish Free State as a senator for two years. Butler's most notable works include *The Countess Kathleen*, *Deirdre*, *The Tower*, *Words for Music Perhaps and Other Poems*, and *The Wanderings of Oisin*. His greatest accomplishment occurred in 1923 when he was awarded the Nobel Prize for Literature.

"Education is not the filling of a pail, but rather the lighting of a fire."
—William Butler Yeats

77

❦ Sydney Tremayne ❧

Hello, there! I am here, present, accounted for. Here you have Sydney Tremayne at your most humble service, as they say! I shall do my best to enlighten you to the triumphs and travails of the most wondrous profession of writer/journalist.

Thank you much for listening to me. I am truly, deeply honored to be here! In true journalistic style, I shall start with a question.

How do you feel about being yourself? Truly being yourself? Have you asked yourself this question lately? Perhaps you have and perhaps you haven't. Either way, it is a most wondrous answer you will get when and how you figure out how to answer it.

Why do I ask such a thing? Isn't this a book about writing and improving your writing and being a writer?

I ask this because us writers, we tend to be chameleons of many sorts, wouldn't you agree? Our writing takes us to great highs and great lows, yes, but it also takes us to other people's lives and other people's opinions and other people's "other things." Of course, this is the case when you are writing nonfiction—yet it is also the case even when you write fiction. For your characters are certainly different from you, aren't they?

All of this that I am babbling on about points out how we writers tend to wander away from ourselves as we write! Even if we are "journaling," as they say, about our lives, we tend to write with an audience in mind. Whereas one who simply journals for the cathartic aspects wouldn't think of an audience, and indeed would shudder at the thought, us writers always think of our audiences as we write, for that is why we write in the first place!

So back to the question asked when I started. How do you feel about yourself? I could ask how you think about yourself, but with this you could most certainly give me a clinical and analytical answer. But when I ask you how you feel about yourself, this brings up an entirely different feeling altogether, now doesn't it?

What on Earth do I wish to say? I am simply trying to get you to see that you as a writer are a most splendid creature able to take on various personas in the name of the craft. You honor the craft of writing and do your utmost to respect the craft and do your utmost to then deliver the most brilliant of words onto the page for all of the world to see.

Am I suggesting you change yourself at all? Most certainly not! Unless you wish to and choose to. I am only suggesting that you acknowledge your ability to be a chameleon, while at the same time acknowledge your ability to be okay with truly being yourself as you change your chameleon suit. This is not an easy place to get to, as they say, but I assure you that you can get to this place.

And when you do.
You will find.
That you access a power like no other.

For you meeting you and embracing you and expressing you while you take on your chameleon suit and express the wants and needs of others creates a most beautiful, synchronistic dance with the Universe that reverberates throughout the Heavens. The result is a siren's call out to readers to read your most magnificent works!

Thank you kindly for listening to the musings of a muse such as me! Do run on to embrace yourself and all of your writing riches.
  Yours Truly,
  Sydney Tremayne

SYDNEY TREMAYNE was a Scottish poet and journalist born in 1912. He died in 1986. Tremayne spent most of his working life living in London and working as a journalist for the *Daily Mirror*. By contrast, his poetry often portrayed the natural world. He spent his retirement years in Scotland.

"Having to deal day by day in prose with what John Betjeman calls 'burning issues,' I was freed from the temptation of opinionated versifying: poetry of any interest to me is more subtle and does not have designs upon an audience."
  —Sydney Tremayne

78

❧ Upton Sinclair ❧

Hello to all of you splendid writers! Upton Sinclair come to "speak." Here we shall go!

Difficult subjects. Do you write about difficult subjects? Do you pull from within and without when you do so? Most certainly, during my lifetime as Upton, I did choose to write about some "difficult" subjects. About subjects that on the Earth Plane are considered quite haunting and troubling and at times, even revolting.

Why would one choose to write about troubling subjects when there are so many other types of writing one could dabble in? Or try. Or write quite thoroughly about? Such as flowers or sunsets or sweet baby bunnies?

Well, for one. As they say in your day, someone has to do it! Someone most certainly has to write about tragedy, wouldn't you say?

Well, of course, that truly isn't the case. The world would most certainly continue to rotate, even if no one wrote about tragedy. In fact, it is quite possible that even less tragedy would ensue, should people stop writing about it. But that is an entirely "other" topic altogether.

Back to the topic here.

Troubling topics. Topics that make you sigh, cry, worry even, or make you angry.

Writers, some writers, are simply tasked with writing about such topics. They/we are!

So how does one go about accessing such topics, and then harnessing their power and then putting it all down on paper or computer screen?

First, embrace not knowing how this will all come about. You heard me right. Embrace your confusion! For when you do this, you will make the road ahead run more smoothly—for the road will run as it should. You won't find yourself hopping from road to road and consulting your map along the way constantly. Rather, you will "go with the flow," as they say.

[I must make an interjection here!! For it is rolling around in Julie's head every time one of us Scribes of the Light uses one. Clichés. You are told to not use them, and yet we scribes are using them. We urge you to remember, however, that we invented clichés! Therefore, we can use them whenever and however we wish!]

Back to my message here about difficult topics. I shall allude now to something I just said regarding clichés. You can do as you wish. Truly, splendid writers, you can write about difficult subjects as you wish in whatever manner you wish. Of course, decorum is most certainly needed at times. There are truly some subjects that your soul would not and could not "touch," so to speak.

But if your soul does lead you to difficult subjects, do tread on those paths to see where they take you. It could be that you wish to try your hand at difficult subjects in the privacy of your own writing realm. Maybe those difficult writings you won't even show to the world! Or maybe, just maybe, you shall share them with the world, and you may just open up the eyes of the world to a current "problem" or "issue" that requires attention.

That is all from me here and now, splendid writing comrades! I do wish you the best as you navigate your way through one of the noblest of professions.

Good Day (or Evening!) to You,
Upton Sinclair

UPTON SINCLAIR was an American writer born on September 20, 1878. He died at the age of 90 on November 25, 1968. He is best known for his muckraking novel, *The Jungle*, which shone a light on the sanitary and labor conditions of the US meatpacking industry. His book was so influential and caused such uproar that a few months later, the Meat Inspection Act and Pure Food and Drug Act were passed. In 1919, he released *The Brass Check*, which covered yellow journalism and "free press" limitations in American journalism. Four years later, the first code of ethics was created. By the time he died, Sinclair had written nearly 100 novels in several genres. During the early 20th century, Sinclair was popular and his work widely known. He was a Pulitzer Prize winner for Fiction in 1943. Some of his other well-known novels include *Oil!* and *Dragon's Teeth*.

"I aimed at the public's heart, and by accident I hit it in the stomach."
—Upton Sinclair

79

➤ SINCLAIR LEWIS ➤

Greetings writers!! Sinclair Lewis at your most humble service. I do say that I am honored and a tad bit gleeful that I am here! Okay, a lot gleeful. For this is a most high honor to present here and to have my words harkening over the airwaves from the Light to the Earth to be put down to posterity. On we shall go!

Where, oh where, did your muse go? Where, oh where, did your verve and zest for writing go? Are you blocked? Do you sometimes get blocked? Darn, darn, darn. It is quite a long, hard, arduous road when you do become blocked, wouldn't you say?

Am I here to tell you about writer's block? Yes and no, as they say!

Yes, for it is a most annoying, so to speak, thing that blocks you from expressing your true self and your words of truth, so to speak.

No, because truly, writer's block is not a block at all. It is meant to come forth at times. To save you, to help you, to comfort you, and to make you even more creative.

More creative? You may ask. How is that so? If I am blocked like a tunnel is blocked when it is full of too many cars, how can I be productive and go forward, even a little bit?

Well, think of this. Perhaps the block is causing your subconscious to think of alternative routes to traverse your plot? Have you thought of that? Most likely not, because you're too busy thinking about how to unstick your cork so that the words can then flow forth with abandon.

Abandon is a most telling term, isn't it? Do you truly want your words to flow forth with abandon? True abandon? For abandon is a bit chaotic, wouldn't you say? Abandon doesn't always pave the road, so to speak, in the right direction. It may take you on a crash course off a cliff. Truly, I say, abandon isn't all "it's cracked up to be."

Okay, you are thinking by now. Is this fellow *ever* going to tell me how to unstick my cork so I can write with fluidity and ease?

I shall.

If you so like.

Here we go.

Sit down. Shut up the stirrings and back talk in your mind. Lift your fingers to the computer keyboard or pick up your pen or pencil and begin.

Yes, you saw that right.

Begin.

Before you ask begin what? Don't.

Simply begin.

With whatever flows from your fingertips onto the page or screen.

Watch it unfold.

Will it be gibberish?

Perhaps.

But most likely it will be quite glorious.

Because your subconscious has had time.

To unwind the rhymes of your plot.

In ways that you most certainly won't understand consciously.

But will delight you.

I do hope this helps you, dear writers! I shall end here. Giving you some "food for thought" and "thought for food," as another writer here most certainly has already said!

Good Day to You Always,
Sinclair Lewis

Sinclair Lewis

SINCLAIR LEWIS was an American novelist born on February 7, 1885. He died at the age of 65 of a heart attack, on January 10, 1951. He was best known for his satirical novels and being the first US writer to win the Nobel Prize in Literature. His novels were satires about small town life. His most notable novels are *Arrowsmith*, *Main Street*, *Babbitt*, and *Dodsworth*. He was also a journalist and studied at Yale.

"When facism comes to America, it will be wrapped in the flag and carrying a cross."
—Sinclair Lewis

80

⇒ W. E. B. Du Bois ⇐

(William Edward Burghardt)

Greetings, always, Dear Scribes of the Earth Plane. A most honored Scribe of the Light at your humble service. Here we shall begin!

Of what can I impart that others here have not? Truly, is there anything at all left to say? You may even ask yourself this when you sit down to write. When you sit down to write something absolutely magnificent!

And yet.

And yet.

You cannot find something significant, even, to say! What to do? What to do?

Well, first of all, as they say, breathe. For truly, you will find something to say. Most likely many something's to say.

That is the greatest fear of the Earth Plane Scribe, isn't it?

Not that you would say the "wrong" thing. Or too much of something. Or too little of something. Or it won't sound "right."

No. The scribe's biggest concern, truly, is not having anything to say.

For truly, if an Earth Plane Scribe has nothing to say, then he or she couldn't possibly be a writer, right?

Not necessarily.

But do let me explain. It is not that you don't have anything to say. For truly, you do. In fact, even those souls who aren't writers have something to say. Some are other creative types and they "have their say" in different ways—through music, for instance, and art.

So remind yourself of this as you stare at the blank page or computer screen—while you breathe and repeat. You do have something to say. You do have something to say. You do have something to say. Most certainly, you do!

So how to access what you have to say? How to bring it forth so that it shall become one with your fingers and mind and express itself perfectly, or near perfectly?

Here are a few "tips," if you will:

After you've assured yourself that you do indeed have something to say, walk away for a while. I know this seems counterintuitive, but it is truly a good move!

Once you've rested sufficiently, and your breathing is steady and even, and you believe to the depths of your soul that you have something absolutely magical to share.

Sit and take another deep breath.

Begin. Wherever you feel like beginning, begin. However you feel like beginning, begin.

Continue. Though things may seem clunky, and the words come out in a chunky, crude way. Continue. Don't stop until you utterly can no longer write.

Walk away again.

Breathe while away. Put the work out of your mind. Refrain from wondering what you wrote.

When you are breathing steadily again and have put the work out of your mind, return to it.

Read it. You will see kernels, or a whole cob of corn when you read. You will see that you do indeed have something to say that resonates with your soul and will most certainly resonate with the entire Universe!

Thank you ever so much for reading, Dear Scribes of the Earth Plane. I do wish you a glorious writing life!
  All the Absolute Best, as they Say!
  W. E. B. (William Edward Burghardt) Du Bois

WILLIAM EDWARD BURGHARDT DU BOIS was an American writer born on February 23, 1868. He died at the age of 95 on August 27, 1963. He is best known as a spokesperson for African American rights. In 1909, he co-founded the NAACP (National Association for the Advancement of Colored People). His most notable works are *The Souls of Black Folk*, *The Talented Tenth*, and *Black Reconstruction in America*. Du Bois was also a sociologist, historian, and the first African American to receive a PhD from Harvard University.

"To be a poor man is hard, but to be a poor race in a land of dollars is the very bottom of hardships."
  —W. E. B. (William Edward Burghardt) Du Bois

81

❊ Mary Shelley ❊

Thank you ever so much for listening to me, Dear Writers! I am most honored to present here. Mary Shelley at your humble service. Here we go, as they say!

Memorable characters. Most certainly my character, Frankenstein, is one of the most memorable characters of all time! For he truly was a compilation of multiple characters in my head and heart, and then in the heads and hearts of many.

Why do I mention this, do you think? To tell you how to create a memorable character? While that would most likely be helpful, I rather would like to talk about what happens when you become married, in effect, to your character. This often happens with one character in particular, and it can cause some trouble for you as a writer.

I shall explain.

Though it is a most glorious achievement when you can access a splendid, memorable character who resonates, it can eventually limit you. For you become known for this most magnificent character and are expected in the future to come up with more splendid characters. And indeed you probably do.

The trouble is, however, that many readers are measuring any new characters against your famous character. This will make the new characters—though they may be wonderful in their own right—not shine as brightly against your famous character. I think you see of what I speak here.

Your new characters simply can't measure up to your famous character—no matter how hard they try. Or you try.

So what to do about this?

Well, different people have dealt with this conundrum in different ways. Some have embraced a certain character and continued to write about the character. This can sometimes work, providing the character is meant to return again and again. At times, however, writers would like to make a statement about a particular character and then have that character remain frozen in posterity in that particular work. At that point, what shall the writer then write about? How can the writer sustain this?

It is not easy, I will say.

Does this mean that you should avoid creating a memorable character that will put you "on the map" and keep you tied to that character?

No.

For if you are meant to create a memorable character. If that character is meant to bond with you at a certain point in time, then you are meant to do just that. Embrace the character and run with him/her/it.

At the same time, know that any characters you create after the first will be just as grand in their own rights. So, just create them and run with them, as well!

I hope this helps more than a little bit, Dear Writers! Get to your wonderful characters!
   Sincerely Yours,
   Mary Shelley

MARY WOLLSTONECRAFT SHELLEY was an English novelist born on August 30, 1797. She died at the age of 53, due to a brain tumor, on February 1, 1851. She is most famous for her gothic novels, *The Last Man*, *Mathilda*, and, most notably, *Frankenstein or The Modern*

Prometheus. Shelley was also a travel writer, biographer, short story writer, and essayist. She also spent a large amount of time helping her husband, Percy Shelley (#73), editing and promoting his romantic works. The inspiration for the iconic novel, *Frankenstein*, came from a competition between Mary, Percy, and Lord Byron (#111) to see who could come up with the best horror story. Both of her novels, *Frankenstein* and *Mathilda*, were so wildly famous that they have been turned into movies and even plays. Fascination about Mary and her life even inspired a 2017 movie about the author.

"Nothing contributes so much to tranquilize the mind as a steady purpose—a point on which the soul may fix its intellectual eye."
—Mary Shelley

82

⇻ E.B. White ⇺

Greetings to you, Dear Fellow Scribes of the Earth Plane or E.P., if you will. I am E.B. White at your most humblest of services. Here I shall share my thoughts.

Of what do you yearn to hear and say? Of what do you yearn to experience? Look closely at these questions and you may notice that they can most certainly be addressed should you write about them. For truly, Dear Scribes, you can access all of the places you wish to explore through your writing.

Of course, some of you may say that you wish to experience things "for real" on the Earth Plane. That sentiment is most certainly understood and to be commended. For that is a most glorious occurrence—when you experience something in person and are then able to write about it.

And yet, there are certainly instances that you most certainly can't easily experience. For truly, this occurred for me when I delved into the rather intimate and entrancing world of animals in my books, *Charlotte's Web*, *Stuart Little*, and *The Trumpet of the Swan*. There are brave souls who go to live with lions, yet that isn't always feasible or even recommended. But for the most part, there are areas of the Earth—though they may be on the Earth—that aren't easily discovered or explored.

So does this mean that you should shy away from writing about those items on the Earth that you can't taste, touch, or feel? No, of course not. For there are many other ways to touch, taste and feel those things of which you wish to write!

The imagination, of course, it starts here. And it shall go on from here, as they say, into the Light. For once you take a "trip" into your imagination—a door to the Light will most certainly creak open. You will then be able to follow a most miraculous path to the writing riches that pour forth when you look into the interior of an Earth Plane existence from the Light. Up here in the Light such vantage points are quite remarkable. They can and will show you, if you ask, the most remarkable of characters and plot points and ways to describe that you would not get should you even try to enter the world on the ground or lake floors, such as that of the magnificent swan.

Is it required that you are asleep or in a deep meditative state or "drugged," as they say, to attain this "bird's-eye view" from above?

You could, if you so choose, but it most certainly isn't necessary. Truly, you just need ask the Light Plane to send you ideas from this vantage point. Ideas and inspirations, and it shall be so. Is it that easy? It most certainly is. But as you can see, you must be open to this way of working. Once you are, you will be astounded at the material that will come washing down on you. At the same time, remember this. It is imperative that once you ask for help, you take it and are a good steward with the material. For the Light is happy to hand over the keys to the kingdom, so to speak, providing that you are responsible with those keys, and that you open the agreed upon doors and hand back the keys for others to use wisely.

> *I do hope this does help you in your most magnificent writing journey! I do hope that I soon see you asking for the keys. I will be happy to hand them to you temporarily. And then I do hope to see you writing down the riches you have gathered from this special place within the Light. This place of writing riches that is*

visited by many daily. A library of writing riches! Soon to welcome you!

Thank you. And I bid you a most glorious day!
Yours Truly,
E.B. White

ELWYN BROOKS (E.B.) WHITE was an American writer born on July 11, 1899. He died at the age of 86, due to Alzheimer's disease, on October 1, 1985. He is best known for his classic children's books, *Charlotte's Web*, *The Trumpet of the Swan*, and *Stuart Little*. When he attended Cornell University, he received the nickname Andy, as was the tradition for anyone possessing the last name White. This came about because the co-founder of the college was Andrew Dickson White. It turned out that White was quite fond of his nickname, using it for the duration of his life. He said about the name: "I never liked Elwyn. My mother just hung it on me because she'd run out of names. I was her sixth child." Five years after graduating from Cornell University, White started working for *The New Yorker* magazine, where he stayed for more than 50 years. He was also co-author of the writer's advice book, *The Elements of Style*, more commonly known as Strunk and White. His children's books are classics and have been made into many movies and plays. White won several awards in his lifetime for his work, including the Pulitzer in 1978 for his body of work.

"I arise in the morning torn between a desire to improve the world and a desire to enjoy the world. This makes it hard to plan the day."
—E.B. White

83

⇒ John Updike ⇐

Hello Dear Writers! Very excited and honored to present here. I so enjoyed my "gig" as John Updike on the Earth Plane, so to come back as him is a most glorious opportunity, which I, of course, jumped right on! On to the messages I wish to impart!

Pacing. This has been mentioned, but not over-mentioned here, and I feel that this topic bears repeating, so to speak, with another lesson to bolster the first.

How important is pace/pacing? Well, consider this. If you are walking along on a journey throughout a most magnificent forest and you are moving along just fast enough to soak all in and enjoy it, how would you feel if it suddenly came to an abrupt stop? Most likely you would be annoyed and irritated and even exasperated, wouldn't you?

This is what occurs with good plot pacing gone bad or backwards. You are clipping along, eager to turn the page or poke the button on Kindle and then things come to a screeching halt. (I so love to not have to worry about Earth Plane rules regarding what you call clichés! Quite freeing!) I digress. Back to the matter of pacing. But herein you can see what I purposefully did. I stopped the momentum for just a moment and stuck in another element. That most certainly affected the pacing, didn't it?

On closer look, what did my stopping the pacing do for the "story" here? Did it make you a bit more intrigued by what I was about to say?

Most likely! And it wasn't too long of a pause, was it? Indeed, it was just long enough for you to swallow, or take a breath, and then I plunged on!

Pacing. I have to say that I was most pleased with my pacing in the short story I wrote, "A & P." In that dear short story I did keep you reading with a kind of pacing you'd find on a slow, yet surprisingly quick summer afternoon, which is when the little short was set.

I say slow, yet quick, for the hazy days of summer do seem quite long, and indeed are, yet the days of summer one can enjoy in one's lifetime here go quickly in the scheme of things. For once you enter adulthood, you do lose your summers, generally speaking—unless you choose a career in which you can grasp them, like teaching, but that is most definitely a different story altogether.

At any rate, pacing is the key to great work. Pacing works well in short stories, of course, because they are short. It can also be used quite well in novels. Most certainly, it can be used in any kind of writing that you would like to use it—even advertising! And actually is quite effective, and used most often to great effect, in copywriting. Pacing is indeed the tiny place between the what is this product and the why do I absolutely, positively need this product to make my life glorious! To make my life better! To make my life a near Heaven on Earth!

So do concentrate on your pacing, and yet do not. For when you strain to create the right type of pacing, it will not come as a surprise to you that the pacing will quite literally jump out the window! Rather, do a little meditating before you write, or whatever it is you do to get into the right writing "place." Then jump on the horse or rabbit or car or aeroplane that comes for you. For the vehicle you do alight onto will have the exact right pacing for your work!

> *I must say goodbye for now, for I am running out of space, as they say! I do thank you for listening to my ramblings and revelations. I do! Most glad to have "met" in this time and space, and I do wish you the most splendid of writing travels!*

John Updike

*Yours Forever and a Day and a Night and a Day and a Night
(You get the picture—and don't you just love my pacing!)*
  John Updike

JOHN HOYER UPDIKE was an American novelist born on March 18, 1932. He died at the age of 76, due to lung cancer, on January 27, 2009. He is best known for his short stories, novels, and poetry that were realistic depictions of the middle class in an American protestant small town. His best-known novels are *Rabbit, Run*, *Rabbit is Rich*, and *Rabbit at Rest*. He was also an art and literary critic and won 19 literary awards, including two Pulitzer Prizes in 1982 and 1991 for his novels *Rabbit is Rich* and *Rabbit at Rest*. He was also the author of *The Witches of Eastwick*, which was turned into a movie and television show.

"What art offers is space—a certain breathing room for the spirit."
  —John Updike

84

⇾ C.S. Lewis ⇽

Scribes, Scribes, Scribes! So nice to meet here and greet, as they say. I am truly honored and do wish to use up every possible morsel of space I have here to fill you with writing wisdom that is quite literally "out of this world!" C.S. Lewis at your most humble service.

Writing travels! My, oh, my, oh, my, how grand can be a writer's writing travels! For truly, writing takes you to worlds that you would not access if you were not writing. Most certainly, literally, writing takes you to the edges of the Universe and back again and again and again! It is a most wondrous and glorious life, this life of the scribe.

How shall I "help" you with my writing advice, as they say? First of all, let us do look at the word help. For help suggests that you indeed do need help. And while it is most certainly true that whenever you listen to another writer you will come away with new nuggets of wisdom, it truly isn't necessary to believe that you are in great need of help. For truly, dear scribe, the fact that you seek wisdom means that you are indeed helping yourself! You are!

So if you need no help, then we can just end here, correct? We could just thank one another and part ways?

I know. I am not seeming to say much, and yet, if you read between the lines here, I would suggest I am saying quite a bit.

First, I would like to suggest that you grasp ahold of your mightiness when it comes to the pen. For truly, the pen for you is much like the sword is for a warrior. Does this mean that you must do a bit or a lot of muckraking with said pen (or computer keyboard)? No, that isn't necessary. Although if that is your goal and lot in life, then by all means muck around with your words so that you give the world the messages they've been waiting to hear.

If you aren't into muckraking, then how shall it help you to use your written words as a sword? Let me suggest this. Use the pen or computer keyboard "sword" to cut through the bull surrounding your words so that you can truly get to the heart of the matter! Take this time to truly cut through the nonsense so that you can get to your own truths. When you do this—when you cut through all that doesn't mean anything for you in this time and space, you will have arrived at your most splendid of truths. These truths form the basis of your work, and your work will take you quite far as you travel and take on all of the various assignments you had decided to take on prior to coming.

You will see now, as I speak, that you most certainly have all that you wish to have and all that you need to give people hope and healing with your "sword pen," including understanding and unconditional love. For as truly as you read this, I assure you that you wish to spread joy amongst other writers and amongst the "common folk." You wish to share of yourself, and you most certainly can do that in any manner you choose.

Do you need help? Truly ask yourself that before you ask for help. If you do require help, as all Earth Plane dwellers do at times, take the help offered and run with it! And remember to always thank the helper. This will create an attitude of gratitude between you both that will continue to create a most glorious cycle of give and take in terms of the written word and life in general.

I do realize that I was quite otherworldly in my explanation here. That is to be expected, I think you would agree, considering my work as C.S. Lewis. At the same time, it was something that the Universe wished for you to consider regarding yourselves as Earth Plane Scribes!

That is all for now! Onward and upward, as they say!
Yours Sincerely and Appreciatively,
C.S. Lewis

CLIVE STAPLES (C.S.) LEWIS was a British writer born on November 29, 1898. He died at the age of 64, due to kidney failure, on November 22, 1963. He is best known for his novels, *The Space Trilogy*, *The Screwtape Letters*, and most notably, *The Chronicles of Narnia*. He also wrote the Christian nonfiction apologetic novels, *The Problem of Pain*, *Mere Christianity*, and *Miracles*. Staples held positions of English Literature at Cambridge University and Oxford University. His series, *The Chronicles of Narnia*, has been turned into plays and even a series of highly popular movies. As a young child, his favorite books were by Beatrix Potter (#48), like *Peter Rabbit*. Young Staples was fascinated with the idea of talking animals. Some say that the books he read as a child and the plight of children evacuated from London during WWII inspired him to write *The Chronicles of Narnia*. He was also a popular BBC broadcaster during WWII, speaking about morality and religion. During the war, he hosted 4 children evacuated from London. Upon the loss of his wife, he wrote the book, *A Grief Observed*. Lewis was also best friends with J. R. R. Tolkien (#93).

"Friendship is born at that moment when one person says to another: What! You too? I thought I was the only one."
—C.S. Lewis

85

❧ James Baldwin ❧

Hello fellow writers! James Baldwin at your service here. Come to give you a few tips from "beyond."

Writing about conflict. Writing through conflict. Writing despite conflict. Simply writing for the sake of writing. You may wonder, I would think, at times, if writing for the sake of writing is truly worthwhile. If writing for the sake of writing is something that you should "bother" with. I tell you here, as I may not have told you there, that indeed, writing for the sake of writing is a most time-honored pursuit. And so I will encourage you to write for the sake of writing. And if you so choose to write for the sake of a statement, then do that as well!

How should you write, really and truly? This sounds like a somewhat odd question, doesn't it? You may think, I'll write like I always write. I'll sit my tush down, and I'll simply write. And when I am done, I'll arise and walk away from my writing pen or my computer and be done with it. For the moment I'll stay away, until the urge to write—the need to write—calls again. And then I'll continue the cycle.

Examine what I've said here, and you may see that this is indeed a way of writing for the sake of writing. Indeed, writing for the sake of writing is most certainly just about the "only" way to go.

What exactly do I mean when I speak of writing for the sake of writing? Let me tell you.

When you dig deep and you write
Just because
You want to write.
Just because you want to express yourself.
To have the chance to express your very essence through the written word.
And all that you believe in.
Then you are writing for the sake of writing.
Yet writing will then give you all that it can and may.
For writing will shout important topics from the rooftops.
And writing will open eyes that were closed and mouths that didn't want to talk.
Writing for the sake of writing can be earth shattering.
It can open hearts and minds and even pocketbooks.
So go ahead and write for the sake of writing and see what comes forth.
I guarantee you that you will be utterly amazed.

> *I think that sums it up for me here and now fellow writers! I'm happy to have had this opportunity and do wish to tell you that I look forward to what you will soon create now that you will be writing for the sake of writing!*
> *Good Day to You!*
> *James Baldwin*

JAMES BALDWIN was an American author born on August 2, 1924. He died at the age of 63, due to stomach cancer, on December 1, 1987. He is best known for his novels, plays, essays, and public speeches about racial and social issues during the 20th Century, specifically the struggles of black Americans. His most notable works are his first novel, *Go tell it on the Mountain,* and *The Fire Next Time,* and *Notes of*

a Native Son. He was the oldest of nine children, growing up in Harlem, New York. After spending nine years abroad, Baldwin returned to the US and quickly became "known as the most eloquent literary spokesperson for the Civil Rights of African Americans." After the assassinations of his friends and fellow Civil Rights activists, Malcolm X, Martin Luther King Jr., and Medgar Evers, Baldwin decided to return to France. His works give readers a psychological perspective of what life was like as an African American during the 20th Century.

"Not everything that is faced can be changed, but nothing can be changed until it is faced."
—James Baldwin

86

⇉ Dorothy Parker ⇇

Hello there, fellow writers. I am most honored to come and present here. It is a most glorious opportunity. If I were in human form, I would most certainly cry with joy! Fortunately, for you dear folks, I am not in human form, so I will spare you the waterworks. Although waterworks from the Light might be a bit entertaining. Lest I forget—Dorothy Parker here. At your service, as I've seen many of my fellow Light Scribes say!

Where, oh where, did my little lamb go? Where, oh where, did my little darling go? You might wonder this after your work has been edited. And if you're like me when I was Dorothy, you might have a few choice words to say when you notice that your favorite passages have been edited out of your work.

I'm not here to admonish you to not use choice words, for they are quite entertaining on the Earth Plane. Rather, I've come to let you know that there are times when editing is warranted, and then there are times when it is unwarranted.

Is this truly of that much significance, you may be asking? In my mind, such as it is in this ethereal place, yes, it does matter a great deal.

For if you are edited and it resonates with you, then that is certainly okay, and better than okay, because your prose will most likely sound fabulous! But if you are edited and it doesn't sound so grand, then that is not necessarily a good thing.

Of course, there are varying degrees of editing. An editor could simply move a few words around, and you could think, that truly is "no biggy," as you say today.

Or the editor could rip apart your work—the manuscript you sweated and slaved over—just for the sake of ripping things up and throwing words here and there.

There are editors like that. Editors who can't quite control themselves and must make their mark—literally and figuratively—on a writer's work. They are somewhat like a buffalo, charging through the tundra known as your manuscript.

While the above editors are most certainly problematic, even more so are the sneaky editors. Those that make a crafty, odd change here and there in your work and then complain about the changes they had to make and allude to changes they might make.

Okay, okay, you may think. I've had all of these editors at one point or another. If your advice is to run as fast as possible from them, I did try, but I seem to find myself under their "not so good" graces again and again.

That is what I wish to "talk to you" about.

What are you accepting when it comes to criticism of your work? What do you brush aside when others speak of your work or edit it?

It may be time to look closely at the ideas you have about your own work that you hold close.

Do you believe that your writing is indeed spectacular and that it only needs a few tweaks here and there?

Then believe that. Embrace that. And move on away from those who don't feel the same way.

It's that easy. For truly, dear writers, there will always be those who wish to meddle, and twist and turn upside down your words.

When you know that you are on the right track, simply stay on that track. Don't let anyone sway you. I tell you this now, as I would tell you this when I was on the Earth Plane. I did stand my ground when

CHANNELED WRITING TIPS

writing as Dorothy Parker. Did it "cost me" as far as my career? Perhaps some. But what it didn't cost me was a deal with the proverbial guy with the horns and red face. I instead kept my composure, and I kept my dignity. For I wrote what I wrote when I wrote it with absolutely no apologies and no red pen or pencil in hand.

Thank you most kindly for listening, fellow writers. I do bid you a most wonderful day and night and night and day writing, writing, writing.
    Yours Sincerely,
    Dorothy Parker

DOROTHY PARKER was an American poet born on August 22, 1893. She died at the age of 73, due to a heart attack, on June 7, 1967. She was best known for her humor and wit and her ability to point out 20th Century urban flaws. She wrote and edited for various magazines, including *Vanity Fair* and *Vogue*. In the 1920s, she and writers Robert Benchley and Robert Sherwood, formed "The Vicious Circle," a group of critics, actors and wits, who met for lunch at New York's Algonquin Hotel. She moved to Hollywood with her second husband, Alan Campbell, and wrote screenplays, including, *A Star is Born*. After her death, the NAACP designed a memorial garden for her outside its Baltimore Headquarters. For her epitaph she suggested, 'Excuse my dust'."

"The cure for boredom is curiosity. There is no cure for curiosity."
    —Dorothy Parker

87

⇢ Gabriel García Márquez ⇠

Hola, y como estas, escritorios! Gabriel Garcia Marquez presente! Mucho gusto! Es un honor presente aquí en el mundo! Vayamos!

I'm honored to present here in English. Here I offer you some crumbs of knowledge in the hopes that they will give you a great meal about the writing life. Let us begin.

Action and adventure! That's what every book needs, correct? Maybe. For though *loco* times move a story along, they don't necessarily give you the meat of the story—the essence, as they say, or the *corazón*, as we say in *español*.

For truly, dear writers, the heart is the central part of everything you write. Forget about your brain—rational thought. It's the emotions that rule when you write, and it's the emotions that rule when readers read.

When a reader tears up at a particular scene in your novel, or cheers when your book's "bad guys" get what "they deserve," you know that the reader has been touched. Touched readers don't come along every day, as you know, but they do come along. And when they arrive, they find themselves in the "thick" of things, as they say. And then they find themselves adoring your work and clamoring for more!

Of course, you want your readers to clamor for more. You want them to buy all of your books, because they love what you write!

First, though, it's important that you catch them in your net. That you get them caught up in your fisherman's net. You do this with passion, as I mentioned.

Passion.

How do your create passion that lures readers? That gets them to travel across vast oceans of time and stop and sit down and read what you've written?

For one, you make your readers feel as if they are a lover—a treasured lover. That they are the only ones in your heart and mind and eyes. When they feel this way—when they feel your impassioned connection with them, they will follow you anywhere.

For those who are impassioned tend to be dedicated, and they tend to be the kinds of readers you want around to read your work and tell the rest of the world all about your prose.

So go ahead and put passion into your work. Infuse it with passion. You can "find" your passion, as they say, by looking deep within to what once excited you. Pull out those latent feelings and infuse them with the here and now. Then you will access passion like you haven't ever experienced it here before.

Then your readers will come in droves. Impassioned about you and your writing and your various purposes.
Buenos días o Buenas noches!
Con respecto,
Gabriel Garcia Marquez

GABRIEL GARCIA MARQUEZ was a Columbian novelist born on March 6, 1927. He died at the age of 87, due to pneumonia, on April 17, 2014. He is best known for his Magic Realism and his Nobel Prize-winning novel, *One Hundred Years of Solitude*. His other well-known works include *Love in the Time of Cholera* and *Chronicle of a Death Foretold*. Marquez was also a journalist, short-story writer, and screenwriter, whose popularity was so great in Latin America that he was widely known as Gabo or Gabito. He is considered one of the greatest Columbians who ever lived, because he is credited for defining the genre of Magic Realism. In 1948 at the age of 21, he quit school to become a journalist. Marquez worked as a journalist for nearly a decade before moving to Mexico to focus on writing novels. After the publication of his first novel, *One Hundred Years of Solitude*, Marquez was an instant international sensation. He went on to write more than 25 books in his lifetime.

"Ultimately, literature is nothing but carpentry. With both you are working with reality, a material just as hard as wood."
—Gabriel Garcia Marquez

88

⇝ Theodor Seuss "Ted" Geisel ⇜

Well, my, my, my! What do we have here! Dr. Seuss here to tell you that I do so adore you dear, dear Scribes of the Earth Plane! I am happy to offer my kernels of "wise wisdom!"

A cat
Borrowed a hat
And then spat
On the cat
That came to get
His most auspicious can
Out of the flim flam
Of his desk drawer

Oh, my, oh, my, what have we here? A rather odd rhyme, wouldn't you say? I would say so myself, yet am I myself, do you think? Or am I one of you, or you, or you? Talking in riddles; talking in rhymes; who indeed has the time for such silly, silly prattle? (Here I will not mention a child's rattle!)

Have you done this, do you think? Borrowed another writer's words? Have you worried yourself over this quite human, yet perplexing of circumstances? I'm here to tell you right here and right now that there is certainly nothing at all to worry about here! I do promise you. For as has been mentioned again and again, we are all quite interconnected—us Scribes of the Light and us Scribes of the Earth Plane! We most certainly are.

So, if you find yourself making utterances you feel might belong to another writer, yet you know in your heart of hearts that it is also coming from a place within you, just breathe. Know that indeed, the voices do become intermingled. This occurs as us writers all go about chatting, as all writers do, with other writers and ourselves, and the milkman and the mail delivery guy, if we've been alone too long with our own thoughts and our writing.

What, truly, am I trying to say? That you really can't, unless you sit down and copy another writer, copy other writers. For we are all busy copying one another—truly. Like a giant mimeograph machine we are, us writers! At the same time, we are also creating our own imprints, our own images, our own impressions—that we then throw into the giant writing pool for others to sort and sift through.

Am I saying that what we write, us Scribes, is not unique and all our own? Yes and no. Yes, our words are most certainly coming from our souls and our soul callings. No, our soul callings are not always making pronouncements, if you will, that are unique all on their own. For we take a bit of that and a dab of this and a squirt of that from the atmosphere when we write—and we make our own Alphabet Soup, if you will! Is this bad or good, as they say? It is neither. For truly it just is. And that is the way of the Universe! To be or not to be? (Yes, another "borrowed" phrase!) Well, we shall always be. There is no other way!

And if you have noticed that my message here is similar to another's, you would be quite correct. Of course, it also proves my point here, doesn't it?

Skip on
Dear Scribes of the Earth Plane
For your work is most certainly

Not done
Nor shall it ever be
But just remember
You are indeed free
To be
As you are and will always
Be!
(This little rhyme does so deserve a Tee Hee!)

Yours Truly, Truly,
Dr. Seuss

THEODOR SEUSS "TED" GEISEL was an American writer born on March 2, 1904. He died at the age of 87, due to oral cancer, on September 24, 1991. He is best known for writing/illustrating more than 60 children's books, such as *The Cat in the Hat*, *The Grinch*, and *Green Eggs and Ham*. Geisel got his big break by chance. He was just about to give up trying to sell his books when he ran into a former Dartmouth friend, who was an editor of the children's section of a publisher.

"Today you are you! That is truer than true! There is no one alive who is you-er than you!"
    —Dr. Seuss

89

✤ Sylvia Plath ✤

Hello, Fellow Scribes, Sylvia Plath here. Pleased to come here today. Thank you for "listening."

Before I start, I would like to remove the elephant—or at least place her in the corner of the room. Yes, my death was intentional, as it was the way it was supposed to be. Just as my appearing here is just as it should be. And that is all that I will say on this matter for now, as I wish to get on to my writing tips!

The lonely life of the writer. The quite quiet life. The life of the writer is a most bereft one at times, and then at others it is a most glorious one! For the writer life is certainly like a roller coaster of highs and lows and lows and highs.

But where do these highs and lows come from, do you think? From the act of writing itself, or from the state of being a writer?

I would have to say a little of both. For you can't help but tap into the writing life when you write, and that of being a writer.

I say this now to you, because I wish to let you know that the deep lows and the high highs are most certainly a part of life when one is a writer. If you are a chipper, upbeat sort who rarely has a bad day—I do commend you, I do! For I and other writers who tend to dip, most certainly see you as a bird in flight—a lark or hummingbird that rarely plummets, as they say. And that is well and good as well!

But back to the "other" matter. That matter of the dips that do indeed threaten the work, don't they?

I will say this. Just know that you are not alone. Just know that you are "normal." And most importantly, just know that "this too shall pass." That is all.

And what will most certainly make it all pass?

More writing, of course.

The more you write, the more you tap into your soul and very essence, and the more you will know that you are on your exact right writing path accessing all of the riches in the rainbow of words that are spilling forth.

Does this mean that you must always write, write, write when you are feeling a bit or a lot glum? No. It may be that talking to another or getting out and getting some sunshine is in order. The point is to continue to live your Earth Plane existence just as you are. The written words of wisdom will most certainly flow towards you in such a way that you can't help but gobble them up, or inhale them, at which point you must then regurgitate them onto the page or the computer screen.

It is most certainly so.

This path of resistance at times, and joy at others.

For the path does take you to all that you wish to and are meant to say with your written words.

Thank you again, Dear Fellow Scribes. I am most honored to have presented here. I do hope that my words have given you some comfort as you go about your days as the writer living the writing life!
  Yours Sincerely and Truly,
  Sylvia Plath

SYLVIA PLATH was an American poet born on October 27, 1932. She died at the age of 30, due to carbon monoxide poisoning, on February 11, 1963. She is best known for her novel *The Bell Jar*, and for her poetry collections *Ariel* and *The Colossus*. In 1982, she was the first person to win a Pulitzer Prize for her work after her death. Her most well-known confessional poem is titled "Daddy." Plath had a mental breakdown and fell into a deep depression following the betrayal of her husband, poet Ted Hughes, who left her for another woman. *The Bell Jar* was a way for her to process her emotions, because it was based on her own life, more specifically about the mental breakdown of a young woman. After the completion of her one and only book, her depression became too much to bear and she took her own life by putting her head in the oven. Her confessional poetry is still cherished and studied to this day, and there was even a biopic (biographical movie) made of her called, *Sylvia*, played by Gwyneth Paltrow.

> "Dying is an art, like everything else. I do it exceptionally well. I do it so it feels like hell. I do it so it feels real. I guess you could say I've a call."
>
> —Sylvia Plath

90

⇾ Franz Kafka ⇽

Good to be here today, Scribes! Very honored and most humbled! I shall begin. But first, may I introduce myself? Franz Kafka at your service.

Civility. Quite a concept, is it not? Something to ascribe to, certainly. An ideal whose time has come, as they say!

Why do I speak of civility? And what on Earth does it have to do with writing? Well, as it turns out, quite a lot! For civility is an ideal that is most certainly a good precursor to writing and to sharing one's writing, most definitely.

From our vantage point "up" here in the Light, us Scribes do watch today's Scribes and we sometimes wonder.

Not about your writing, for it is quite grand and fabulous!

But about your manner of sharing said writing.

Of getting said writing "out there," if you will.

Am I suggesting that you might not be doing "a good job" of getting your writing out there?

While I won't venture to say that anything is "right" or "wrong," I will say this—we in the Light, us Scribes here, do love to see it when you let your work take flight. When you give your words the permission to sprout wings, if you will, and fly, fly, fly!

If we see anything from here, it is this: You might be holding too closely to your words for fear of them taking a brief flight and then thumping to the ground to die a slow, painful death. Or that your words will get swooped up in a windstorm of sorts and make their way into the clouds where you can't retrieve them, no matter how hard you try. Indeed, up in the clouds, you fear that those words will get stolen and then reiterated back to the Earth under the name of another.

While this plagiarism is most certainly a valid concern, there are safety features, as they say, you can use to avoid such a problem.

At the same time, we urge you to shout your words from the rooftops. Once you feel secure in the fact that your work is protected, do get your work out there!

Now, you may be thinking, how does this have anything at all to do with civility?

It does in that you are urged to treat your work with civility. (I know! You'd thought I was referring to other people! While it is certainly suggested to treat others with civility—here I wish to talk about how you treat your words.)

Do you treat your words with civility? Do you treasure them and talk to them as if they have their own legs, and in some cases wings? Do you assure them that you know they know exactly where to go? They know exactly who would like to read them and enjoy them and savor them?

When you are civil with your words; when you trust them to go where they need to go, and release them to go, they will most certainly land where they are supposed to.

So go ahead and send your words out into the Universe. Give them a civil send off. Then watch as they land where they may and resonate where they may and enlighten and heal hearts where they may.

You will know at this point that your work is done, so that you can continue on with your next task and your next and your next.

Thank you for listening to the ramblings of a Light Scribe such as I!
I do wish you a most civil day and night!
   Yours Forever Truly,
   Franz Kafka

FRANZ KAFKA was a German speaking Bohemian Jewish novelist born on July 3, 1883. He died at the age of 40, due to tuberculosis, on June 3, 1924. He is best known for his short story, "Metamorphosis." His works are complex and bizarre. So much so that a literary term was coined for his style—Kafkaesque. He went on to write many other successful short stories, including "The Trial," "The Castle," "Amerika," and "The Judgment." His writing explored the ideals many people strive for, such as security and understanding. He grew up in an upper middle-class Jewish family, studied law at the University of Prague, and worked for an insurance company, leaving him only time in the evenings to write. In 1923, Kafka in an effort to dedicate all his time to writing, moved to Berlin, although he died shortly after, due to tuberculosis. A trusted friend went on to publish most of Kafka's work, such as *The Castle* and *Amerika*. Although he had a very short literary career, his writing style has inspired many and secured him a spot in literary history.

"A book must be the ax for the frozen sea within us."
   —Franz Kafka

91

❧ Marcel Proust ❧

Greetings, Dear Writing Pupils! I am Marcel Proust. And I have come down to Earth to speak with you, so here we shall go!

What drives you as a writer? What makes you go tick-tock? What does feed your muse? What does make you want to write, write, write?

Have you identified these sources, and truly, is it necessary?

I am here to tell you that yes, it is indeed necessary. For when you access the riches of the Earth's mighty kingdom and all you could draw from here, you most certainly will discover your muse and draw from its well of knowledge.

How does one figure out what drives one?

How does a writer determine his or her reason for writing? Indeed, his or her reason for living the writing life? For accessing the writing riches?

Have you thought to look inside? Truly inside? To cast a light on the inside of your soul? To ask yourself as you do so for answers, if they choose to come forth?

I know, I know. This all sounds rather vague and quite ethereal. You are perhaps thinking that I am indeed drinking from the "wine of the Light." In fact, I've consumed too much of that wine—too much of the Light.

Truly, I have not. For I wouldn't be in my right mind, as they say, to tell you that you know what drives you. You need only ask yourself, and you will most definitely find that what drives you is what feeds you. What feeds your soul. What feeds your mind. What feeds your very being. That is what drives you, and that is indeed why you write.

A few adjective phrases, if you will, that will most certainly give you a clue, as they say, as to why you might be driven to write.

A need for attention

A need to please

A need to express

A need to undress—to expose yourself and the secrets of the Universe

An urge to explore the yet unknown

A feeling that you must, simply must, express via the written word, or you shall quite literally burst!

A knowing, deep knowing, that you most certainly have the answers to some of life's questions inside of you, and that with a few, or a lot, of words, you can express those secrets, those answers to life mysteries.

And so you write. You write for some or all of these reasons—but you write. And you can be assured that as you write, all of your answers will eventually come forth, and the answers to questions of those with whom you share your writing, and with those whom you are yet to share your words of wisdom.

So go ahead and write, write, write, Dear Writing Pupils—who are certainly Scribes—Divine meets Earthly—in their own right!

I do bid you a good day or good night! Now do please write!
Yours Always and Forever,
Marcel Proust

VALENTIN LOUIS GEORGES EUGÈNE MARCEL PROUST was a French novelist born on July 10, 1871. He died at the age of 51, due to pneumonia, on November 18, 1922. He is best known for his seven-volume

novel, *In Search of Lost Time*, which is based on his own life told allegorically and psychologically. The book is in the top ten list of longest novels ever written. His other famous works include *Swann's Way* and *In the Shadow of Young Girls in Flowers*. He was greatly influenced by Gustave Flaubert (#39) and Honorè de Balzac (#40). Proust grew up in a wealthy French family. His writing career started with his writings about the exclusive Parisian drawing rooms. After the death of his beloved mother, he voluntarily isolated himself. Doing this drove him to start on his masterpiece, *In Search of Lost Time*.

"*The real voyage of discovery consists not in seeking new lands but seeing with new eyes.*"
　—Marcel Proust

92

✤ Anton Chekhov ✦

Greetings writers! Anton Chekhov reporting here. At your most blessed and humble service. I shall begin my foray into explanations about the writing life and writing—most glorious writing!

Country. Homeland. Of what do I speak? I speak of a sense of place, true, and yet it is more than that. It is a sense of grounding, as well, and a sense of knowing where you belong.

And yet.

Here in this work, many are speaking of how we are all intertwined and interconnected, aren't they—even in the Light? So why would I then talk to you of country and homeland and belonging to a certain place in time?

Because it most certainly is what occurs when you place a novel. When you "plunk" that story, to use a modern turn of phrase, right into the center of wherever it is you have decided that the novel should take place. Or to be a bit more accurate here, wherever your characters have decided they shall set down roots. For truly, the characters do drive the story, and they drive the plot, and they drive what occurs amongst themselves. However, that is another story—and it has been covered here in this book quite well.

Back to homeland. Back to roots. Yes roots. For roots do tie you to certain things—to certain places. At the same time, they do ground you so that you can then write and get the story out for all the world to see.

So are your country and city and even neighborhood roots of significance? Yes, they are. For when you feel a sense of connectedness, a sense of place, you can then give your characters that same sort of sense of connectedness, that same sort of place.

Is this always necessary? For certainly, haven't great works been done on the move, so to speak? Yes, they have. But even then, I ask you to consider this. The author himself or herself most likely felt a sense of place and grounding with one place in particular. And so he or she was most likely tapping into that sense of homeland while the writing occurred.

Some call this place home.

Some call this the place where one goes when one has nowhere else to go. Truly, when you are writing and you wish to feel grounded so you can continue writing, you do go to the only place where you feel a sense of security.

Some would also call this a safe place.

Why, oh, why, is this of significance? For one, because it is important to ground yourself on the Earth Plane as you express your truths in your writing, and the truths of your characters and plots. At the same time, it is also important to have a sense of comradeship, of kindred spirit, with some section or subset of people. This will give you a compass, so to speak, a way to find your way back home to a safe place where you can truly express yourself.

Of course, there are those countries where unrest is in the air—indeed where the country is a literal and figurative jumbled up "mess," as they might say—mixed with tragedy, most certainly. Those writers who work to give the rest of the world a bird's-eye-view of such tragedy are to be commended.

And yet…I would venture to say that as they write—from war-torn areas and those ravaged by Mother Nature's eventualities—that they access a safe place in their mind's eyes that calms them to the core so that they can be effective Scribes and record what they see for all the world's enlightenment.

That is all for now, Dear Fellow Writers! I wish you the best times with your writing.
Always,
Anton Chekhov

ANTON PAVLOVICH CHEKHOV was a Russian playwright born on January 29, 1860. He died at the age of 44, due to tuberculosis, on July 5, 1904. He is best known as a master playwright and a genius modern short story writer. His most notable plays are *The Cheery Orchard*, *The Seagull*, and *Three Sisters*. His most notable books are *Fat and Thin*, *The Lady with the Dog*, *The Bet*, and *The Man in a Case*. Chekhov famously advised book writers by saying, "If in the first act you have hung a pistol on the wall, then in the following one it should be fired." This quote became so well-known and accepted that it was turned into a literary concept called Chekhov's Gun, which states that "every element of a story should contribute to the whole." Chekhov was also a licensed and practicing physician and considered it his primary occupation, even going so far as to treat the poor free of charge.

"Medicine is my lawful wife and literature my mistress; when I get tired of one, I spend the night with the other."
—Anton Chekhov

93

❈ J. R. R. Tolkien ❈

Greetings Earth Scribes! It is I, J. R. R. Tolkien, come to give you words of wisdom from the past and present regarding the written word!

It is quite a wondrous occurrence this!! Hailing you from the Light. Indeed, this is a bit like my time on Earth, for I was quite often hanging about a bit or a lot in the Light as I wrote. You may note that from my writing, and that is quite good, I should say!

Characters. Creatures. Characters and Creatures. Oh, my! It is a most wondrous life, this writing life. For one can do just about anything one wants to on the page, and the audience, should they connect with your prose, will most certainly accept, even "swallow," anything and everything you serve up!

Should one, this point comes up with my last turn of phrase, but should one think this through before serving up what one serves up? For, truly, isn't there a bit of ethics and morale latitude that must be considered? For truly, writers are tasked with a quite big and brave mission, wouldn't you say?

Of course, we do entertain, and we do a right mighty job of that, I do say! But at the same time, we also are often listened to, aren't we? And some may even take to heart what we have to say. Oh, my! That does put a writer into a bit of a quandary, does it not? For it is difficult to warn one's readers: "Read what I've written, but please take it with a grain of salt, as they say." For truly, you may also have something you quite wish to say!

Oh, bother. What is a writer to do? How does a writer know when to say what and what to say when?

How about this? When you do write and when you do consider that writing, how does it truly make you feel? For in your feelings, in those stirrings that surely will play a bit with your soul, you will find the kernels of wisdom that tell you if: A) what you have said is exactly what you would like to say and it is quite grand, or B) what you have said is a bit off the mark and doesn't quite ring true, and then there is C) you are quite confused and have no idea if you've said what you wish to say or how it might affect others.

Of course, you do want to express your truths. You most certainly do! But on the other hand, you also want to ensure that what you put out there is truly something that the Universe will certainly find some solace with—or comfort—or knowledge—or entertainment. Something, as they say, worthy of being published.

How does one make sure? Well, I would suggest going with A every time, if you so choose. For A will never fail you. If you do find yourself at B or C, perhaps sit back and examine what you've written and then do give it a break. Let your subconscious (AKA window to your soul) work on it a bit and then go back to it and see what you see when you see it. After some rest and rejuvenation, you may very well see that you need only make a few tweaks, and your message, your writing wisdom, is perfect and says exactly what you wish to say. At that point, you can most certainly give it another polish or two and then send off the manuscript via your computer while you give it a big tallyho!

That is all for now, Dear Earth Scribes! I am, once again, quite honored to have presented here, and so grateful for your attention.
As Always, Honored Truly,
J. R. R. Tolkien

J. R. R. Tolkien

JOHN RONALD REUEL (J. R. R.) TOLKIEN was an English writer born on January 3, 1892. He died at the age of 81, due to a stomach ulcer, on September 2, 1973. He is best known for his wildly famous fantasy books, *The Lord of the Rings* trilogy, *The Hobbit*, and *The Silmarillion*. His trilogy books, *Lord of the Rings, Fellowship of the Ring,* and *The Hobbit,* were all turned into movies. His work inspired a whole series of related films. Born in South Africa, the author grew up in England where he attended Exeter College and ended up teaching as a professor of literature at Oxford University while he published his most famous fantasy novels, *The Lord of the Rings* trilogy and *The Hobbit*. While at Oxford, he started a writing club, The Inklings, whose members included the likes of C.S. Lewis (#84) and Owen Barfield. His earning a first-class educational degree in Anglo-Saxon and Germanic languages enabled him to create entirely new languages in his fantasy books. Tolkien also served as a lieutenant for the Lancashire Fusiliers during World War I.

"All we have to decide is what to do with the time that is given to us."
"Not all those who wander are lost."
—J. R. R. Tolkien

94

↠ Geoffrey Chaucer ↞

Greetings, as they say. Geoffrey Chaucer at your most humble service. I shall begin!

Perspective. I've seen writers here delve into this, and yet, I have something different to say. Something different, even, to impart overall. But isn't that the way it is with perspective? In fact, perspective is just different opinions and different viewpoints.

I can hear you sigh. It's a collective sigh here. For truly, we all know that we all have varying viewpoints, don't we? And I daresay at times that gets rather exhausting, doesn't it? For trying to keep those viewpoints in mind and trying to be mindful of those viewpoints and trying to respect those viewpoints can wear one out. At times it makes a writer wish to hole up and well, just write.

And that is what I urge you to do. Today I come to you to urge you to simply hole yourself up and write. And then write some more. And then write some more. For when you do, you will express your perspective, and something else quite lovely shall ensue. Your worries and concerns about others' perspectives will literally fade away.

How is that possible, you wonder, and perhaps even more important, why is it important?

Here is the reason, Dear Scribes. Perspective is necessary. Yes. Perspective is called for in all writing. Yes. Perspective colors a work and makes a work what it is. Most certainly. But you can't, no matter how hard you try, control or corner your perspective. For it has a life of its own. Writers don't realize this, but perspective tends to overtake a work if you let it. At the same time, you can't help but let perspective settle in and take over. For, as I mentioned, all work requires perspective.

So what is a writer to do with perspective? Simply embrace it. That is all. Know that when you start a work that you will be starting with a certain perspective. That perspective may even change during the writing of the work—as mentioned. Truly, it can take on a life of its own. But one thing you can be sure of. There will be perspective in your work. That is something you cannot ignore and avoid.

Is it necessary to tweak your perspective? You could try. But I daresay you'll find yourself struggling a bit to even modify perspective, for it may kick and buck at the attempt, and you'll just end up with the same perspective as when you started.

Giving in to perspective is your best choice. When you do, you will find that the work takes you on paths and down highways and byways that you might never have imagined had you tried to kick and buck the perspective. Take the ride with perspective and delve into the deep end with it, even. And know to your very soul that the perspective from which you are relaying the story or saga is the absolute perfect perspective. In fact, you could not write this story without this perspective. Once you accept and embrace this fact, you will most certainly be ready to thank the work for coming to you and move onto the next with its quite different perspective.

Thank you Scribes, for listening to me over the many ages! I do thank you also for reading my work, as that is a high honor!
  Yours Truly,
  Geoffrey Chaucer

GEOFFREY CHAUCER was an English poet born sometime between 1340 and 1344. He died on October 25, 1400. He is best known as the Father of English Literature and praised as the greatest English poet from the Middle Ages. His most famous works include *The Canterbury Tales*, *The Wife of Bath's Tale*, *Troilus and Criseyde*, and *The Legend of Good Women*. His primary job, which he held until his death, was as a public servant to Countess Elizabeth of Ulster and for the British Court. As a teenager, he fought in France's 100 Year War and ended up being captured and held for ransom. Due to his royal connections, his ransom was paid with the help of King Edward III, and he was released. After his release, he joined the Royal Service where he did much traveling through France, Italy and Spain as a diplomat. He continued to work in that capacity while writing in his free time.

"Time and tide wait for no man."
"The greatest scholars are not usually the wisest people."
—Geoffrey Chaucer

95

❖ Flannery O'Connor ❖

Hello dear Fellow Scribes! I am most honored to be here! Flannery O'Connor here. At your most humble and Divine service!

What's in a name? Truly, I ask you, what is in a name? For names do define us, wouldn't you say? And they most definitely help to define our characters. On the Earth Plane as Flannery, I did have a most unusual name. Of course, it was my "middle" name, as you say on the Earth Plane, but I did adore it and was happy to adopt it as my first. For truly, what is more flamboyant than an unusual name? A name like no other—or nearly like no other.

How do you choose your characters' names? Do you have a method? Or do the names simply step out of the flames of the seeming madness of the creative process? And just how important are names to your characters?

In my mind (such as it is in the Light!), I do think that names are quite important. For they help to characterize your characters. They help to define your characters' behaviors and they help to define, even, the situations in which those characters find themselves. So, yes, I am talking about plot being affected here, as well.

How is it that names are that important? How is it that names can and do affect and even drive a story? Perhaps a little example will help me explain this idea.

Let's say that you've named your character Rosebud. Let's also say that dear Rosebud works in a florist shop. Now that is a name that seems to be made-to-order for Rosebud, isn't it?

I can hear you thinking that my prior example was quite a simple one. Okay, fine, then. Here is another. Say that your character's name is Gumphrey. An odd name, I know, but I am trying to prove a point here. And let's say that Gumphrey is faced with a most startling and harrowing situation in your book. He finds himself under many beams and bricks after he is in a building that collapses due to an earthquake.

Gumphrey must dig his way out to save himself, for the rest of the city is in an uproar, and no one even knows Gumphrey is trapped. If you look closely at his name, it could hint at the word gumption. It would take quite a bit of gumption to dig oneself out of a building's rubble, so it's no surprise when Gumphrey does indeed remove himself from the building.

However, what if Gumphrey's name was Pigeon or Patsy or Slim? I do know that these names are quite odd—all of them—but then they are most likely getting the point across.

So when you choose your names for your characters, do consider a few factors as you do so.

1) What does this name say about the character? What might one infer from the name?

2) Does the name indeed fit the character? Of course, the story could revolve around a character not fitting his or her name. Or the name could be used for effect. Either way, the name itself does certainly matter and affect the story.

3) Are you able to pronounce the name without tripping over your own tongue? I say this, because if you do a reading, as they say, you most certainly want to pronounce your character's name correctly.

4) Do you like the name? Does it resonate with you and the story and the character himself/herself? Does it make you want to turn the page in order to find out, for instance, what Stormy is about to do with her late grandmother's tea set. Perhaps Constance, her sister, would be a better caretaker of the antique set?

That is all, dear Fellow Scribes. I do wish you much luck choosing your characters' names and enjoying the most splendid process of writing. For writing is truly one of the most treasured and honored of professions! Good day or night to you!
  Yours Truly,
  Flannery O'Connor

FLANNERY O'CONNOR was an American novelist born on March 25, 1925. She died at the age of 39, due to lupus, on August 3, 1964. She is best known for her Southern gothic style of writing where the characters are flawed or disturbed and oftentimes depicted in sinister situations or settings. There are often romantic and supernatural elements. She wrote two novels and thirty-two short stories. Her most notable works are *Wise Blood, The Complete Stories, A Good Man is Hard to Find,* and the short story "Everything That Rises Must Converge." She is widely regarded as one of the best 20th Century short story authors writing about Southern life and religious themes. She won many awards for her works, including the O. Henry Award in 1957 and the National Book Award in 1972.

"The writer operates at a peculiar crossroads where time and place and eternity somehow meet. His problem is to find that location."
  —Flannery O'Connor

96

➤ ÉMILE ZOLA ➤

Hello, there, as they say today! Émile Zola at your most humble service. Here to offer my "take" on the writing life and writing for you in this time and space!

Time and space. Space and time. When you turn those two statements around, as I did, it does give a quite different meaning, doesn't it? How often do you meddle with your words, turning them backwards and forwards and sideways and upside down, even? How often do you take them out of order and put them back in order?

Besides expediency, does this matter, really? How does it matter how you go about forming your prose and then editing it?

It does matter. This is not to say there is any "right" or "wrong" way, but your process does matter. To you, of course, and also to your characters. For how you go about putting all of the pieces together, including finding a setting and deciding on plot points and deciding on the cast of characters, that all affects the final work.

Is there a correct or prudent way to do this? No. Then, why, you may be wondering, am I pointing this out? Because the process does matter. It may not be right or wrong, but it indeed affects your flow. It affects how much you enjoy the process of writing, as well.

So what fantastic advice will I give you about process? To go with the flow. To use whatever process comes naturally to you. For here in the Light, and even when I was there on the Earth plane as Émile, I did notice many writers very concerned about process. Fretting about if their processes are indeed proper. If their processes will lead them to where they want to go. You may find yourself asking other writers about their processes, and then comparing yours to theirs.

While this is all well and good, as they say, it may not be necessary and indeed could disrupt the entire process for you. It could make the process go much more slowly and certainly not with fluidity.

So what is the answer with the processes? Just go with your own flow, as was mentioned prior. Don't, if you choose, worry about another's processes. You might want to find out about another writer's processes out of curiosity, and then you might even "steal" some of that writer's processes for your own good. And that is quite grand as well. You would be, if you see where this is going, going with the flow when you choose to find out about another writer's processes because you wish to, not because you think you have to.

If this all sounds quite a bit like doing your own "thing" in whatever manner you choose for yourself, you would be most certainly correct! For processes are just that—processes. They can be different or the same or similar or diametrically opposed. A process that works for one writer may not work for another, while a process that works for one book may not work for another book—even for the same writer!

So go ahead. Create your books as you see fit. Flow along on the river of creation, as they say, and do enjoy the creative process journey! For it will be like no other—truly. And that is a most blessed thing!

Good day to you, Fellow Scribes. Do enjoy your writing journeys, wherever they may lead!
    Always,
    Émile Zola

ÉMILE ZOLA was a French novelist born on April 2, 1840. He died at the age of 62, due to carbon monoxide poisoning from an improperly vented chimney, on September 29, 1902. His most notable works include *Germinal*, *Nana*, and *Thérèse Raquin*. He was also a playwright and journalist. In 1865, he published his first novel, *La Confession de Claude*, which was highly controversial at the time and ultimately cost him his job as a journalist. The book was a semiautobiographical novel about a man who falls in love with a sex worker. In the two years to follow, being undeterred, he published two more novels, *Thérèse Raquin* and *Madame Férat*. In 1868, he wrote *Les Rougon-Macquart*, which is a large-scale series of novels consisting of 20 volumes. Zola, who founded the Naturalism Movement in literature, went on to explain his theories about art though several published treatises. His writing was considered scandalous and groundbreaking.

"If you ask me what I came into this life to do, I will tell you: I came to live out loud."
"The artist is nothing without the gift, but the gift is nothing without work."
"There are two men inside the artist, the poet and the craftsman. One is born a poet. One becomes a craftsman."
　—Émile Zola

97

⇥ Harriet Beecher Stowe ⇤

Hello, Dear Scribes!! Happy greetings to you! I am Harriet Beecher Stowe, and I am so thrilled to be here! My message for you ensues.

Where, truly, does your heart lie in relation to your writing? Are you happy when you write? Are you sad? Do you wish for joy when you write, or will you "settle" for contentment?

Why do I ask these questions of you? Most certainly, what on Earth does this have to do with becoming a better writer and improving one's craft?

I do say here that it has quite a lot to do with that! Most certainly, you will find that how you feel truly does color your writing. It not only colors it, but it infuses it.

So does this mean that you should only feel joyous when you sit down to write? No, of course not. For if we writers all waited until we were joyous, we wouldn't write nary a line—hahaha—as you say on the Earth Plane now—but truly you know what I mean!

How should one feel when one sits down to write? Like writing, you would think, although surely, you know this, that you don't always feel amenable to the process, do you?

Okay, okay, I can hear you saying; get to it already, Harriet!

I will.

I feel—and this is all up to you, of course—but I feel that you should feel like you want to express in your writing. You should, therefore, take on the feelings of whomever you are writing about—that character's or characters' feelings, and the mood of the plot and the time and space in which you are writing. Truly, it works best if you can "become one" with the tone of the story.

Yes tone! I am talking about tone, and I am referring to how one arrives at the tone that you wish to impart. For truly, it is necessary to access the tone you would like by feeling and being at one with that tone.

So, if you are writing a rather frightful scene, sit down in your writing chair with trepidation. And if you are writing a love scene, sit down with love flooding your heart. I think you see what I mean here.

The tone is truly very important to a work—ultra-critical, actually. For tone will make the reader, in turn feel, and you, of course, want the reader to feel the "right" feelings for the scope of the work and its theme and message.

How do you go about taking on these feelings that you may not be feeling? For hopefully, you aren't going about your days carrying undue trepidation. Or horror, or dread.

It may seem like a no-brainer, and yet it does require some brainpower—but go ahead and think of the situations in which you will be putting your characters. Become your characters and imagine that the situation is indeed bearing down upon you. Let the emotions regarding this flood in on you. Let them take you out to sea and splash around in them for a bit.

Then sit down speedily and begin to write. As you write, you will be swept along in the wave of emotions, and you will find yourself in the thick of things, and you will find that the tone is most certainly right on point!

That is all from me now, Dear Scribes! I will bid you a nice day or night and a most splendid writing life!
  Yours Truly,
  Harriet Beecher Stowe

Harriet Beecher Stowe

HARRIET BEECHER STOWE was an American author born on June 14, 1811. She died at the age of 85 on July 1, 1896. She wrote novels, poetry, essays, and nonfiction books. She is best known for her novels *Uncle Tom's Cabin*, *Dred: A Tale of the Great Dismal Swamp*, and *The Minister's Wooing*. She is credited for being the most influential woman of the 19th Century, because of her contribution to the Abolitionist Movement. She is even rumored to have contributed to the uprising and outbreak of the Civil War. So influential was Stowe that President Abraham Lincoln was reported to have said to her: "So you're the little woman who wrote the book that made this great war." She was a mother to seven children.

> "It's a matter of taking the side of the weak against the strong, something the best people have always done."
> "Women are the real architects of society."
> —Harriet Beecher Stowe

98

⇻ Kurt Vonnegut ⇺

Yeah, it's me, Kurt Vonnegut. Ready to give you some writing advice, be it what it may be. Thanks for the invite. It's definitely appreciated! Let's get to this, as they say.

Hard lessons. The school of hard knocks. Is that what the writing life has been like for you? If so, not surprising, for many of us writers have dived into the deep end without water. At least it seems like that on those days when you feel like ripping what hair you have in your head out trying to come up with the perfect sentences—the perfect words, even.

Are there perfect words? Yes, there are, and no there aren't. Okay, so you thought I might sit down and give you some straightforward facts here. While that was my way on the Earth Plane as Kurt, for sure, I'm a little different here in the Light. And yet, I'm very much the same.

So what to do about the fact that you may have signed yourself up for the school of hard knocks and you get stuck at times and the words just don't want to spring forth?

Nothing.

Yes, I repeat. Nothing.

For when you start churning and stewing and cussing and carrying on about this, it will only make matters worse.

Believe me.

So should you give up!

Of course, not.

But do walk away for a bit. Get a strong cup of coffee or eat a good meal. Take a walk. Talk to a loved one. Pet your pet, if you have one.

Just know that it'll be okay.

And then remind yourself that you've been here before. This writer's block—which truly isn't a block at all.

In fact, it's a good thing. This stalling. Because it means that your subconscious is working out some bugs that you may not have even known you had.

And when your subconscious is done. You'll know. For you'll feel like sitting your butt back down and churning out the work, finally.

It may take an hour; it may take a day; it may take a month. I know, I know. You don't want to hear this. But truth is, what you do want to hear is the happy clicking away of the keyboard as the words rush forth—the "right" words that you know are coming directly from your subconscious and soul.

So let the school of hard knocks in the "dry well department" be okay. Embrace the silence for a time, and you will soon see that the quiet leads to a crescendo of writing jewels that will come clamoring onto the page and won't stop until you've finished the last splendid sentence.

I do hope this helps you figure out this writing "thing" and live this out-of-this-world writing life!

Keep at it!

Kurt Vonnegut

KURT VONNEGUT was an American writer born on November 11, 1922. He died at the age of 84, due to traumatic brain injury, on April 11, 2007. He is best known for his dark satirical writing style and the science fiction elements in his writing. Vonnegut published fourteen novels, five plays, three short story collections, and five nonfiction works. His most notable works are his bestselling classic novels, *Slaughterhouse-Five*, *Breakfast of Champions*, and *Cat's Cradle*. After studying at Cornell University, Vonnegut enlisted in the US Army and was sent to study engineering at Carnegie Mellon University before being shipped off to Europe to fight in the Battle of the Bulge. After the battle was won, Vonnegut was captured and held as a prisoner of war (POW) near Dresden, Germany. He narrowly escaped harm from the Allied firebombing of the city, because he and the other POWs were being forced to make vitamin supplements in an underground meat locker. When he finally escaped and returned from war, he married his high school sweetheart, Jane Marie Cox. Together they had 3 children. When his sister died, he adopted her 3 children, as well. He worked many jobs until his writing career took off.

"I urge you to please notice when you are happy, and exclaim or murmur or think at some point, 'If this isn't nice, I don't know what is.'"
—Kurt Vonnegut

99

❯ VOLTAIRE ❮

Hello Fellow Scribes! Voltaire here. Most honored, most definitely, to present here. I am ready to give you all that I may to help you with your writing triumphs and travails!

The splendid writing life! Oh, my, it is a glorious one! And it is a life that has always been glorious! Are there times when the writing life is a bit trying? Most certainly! But then, life in general can be trying on the Earth Plane.

I only mention this—this idea of the glorious writing life—to point out to you that in this time and place and space the writing life can be the most glorious of all time!! For truly, in this 21st Century, you scribes have so much latitude! The freedom to say what you wish—for the most part—and to then publish your own writing, if you so choose.

Back in my day, as they say, it was not so. At least in the publishing department, for one could cloister oneself away and write to oneself or a few others. But getting the word out was a much more controlled situation.

So what does this comparison do for your writing? I suggest that you use this comparison to free yourself. Remind yourself of the freedoms that you do experience in this lifetime to express yourself as you wish in whatever manner you wish!

We Fellow Scribes in the Light are here to help you with this journey. With this mission. We are! We are so excited when we see the freedoms that you do indeed experience, and we are most happy and enthusiastic and eager to help you help yourselves.

How might this be done? I will give you a few "pointers," as you say in your day now!

1. Listen. Heed the messages you will most certainly hear coming in the sound of the birds in the trees and the breeze and the ocean's waves. Or those messages may come over the airwaves via your television or your radio. Or the messages may come from a friend or a family member, or another Fellow Scribe!

2. Follow the breadcrumbs. We in the Light are ever efficient at sprinkling crumbs of knowledge and clues to what you may write and how you may write it and even how you may publish. Look for those breadcrumbs always.

3. Believe. Believe that you can indeed access the Light in less than a second, if you wish. And that an Army of Fellow Scribes is at your service—at your beck and call, always.

4. Have faith. That you have all that it takes to be a most renowned Fellow Scribe. That you have what it takes to be a "bestselling writer." For truly, I tell you now, you already are!

5. Know. Know that all is going and will go in Divine right order in Divine right time. Always! Your reading this at the Divinely right time is a perfect example!

Well, that is all Dear Fellow Scribes. I know this is a bit on the "short and sweet" side, as you say in your day, but that is as it should be. For truly, you know exactly what you want to say and exactly when you want to say it. And you know that what you say will most certainly ring true for many!

Good Day to You Always!
Most Humbly,
Voltaire

Voltaire

FRANÇOIS-MARIE AROUET, penname Voltaire, was a French writer born on November 21, 1694. He died at the age of 83 on May 30, 1778. He is most famous for his wit and his verbal attacks on the Catholic Church and Christianity as a whole. He was also an advocate for freedom of speech, freedom of religion, and the separation of church and state. Voltaire was a French Enlightenment writer, philosopher, and historian. His most famous works include *Candide, Zadig, Oedipus, Mahomet,* and *Dictionnaire Philosophique.* Despite the controversy surrounding his views and beliefs, he is still considered one of France's greatest philosophers and writers. Voltaire's concepts of social reform were what the founding fathers of the American Revolution built upon to build a new form of government.

"*Those who can make you believe absurdities can make you commit atrocities.*"
—Voltaire

100

❖ Albert Camus ❖

Well, well, well, I am most honored to present here! Albert Camus at your service. Let us begin.

Subterfuge. Intrigue. Suspense. These are most certainly helpful aspects to include in your work so that it might keep readers turning the page, as they say. But is it possible to get readers to turn the pages by simply relaying everyday life to them? You may question this and even ask yourself, how can boring, everyday life be anything but boring and everyday? And how on earth could I make it otherwise?

Of course, many writers have done so. Most certainly, some of the greatest works ever created relate aspects of the mundane. Aspects of the ordinary, if you will. But what those works do so well is show the absurdity, truly, of the human condition. They bring up the little points and the not so little points along the road of life that humans tend to come up against or simply roll over without notice. And then those plots/stories do show the readers how those actions or non-actions affect all of the characters involved.

For some the involvement and the reactions are quite minimal. In fact, some characters do little more than roll over and go back to sleep when faced with life's little and big challenges. While other characters do tend to overreact, even to the littlest of things. Truly, there are those characters who have mastered the art of crafting mountains out of mole hills. Of hills out of mere dips in the road.

So why is this of significance? Well, for one, it shows you that indeed your story—even your own life story—could indeed be a most wondrous one, depending on how you depict it. Your treatment of the hills and valleys and mole and ant hills of your life will certainly color the story and make it either a page-turner or a snore-fest, as they say.

How does one make "little" stories "big?" I had mentioned absurdity. And I suggest that you take ahold of this concept and that you run with it. For truly, showing readers the absurdity of the human condition most certainly makes for a rather large story, if you will. For when you see the irony in the fact, for instance, that the milkman ran over a cow accidentally on his way to work, or the postman delivered a letter to the wrong address and then cuts his finger trying to retrieve it from a person's mailbox, these are most certainly "little" things, in the scheme of things, and yet they can become quite big stories as the yarn unspools, for lack of a better term.

For consider this. What if the owner of the cow is the milkman's boss? And the cow was his best milk producer? And what if the letter the mailman is trying to retrieve is a love letter from his wife to the man who resides in the house next door? And the mailman's blood on the envelope, which he never does retrieve, gives him away later when the man next door is found to have had an untimely demise. Of course, the latter is a bigger item, but it did start with a quite minor one. This is another tactic you can take—to juxtapose "large" life issues with "tiny" ones.

> *I do hope this gives you something to mull over and consider as you plan your most glorious works and then write them! Do find yourselves in the depths of writing, dear Fellow Scribes, at least once a day—for doing so will give you a great vantage point from which to view life's little and big absurdities.*
>
> *Yours Always,*
> *Albert Camus*

ALBERT CAMUS was a French-Algerian writer and philosopher born on November 7, 1913. He died at the age of 46, due to a traffic collision, on January 4, 1960. He won the Nobel Prize in Literature in 1957. His most famous novels are *The Stranger*, *The Plague*, and *The Myth of Sisyphus*. He also wrote many plays, including *Caligula*, *The Just Assassins*, *The Misunderstanding*, *The Possessed*, and *The State of Siege*, to name a few. He was also an essayist and journalist and a strong supporter of individual rights. Camus believed in the philosophy known as Absurdism, which is where one embraces "the absurd condition of human existence while also defiantly continuing to explore and search for meaning." In his essay, *The Rebel*, he wrote that he would devote his whole life to the opposition of Nihilism. He was divorced twice, with one of his marriages ending because of infidelity. Later he stated that he strongly disapproved of the institution of marriage, which he saw as an unnatural state.

"The only way to deal with an unfree world is to become so absolutely free that your very existence is an act of rebellion."
—Albert Camus

101

⇝ Alexandre Dumas ⇜

Well, hello, Dear Fellow Writing Scribes. Pleasure to meet you here and now! On to my message, as it is! Highly honored to be "here." Alexandre Dumas at your service.

Service. What a word, eh? For service does bring up many thoughts, and even feelings. Service can of course mean many things within the English (and French) language—for there are nuances to the word.

When we talk about the word service when it comes to writing, of what do we speak? Do we speak of how the written word may help and heal, yes, I think we do. Do we also speak of how the written word can be of use to many? Yes, I think we do.

Do you feel that your writing will indeed be of service to those for whom you write? Do you also think that it could potentially be of service for those in your life who may not read what you've written? Yes, that is also the case. For as you are of service with your words and spread them out there for all of the world to see and gain from, you also do a good deed or two or more for yourself.

For helping with the written word truly helps all of humanity—even those who may never consciously read your words. Your words do make themselves known to some, who then talk about them with others, who then act upon what they've read. You see how the daisy-chain effect does ignite and then spread like a weed, so to speak, don't you?

As you are guessing, this spreading through the written word of service is most definitely a service in its own right. The written word can be of service to those who read it and then be of service to those who write it. For truly, when you write you absorb what you have written, and in many ways it becomes a part of your soul. This does refer to the good and the "bad," but have no fears, for it is as if in a library, this bad, so that you can take it out and spin it around and analyze it from every direction, and then you can put it back where it belongs in the library.

Service. Do you wish to be of service with your writing? If so, you are not alone. For many writers have expressed their interest in being of service to the Light and Earth Plane through their work.

It is most easy to be of service using the written word. Truly, all you must do is write about something of interest to people. Truly, Divine Timing and Divine Orchestration will take care of the rest and make certain that all of those who could use your Divine service will be showing up in record time.

At times, service can become quite wearying. We in the Light know this and see this in all of the caretakers on the Earth Plane, and indeed for Scribes. We do remind you of this, however. When you do the service your soul calls you to do and write, you most certainly elevate your soul, as they say, to a new status, so to speak. Actually, you elevate your writing status. The more you write, the more you help, the more your writing is helped and your soul is helped.

Do you have to impart clearly visibly "helping" words when you write to be of service? No you don't. For you can simply entertain and that will be of service. Most definitely, giving readers a good laugh is a right grand service! Just as giving information is of service, and just as buoying readers up with your words is of service.

That is all for now, Dear Fellow Writing Scribes! I do hope that my words were of service to you so that you may then be of service to others, and so forth! Do have a grand writing life!
  Yours Always,
  Alexandre Dumas

Alexandre Dumas

ALEXANDRE DUMAS was a French writer born on July 24, 1802. He died at the age of 68, due to a stroke, on December 5, 1870. He is known as one of the most recognized and widely read French authors of all time. His works have been translated into more than 100 languages. His most notable works include *The Three Musketeers, The Count of Monte Cristo, The Man in the Iron Mask, The Black Tulip*, and *Twenty Years After*. After becoming a successful author, Dumas built the Château de Monte Cristo in Port Marly, Yvelines, France as a sanctuary where he could write and entertain guests, which is what he did until he became overcome with debt that forced him to sell the property. He then fled to Belgium before settling in Russia. He continued to write and publish travel books about Russia. Many of his bestselling novels were turned into films.

"All for one and one for all."
—Alexandre Dumas

102

❖ RAY BRADBURY ❖

Greetings, Earth Scribes! How utterly out-of-this-world is the fact that I am presenting here and that you are reading this! There truly are no coincidences! This I knew as Ray Bradbury on the Earth Plane, and this I know now, most certainly, from the Light!

What do I wish to impart that hasn't been imparted here, being that I'm number 102? What a number, wouldn't you say? A number that does make me feel a tad old, even from the Light! But I do say that in jest! For we are all eternally young here in the Light!

Youth and the lightness of this state. It is a quite lovely place to be. As is the state of being a writer! Of being able to express yourself in whatever manner you wish.

Switching genres. That is what I wish to speak about. In a sense, switching genres when you so choose is a lot like being born again, wouldn't you say? For when a writer jumps from one genre to another—say fiction to nonfiction—a writer does feel a freeing sense of starting again. And that is a quite freeing feeling. And that freeing feeling will indeed help you as a writer to soar with the writing, whatever writing it may be.

You may have heard said that it's best to "stick with one genre" and get to know that genre through and through, so that you can master the genre. Indeed, it may even be inferred, depending on when you start writing in your life, that you should go to your grave, to use a rather dreary term, writing the same genre. Certainly, this is a bit extreme. For who wishes to put on their epitaph, "He/she wrote only in one genre!"

Of course, there may be some of you who wish to do this, and so I say, please do! However, if you choose to dabble here and there with genres, I invite you to do so. In fact, I encourage it! For switching genres—even jumping here and there as an excited rabbit with the writing—is certain to give your words a spring in their proverbial steps. At the same time, it will give you quite a writing education. For when you write in different genres you learn so many new methods and techniques. You most certainly do!

What would be my advice should you choose to write in certain genres, as I did as Ray Bradbury? Here is a list. These lists are quite handy!

1. Do switch as you wish. Rather than fearing that you appear to be bit chaotic, and as if you don't quite know what you're doing—just switch genres and write, write, write.

2. Know that you are on the right track when you have the urge to switch genres. If you have just finished a piece of fiction and you learned of a technique while writing the work that would then flesh out to be a magnificent magazine or blog post, as you now say, then most certainly write what you know! For certainly, the urge to write is the most important urge of all and something you would be wise to heed!

3. Breathe a sigh of relief. This is especially appropriate if you have been told to "make up your mind already" and stick to one thing. I am officially giving you the go-ahead to switch!

4. Look for synchronicities. For there will be parallels between the various themes and subjects that you write about amongst the various genres. When you see these synchronicities, do two things. First, pat yourself on the back, for this certainly is a sign that you are on all of the right tracks! Second, look for even more synchronicities. For as you notice some synchronicities and acknowledge them, others will soon follow!

5. Expect that your writing will ramp up several notches, as they say. For being a jack-of-many-trades in the writing realm is certain to

strengthen your writing skills and to make you even more prolific. This may be contrary to the basic wisdom bandying about regarding the perils of switching genres, but I say that it is quite accurate. And isn't that truly the case with much on the Earth Plane? What appears to be one way ends up being an entirely different way? When you come to realize this, you certainly soar as an Earth Plane Scribe!

Thank you ever so much for listening, Earth Scribes! I do bid you a most glorious life as a scribe and hope that your days and nights are filled with shooting star epiphanies that take you to the moon and back again and again!
Yours Forever and Truly, Truly,
Ray Bradbury

RAY DOUGLAS BRADBURY was an American author born on August 22, 1920. He died at the age of 91 on June 5, 2012. He is best known for his novels *Fahrenheit 451*, *The Illustrated Man*, and *The Martian Chronicles*. Bradbury also wrote short stories, such as "The Veldt," "A Sound of Thunder," and All Summer in a Day." His most famous book, *Fahrenheit 451*, took him a little more than a week to write. At one point, the book was ironically banned. It is about the future and banning/burning of books. Bradbury had a lifelong habit of writing every day. His short stories were praised for being highly imaginative and his novels for blending social criticism, childhood nostalgia, and an awareness of the potential hazards of runaway technology.

"You don't have to burn books to destroy a culture. Just get people to stop reading them."
—Ray Bradbury

103

❥ Harper Lee ❦

Hello, Scribes! Nice to meetcha, as they say! Harper Lee here. At your service, most definitely!

Point of view. I would most certainly like, right here and now, to discuss with you point of view. For point of view is one of your most important tasks in order to relay a story as you would like.

Point of view gives you grace. It gives you latitude. It gives you plot, even. For point of view is most certainly a talisman or woman, so to speak.

How should you choose your point of view, do you think? Is there one "right" way? Not surprisingly, no, there is not. For we are all different beings, and therefore we are all different in our approaches to writing in general, and most certainly in choosing our point of view.

What is point of view, truly, before we go further with this? It is the vantage point from which you are telling the story. It is your lookout point, if you will, and from that lookout point the reader not only sees the land (plot) lying out in front of him or her, but the reader also sees the vantage point. This is of significance, I must tell you.

For if the character reacts to the plot laid out in the great valley from where he or she stands, he or she will also react to those items and people that are up close and personal to him or her within the vantage point location.

If this sounds a bit complicated, it is. For we are talking, in essence, about two types of vantage points. One is the faraway vantage point that the character sees through his or her eyes and into the distance—for instance a scene occurring in the middle of a restaurant as the character eats a solo dinner tucked away in a corner. Then there is the vantage point inside the head of the character as he or she keeps a running dialogue going while eating.

Of course, both of those vantage points might certainly be different—and in fact, they usually are! That is good, of course, because it gives the story depth and interest, and even intrigue.

Such vantage points also give the writer a wide girth from which to stretch and strain the plot lines so that they are of interest and they serve their required purposes. This is another quite valuable benefit of perspectives.

How else may what are certainly two different perspectives help move a story along or give it breadth? When you have these two vantage points meet—or clash even—then you have the makings of quite a good story! In fact, if you are thinking that is what occurred in *To Kill a Mockingbird*, you would certainly be correct. For that reason, alone, the story took wings and took flight and soared. Perspective was an integral part of the work and an integral part of the inner workings of the mind of the main characters.

I do hope that this little chat on perspective has given you some delightful and helpful and filling "food for thought." I wish you wondrous treasures in your pursuit of the writing life.
Yours Truly,
Harper Lee

NELLE HARPER LEE was an American novelist born on April 28, 1926. She died at the age of 89, due to a stroke, on February 19, 2016. She is best known for her novels *To Kill a Mockingbird* and *Go Set a Watchman*. She won the Pulitzer Prize in 1961 for *To Kill a Mockingbird*, which was an immediate success and is now considered a classic of American Literature. Lee's father, Amasa Coleman Lee, was a lawyer and the inspiration for *To Kill A Mockingbird*, told from the perspective of a young girl. Lee followed in her father's footsteps and went to the University of Alabama to study law. She realized, however, that law wasn't her calling, so she left and worked as an airline reservationist until she was fortunate enough to get the financial help she needed from friends to pursue her writing fulltime. One of her most well-known friends was Truman Capote (#107). She took notes for him, which were later compiled and used to write his best-selling novel *In Cold Blood*. She never married or had children, but devoted her life to writing.

"You never really understand a person until you consider things from his point of view."
—Harper Lee

104

➤ Guy de Maupassant ✦

Bonjour Fellow Scribes. Guy de Maupassant present and accounted for! I do thank you for listening to me! On to my message.

Sense of place. Indeed setting. How does one go about setting up the setting, so to speak, so that it indeed seems "real?" And is it vital that it feel real, truly?

I would like to say here that yes, it is indeed important that setting feels real. That setting fulfills its end of the bargain, so to speak, and gives the readers a place for the plot and the characters to experience, learn and grow—devolve even.

How does one ensure that the setting fulfills its various requirements? I shall enumerate for you here, as they say!

1) Do you feel as if you are in your setting? When you are writing and when you are visualizing your setting, do you feel it? For example, if it is a tropical setting with a beach containing crystal blue water, do you feel yourself there? Can you truly feel the rhythm of the ocean waves, the granules of sand between your toes and the humidity in the salty sea air? When you lick your lips, do you taste the salt?

2) Does your setting come to meet and greet you? By that I mean does the setting truly seem alive and spring forth from the page? Does it make itself known in a brassy and bold way so that you are sure that you truly "know" the setting and that you understand it, even?

3) Do you wish to stay awhile—to linger—in your setting? Of course, this would make sense if you are describing a tranquil tropical beach setting with a comfortable seat. But do you also wish to linger even if the setting isn't as pleasant—say the battlefield? The fact that you wish to stay speaks to the effectiveness of the setting. Truly, a setting will mesmerize and entrance if it is well-drawn—to the point where readers and even the writers wish to stay and explore.

4) Does the setting feel as if it fits perfectly? Does it slide into place and lock itself into your plot seamlessly? Is this obviously the only place that the work could take place in order to be the work that it is? Would another setting seem off somehow and simply not right?

5) Do you just know? Do you know deep in your heart that your setting is a beast all on its own and that it has legs and that it is perfectly placed in this time and space in your work? Then, my dear Fellow Scribes, you have accessed the absolute perfect setting for your story! And it will help you to present and create the most glorious of stories to share with readers. Indeed, the setting will be so memorable that it will resonate with readers for a long time. And they will come to meet you again and again in the settings you create in the future!

Thank you, Dear Fellow Scribes, for listening to my various "good reasons" for being mindful of your setting and how your setting will affect your plot points and your characters. I do believe I have said my fill and will now "sign off," as they say.

Yours Forever and a Day,
Guy de Maupassant

GUY DE MAUPASSANT was a French writer born on August 5, 1850. He died at the age of 42, due to syphilis, on July 6, 1893. He is best known as a master of short stories and was a member of the naturalist school of writers. This group of writers was known for depicting human lives, social forces, and destinies in pessimistic and disillusioned terms. His works painted a fascinating picture of 19th Century French life. He published six novels and more than 300 short stories in his lifetime. His most notable novels and short stories are *Bel Ami*, *Une Vie*, "Boule de Suif," "The Necklace," "The Horla," and "Two Friends." He was the apprentice of Gustave Flaubert (#39), who said, "He's my disciple, and I love him like a son." Flaubert also introduced him to other leading writers of the time, including Émile Zola (#96), Edmond Goncourt, Ivan Turgenev, and Henry James (#47). Stricken with grief over the loss of his brother and his advanced congenital case of syphilis, Maupassant tried committing suicide by slitting his throat, although his efforts were unsuccessful. He was admitted to a private asylum in Paris, where he died just one month prior to his 43rd birthday.

"It is the lives we encounter that make life worth living."
—Guy de Maupassant

105

❧ CHARLES BAUDELAIRE ❧

Greetings, Fellow Scribes! Thank you much for showing up, as they say. I, Charles Baudelaire, am eager to give you a few writing advice tidbits, as you do say today! Here we shall go.

How do you go about inspiring yourself? Truly inspiring yourself? For truly, Dear Fellow Scribes, inspiration is the "way to go," as you say in your day. If you were to sit down un-inspired, most likely what you'd have to say to the page or the computer screen would be quite dreary or boring or just not worth saying at all!

This is not to say that at times you most certainly must sit down, no matter what, and write, despite not being inspired. This may happen, as it did to me as Charles, when there are those dreaded Earth Plane tasks, such as bills to pay. Collectors are such a bother—a nuisance, as they say!

But I digress. Back to the matter at hand. Inspiration! What truly does inspire you? What makes your heart sing in a manner that the songs *simply must* come out onto the page?

Sometimes it could actually be an Earth Plane necessity that does inspire. I can remember, for instance, being inspired by the bill collectors, so to speak, or the need to buy coal for heat—you "get the picture," as they say.

Perhaps nature does inspire you? Seeing a great owl at night with his most mighty wingspan and deep, knowing eyes. This could indeed inspire one to great heights to write, write, write! Or perhaps a cold spring morning when the dew is frozen on the ends of the blades of grass that then do droop toward the ground, ready to melt and infuse the earth with the knowledge embedded in the drops once the sun does come out.

Or maybe reading another Scribe's words of wisdom will inspire you! Or watching a film in the cinema, as they might say.

Or maybe you simply get inspired by just thinking—or trying not to think. In some circles, they refer to this as meditating. If you can try this tactic, it most certainly is quite effective. For it forces your mind to quit making lists and counting the money or lack of it or ruminating about how the water closet does need a bit of repair.

How, oh, how do you access inspiration so that you may fly, fly, fly with your writing in such a manner that you can't help but truly soar?

Ask yourself this question—what inspires me? And then quickly jot down your reply to yourself. For surely, whatever you write will answer your question regarding inspiring yourself. It may be a simple word or phrase. For instance, sand or beach. By George, then go to the beach and stick your toes in the sand! Just remember to bring a writing implement and paper, for you will most certainly need it when the words spring forth. Or maybe, you write forest, or field, or horse track, even. Wherever it is that you access from your soul—that is where you will find the jewels of inspiration and the tremendous treasures of the written word. Your written word—your messages for humanity!

That is all for now, Dear Fellow Scribes. I am highly honored to have presented here—n'est-ce pas! (A little addition from my "native tongue" as Charles!) And I truly do wish you a most splendid writing life filled with tremendous inspiration that coats your words with wings of doves and helps those words to soar!

Yours Truly,
Charles Baudelaire

Charles Baudelaire

CHARLES BAUDELAIRE was a French poet born on April 9, 1821. He died at the age of 46, due to syphilis, on August 31, 1867. He is best known for his essays, poetry, and his translation of Edgar Allan Poe's (#8) works. His most famous works include his books of poetry, *The Flowers of Evil*, *Le Spleen de Paris*, and *L'Alatros*. He became notorious after the publication of his volume of poems, *The Flowers of Evil*, due to the themes it contained, including sex, lesbianism, death, metamorphosis, urban corruption, depression, lost innocence, and alcohol. Upon the book's release, he gained many followers, but the experience also brought misfortune to himself, his printer, and publisher. The book was considered offensive to public morality and six of the poems were banned. Baudelaire grew up in a wealthy family and was widely known in the artistic crowds as a dandy and carefree spender. He quickly spent much of his allowance and inheritance. He was also a long-time user of laudanum.

"Always be a poet, even in prose."
"To handle a language skillfully is to practice a kind of evocative sorcery."
   —Charles Baudelaire

106

⇒ WASHINGTON IRVING ⇐

Splendid to present here chaps and ladies of the written word! I am Washington Irving, and I am honored to share my writing wisdom, as it is!

How shall I help you, for you are so advanced, as they say? For truly, writers today have so much information at their disposal. Most certainly with the thing that you do call the internet. And then if you were to go "old school," as they say, you would find thousands of books in a big library, wouldn't you?

Why do I bring this up? Most certainly not to complain for the small collection of books I did gather as Washington Irving—comparatively. Or the fact that research was rather tedious and challenging back in my day. No, I mention this for I do wish to let you know that overwhelm with massive amounts of information is most certainly to be expected, and it is nothing to become concerned about, truly.

For today you writers of the written word have so much information to choose from and sort through, and to be quite candid, to ignore. There is so much at times that it is actually best that you do ignore some or all of the banter. Why? Isn't being well-informed a good thing, as you say? Yes, and no.

Yes, it most certainly is a good thing to be informed about your subject. For surely, if you are writing a novel set during the time of the building of the great American railway, then you would want to be accurate. In that case, research is much needed. The same would hold true if you were writing about foreign espionage via the computer.

But when you don't require additional information is when it is truly time to write. For I say to you now, and you know if you have done this—as many writers have—research is sometimes used to put off putting the pen to the paper or the fingers to the keyboard. For truly, you may and do procrastinate in the form of immersing yourselves in research when you fear that you don't have enough to say. You think that you don't have enough new information to share or gems and jewels to inspire your readers.

I tell you this now that you most certainly do have all that you wish to share with your readers in you right here and now! In fact, you were born with what you had wished and planned to say. You simply had to grow up, as they say, and learn to read and write and think to be able to access what your soul wishes to say.

So do remove yourself from the mire of information, if you feel stuck within it and drowning, and sit down and write. If you are concerned about not having enough information, assure yourself that you can always do additional research later. For truly, it is time when you feel the overwhelm, to unload your treasure chest of words onto the page. This feeling of overwhelm is a feeling of those words knocking at the lid of the treasure chest as it literally bursts at its own seams!

I will close for now, dear writing chaps and ladies, for I do feel and see that you "get" what I am saying here! Do soldier on, as they say, with your writing travels. And I shall "see" you in the Light!

Yours Always and Forever,
Washington Irving

WASHINGTON IRVING was an American short story writer born on April 3, 1783. He died at the age of 76, due to a heart attack, on November 28, 1859. Irving was the first acclaimed American writer considered worthy of recognition by the English literary establishment. His most notable works include his short stories "Rip Van Winkle," "The Legend of Sleepy Hollow," "The Sketch Book," "Tales of Alhambra," and "A History of the Life and Voyages of Christopher Columbus." Many of his short stories are famous internationally and were later adapted into movies and even television shows. He was the youngest of 11 siblings and was named after George Washington. As a child, he received a private education and then went to New York to study law, but barely passed the bar. Realizing his preferred passion for writing, he wrote the book *History of New York from the Beginning of the World to the End of the Dutch Dynasty*, which earned him widespread fame. Not knowing what course to take in life, Irving worked as an editor for *Analectic Magazine*, following this by traveling to England to help his brother with a failing family business (where he wrote *The Sketch Book*). Then he moved to Madrid for research on his next big hits, *A History of the Life and Voyages of Christopher Columbus*, *Chronicle of the Conquest of Granada*, and *Tales of the Alhambra*. Irving was appointed secretary of the US legislation to London, a position he held for three years before returning home just to turn around and spend time as US minister to Spain. When he finally settled back home in the US, Irving spent the rest of his time at his New York estate, Sunnyside. This served as a meeting place for leading writers, artists and politicians of that time period. During this time, he worked on historical biographic works, such as the five-volume *Life of George Washington*.

> "There is a serene and settled majesty to woodland scenery that enters into the soul and delights and elevates it, and fills it with noble inclinations."
> —Washington Irving

107

❧ TRUMAN CAPOTE ☙

Hi there, writers! Honored to have been "chosen" for this project, as they say, and to present here. I am Truman Capote, and I will do my best to be at your service!

Tough subjects. How does one go about treating tough subjects in such a way that readers wish to read about the tough subjects, rather than shun them? I had a bit of this occur for me in my life as Truman, as you know. Especially with the novel *In Cold Blood*. What a doozy that one was!

At the time as Truman, it was widely believed that the novel was in fact difficult, because it was "true." Here in the Light, I must tell you that even your fiction is most certainly true. For in some lifetime or another, you have most likely been involved in a similar circumstance of which you write, or seen it with your very own eyes. Either way, "true" takes on a rather odd tone, even for those on the Earth Plane now accessing the Light.

So what is the significance of this, do you think? And how does it relate to writing about tough subjects? It is simple. For when you are writing fiction and the subject is delicate or quite horrifying, even, know that you most certainly have seen something along these lines at some point in your soul's journey.

Do I tell you this to alarm or horrify you? No, I do not. For that certainly isn't my aim here. I tell you this so that you can be assured that what you feel is most certainly authentic. When you know how the character felt, for instance, after ending another's life or attacking another's person, you have felt similar feelings at some point on one end of the spectrum or the other—so either from the victim's eyes or the attacker's eyes, or both.

I know, I know, this may be going a little too deep for you. You may not wish to think of yourself in such unsavory, difficult circumstances. Then don't. Simply write what you feel in the manner that you feel it, and know that you are indeed accessing legitimate feelings and circumstances.

And of course, do check yourself, as they say, by doing your due diligence. Research what you've written to verify that it is accurate. I tell you now that you will be surprised at how accurate you are! But that is as it should be and is no reason for alarm.

The "good" thing, as they say, about writing about difficult subjects is that you give a true, accurate image of the world as it stands in one place and time. This isn't to say that the entire world always offers up negative or difficult or potentially painful and even deadly circumstances. It only highlights the fact that difficult is intriguing in its own right—because, writers, your readers have also experienced as the victims and perpetuated as the perpetrators. Is this a good thing or a bad thing? It is neither. For truly, you want the authenticity that comes from the inner knowing about what it's like to be in such situations.

I'll leave you with that, fellow writers. I wish you good reading and writing travels!
   Yours Kindly,
   Truman Capote

TRUMAN CAPOTE was an American novelist born on September 30, 1924. He died at the age of 59, due to liver disease, on August 25,

1984. He is best known as one of contemporary American literature's most famous and controversial writers. He is also well-known for not taking notes during his interviews, because of an ability to retain conversations and quote them verbatim. This ability was tested with an accuracy of higher than 90 percent. His most notable works include *In Cold Blood*, *Breakfast at Tiffany's*, and *A Christmas Memory*. He also wrote many successful plays, including *House of Flowers* and *The Grass Harp*, which are his most popular. He was close friends with Harper Lee (#103). It was with her help that he was able to compile the information needed to complete *In Cold Blood*, which became a bestseller. His childhood consisted of absentee parents and all-around neglect, yet he was able to persevere. Many of his novels, plays and short stories have become literary classics and have been adapted into movies.

"To me, the greatest pleasure of writing is not what it's about, but the inner music that words make."
—Truman Capote

108

⇒ L. Frank Baum ⇐

Hello, Dear Fellow Scribes! L. Frank Baum at your service. How wondrous that I should be "chosen" to present here! I am most certainly grandly honored, I shall say! Now, let me begin.

Coining a phrase. A phrase that takes wing and takes flight and finds itself here and there and everywhere. Over vast oceans. Over great distances. Over "long" periods of time. Into the hearts and minds and very souls of many! What writer doesn't wish to do this? To coin a phrase that truly resonates with one and all!

In my life as Frank, I most certainly did coin a phrase. "There is no place like home!" When I wrote the *Wizard of Oz*, which started out as a children's tale, and yet did resonate with people of all ages, this most glorious phrase did come forth.

How did I coin that phrase, which has been used so many times in so many ways since I did utter it onto the page, shall we say? Did I meditate myself into a state where I could pull these jewels of words from the collective consciousness, as if pulling stars from the sky and aligning them in just the perfect order? Yes, I did! But *how*, you may wonder, did I do that? And certainly, how might you do the same? And then again, do you want to do the same?

Well, of course you don't have to coin a phrase as a writer. But it is a most magnificent turn of events when it occurs! For the turn of phrase most certainly lends a sort of longevity to your work, while at the same time it may add a deeper meaning to your work. And the most glorious part of this is that the reader/viewer of the resulting book or script may also come away with a "lesson" or "lessons," so to speak.

It is most glorious when that lesson is something that will in turn feed the reader's soul. How wonderful when that happens!

For truly, "There is no place like home" does mean different things to different people, as they say, yet it also means the same thing to all. For we are all interconnected, we are! This has been said quite often in this glorious work, and I shall say it again. We are interconnected, and no amount of trying to disconnect will un-connect us, shall we say.

Home is many things to many people. Yet home is the same to all. For home is truly here in the Light. And yet home is also those places you call home on the Earth Plane, and home is those people in your lives with whom you feel at home. And the most glorious home for all of us is the home you access when you access your own soul! For truly, that is what Dorothy did connect to when she clicked her red slippers together. She accessed herself while accessing all of those in her life—she accessed the true glory of the Universe, the true glory of our magnificent always interconnected Universe!

So go ahead and try your hand at a turn of phrase or two or more! Coin that phrase by tapping into the vast jewels floating about in the Universe. When you find a phrase that truly rings within your heart—strums your soul to new levels of joy—you will know that you've got a "keeper" of a phrase! Then you can spread your wondrous phrase to all meant to hear it and internalize it and relish it and resonate with it and heal with it—you get the picture!

I shall bid you a good night or good day. I am most honored, as mentioned, to have connected with you Dear Fellow Scribes! Do remember! There's no place like home!
Yours Truly Forever and Ever,
L. Frank Baum

L. FRANK BAUM was an American author born on May 15, 1856. He died at the age of 62, due to a stroke, on May 6, 1919. He was best known for writing one of children's literature's most famous works, *The Wizard of Oz*. He went on to write a collection of Oz books, 14 in total. *The Wizard of Oz* was so popular that it was adapted into films, plays, and Broadway musicals. *The Wizard of Oz* book is still being printed today. He also wrote 42 scripts, 83 short stories, 41 other novels, and more than 200 poems. Baum was admired for his ability to coin phrases in his novels, and his use of them. His most notable, of course, is, "There is no place like home." Baum married Maud Gage, the daughter of Matilda Joslyn Gage, a notable suffragist and feminist. He was secure in his masculinity, so he felt it unnecessary to assert it. Most of his novels depict girls as the main characters and heroes. It was his mother-in-law, Matilda Gage, who convinced Baum to write children's novels. Although he didn't start writing children's novels until he was 40, he experienced instant success. The name of the mythical land OZ came from the letters "O-Z" on one of his file cabinet drawers. He came up with the name after his publisher told him it would be bad luck to have a jewel in the book's title. The book was originally called The Emerald City, but was changed to the Wonderful Wizard of Oz. Baum was also father of 5 boys.

"No thief, however skillful, can rob one of knowledge, and that is why knowledge is the best and safest treasure to acquire."
—L. Frank Baum

109

➤ Ken Kesey ◆

Hey there, writers! Cool, as I said in my life as Ken, (author of One Flew Over the Cuckoo's Nest), to meet you here! Actually, totally cool! I am glad to make your acquaintances, though many of us have already met in one life or another, but that's a whole different story—ball of wax. Here we go with the writing tips. I'll do my best!

Notations. Adding references. Adding viability. Adding soul purpose to your work. What the heck am I talking about here? I'm talking about validity. I'm talking about resonating with reader's when they read your work. I'm talking about you resonating with readers, and I'm talking about your work resonating with readers.

Is this important? Heck yeah! For you do want your work to "stick," as they say. And it'll stick a lot harder if the reader does feel like you "know what you're talking about."

So how do you give your readers what they want in terms of viability? And why did I mention soul purpose in all of that? Is it a part of this, truly? Yes, it is. For your soul purpose for writing what you are writing is of utmost importance to your soul and the souls of others. And so the viability and validity will allow you to then "pass off" your work as valid.

Okay, okay. So how to get down to "brass tacks" here and just do something, anything, really, with these words I'm pitching/hurling at you.

I'm not suggesting that you reference the heck out of your work. That is a little over-the-top and better left for academic works. But I am suggesting that when you feel when you're writing a scene or describing a situation/place/character that it would be good to give some authenticity to that entry, then do so.

How could you do this? Well, for one, a reference notation isn't all that bad of an idea, at times. Though it may be a bit out of place. In that case, put something in your author's note at the beginning of the book thanking the person or institution that you consulted about the work. This will go a long way towards "convincing" some that you are truly accessing what you say you are.

For those of you who aren't too much into all of this jazz in terms of referencing, I do get it. I know when you're tapped in and tuned in and the words are flowing that you are indeed downloading "true" things as you are seeing them—as they are seen within the Universe.

And if you're okay with brushing off comments about the fact that you might not be totally accurate, then this isn't something to worry about, either.

But if you are wishing to not have such comments/questions, then a few notations, annotations, notes in your forward from another writer/expert, etc. are a groovy thing to add!

Okay, so enough of my soapbox talk here. I know that whatever you write, it will be totally cool! I do. And I want you to also know that we're with you all of the time, guiding you, us Scribes of the Light. We love to do it. And we are really "jazzed," as you say nowadays, to see your many writing triumphs and accomplishments!

So, get to it, Fellow Scribes! Write on!!!
Yours Always,
Ken Kesey

Ken Kesey

KEN KESEY was an American novelist born on September 17, 1935. He died at the age of 66, due to a liver tumor, on November 10, 2001. He is best known for his novels, essays and as being a countercultural figure. His most notable works include *One Flew Over the Cuckoo's Nest*, *Sometimes a Great Notion*, *The Sea Lion*, *Caverns*, and *Sailor Song*. He was a self-proclaimed link between the Beat Generation and the hippies. He attended Stanford University and later participated as a hospital aid and experimental subject. He was known for his desire to have authenticity in his writing, which led to his taking a job at a veteran's hospital. Based on that experience, he wrote *One Flew Over the Cuckoo's Nest* in 1962. His next novel, *Sometimes a Great Notion*, and his other proceeding works were based on Kesey's transformation from nonfiction novelist to the hippie generation's most popular guru.

"People don't want other people to get high, because if you get high, you might see the falsity of the fabric of the society we live in."
—Ken Kesey

110

⇾ Doris Lessing ⇽

Oh, my! How grand! To have "squeaked in here" second to last! I am Doris Lessing, and I am truly honored and grateful to present here to you my words of wisdom when it comes to the written word. I shall begin without further ado!

Characterization. What a wondrous thing! To be able to have a hand in the "development" of your characters. Truly in their birth and growth and death, even. What is the "best" way to draw your characters? Not surprisingly, there is no best way. Truly, we all go about this task differently, us Scribes in and out of the Light!

One thing is certain, however. Characterization is the life-bread of the written work. For without wondrous characters. Without characters that shine and do shout from the rooftops their wondrousness, we would not have the great works that we do!

You can most certainly think of many such characters. Bold, brave characters! Or meek and mild ones. Whichever and however you think of them, one thing is certain. They leave a mark, so to speak, on your mind, and your heart, and truly your soul. For these characters that come forth, they are in fact, compilations of all characters. They are composites, in fact, of real characters—real people walking the Earth now and "back when."

So what do I have to add to this wondrous mix of character? Character study, shall we say. How do you go about accessing your most wondrous characters, and how do you go about getting them to "stay" on the page and do the most glorious things that they will do in order to move your plot forward and in order to make your readers turn page after page after page!

Not surprisingly, you can't "make" your characters do anything. For they will do exactly what they wish to! They will! But you can cajole them and convince them, so to speak.

How to do this? By letting them be themselves. By letting them shine! By letting them dance and sing and yell and scream and cry as they wish.

Won't this have your work going all about the page, so to speak, and making very little sense? No, it won't, if you do also ask your characters to act within parameters and reason. For if you give them a splendid plot in which to maneuver and a glorious setting in which to frolic or learn or toil, you will have given them all that they need to then become themselves on the page and live out their own life purposes on the page.

I think this is making a little or a lot of sense to you, isn't it? I am suggesting, yes, giving your characters "free reign" within a controlled setting. Try this, I urge you! You will see the most glorious turns of events, so to speak, you will!

Is there anything else I can give you before I do go back to my writing tasks in the Light? Yes, there is! Do have fun with this, Dear Fellow Scribes! Do let your soul sing as you write and let your hands make happy pitter patter as they type, and smile, smile, smile as you do portray your characters in all of their glory. And, of course, when your characters do suffer, have no compunctions about crying! For they will most certainly appreciate your empathy!

That is all for me right now, Dear Fellow Scribes. Thank you much for listening!
  Sincerely Yours,
  Doris Lessing

DORIS LESSING was a British-Zimbabwean writer born on October 22, 1919. She died at the age of 94, due to a stroke, on November 17, 2013. She is best known as being a feminist role model, librettist (opera writer), biographer, and for her novels, poems, plays, and short stories. Her most notable works are her novels *The Golden Notebook*, *The Grass is Singing*, and *The Good Terrorist*. She wrote more than 55 works, spanning many different genres, including fiction, nonfiction, opera, fantasy, science fiction, and poetry. In 2007, she received the Nobel Prize in Literature. She earned several other literary awards. Lessing worked many jobs before she got married, including as a journalist, nursemaid, office worker, and telephone operator. It wasn't until she moved to England with her son from her second marriage that she published her first book, *The Grass is Singing*. Her novels inspired many films.

"Any human anywhere will blossom in a hundred unexpected talents and capacities simply by being given the opportunity to do so."
—Doris Lessing

111

⇝ Lord Byron ⇜

Greetings to you, Fellow Scribes! Lord Byron here. Highly honored to have been the "project manager" for this most splendid project in this time and space! Hooray, for I am the last to be "channeled," and that is a most splendid thing! I shall give you some kernels of writing wisdom to add to your most massive and splendid list!

How shall one write? How shall you write? How, truly, should you write? Is there a secret? Certainly, there is always a secret. There is always a "secret sauce," as you say now in your day.

Truly, I was a poet in the lifetime as Lord Byron, so I shall give you these parting words of wisdom in a poem—about the writing life—about being a writer—about accessing your soul and pulling out all of the riches so that you might then resonate with what you write and even what you don't write.

For truly, I tell you now, everything you write was meant to be written. And everything you don't write was meant to be unwritten. This may sound rather vague (do forgive me!), but I assure you that what I have just said truly does resonate with your soul.

Sometimes, Dear Fellow Scribes, it is a matter of pure, blind, unadulterated trust in what your soul wants. You may not always know consciously what your soul wants, but truly, I tell you, your soul knows exactly what you want and need and exactly what is best for you with every step you take in this most glorious Earth Plane existence! We refer here to the most auspicious things you do enjoy and the not-so-great things that you endure.

On to my poem now. I know I do ramble!

Forgiveness
Is bliss
If you so wish
To let your spirit soar
You will find great treasures
By looking to the heavens
While you also plant your feet
On the ground
In such a way
That you can hear
The sound
Of Mother Nature
Speaking to you
I do wish you bliss
As you access your soul's calling
I do wish you joy
As you speak to your soul
I do wish you glory
Truly
You shall achieve abundance
All that you yearn for and more!

Yours Always and Forever,
   Lord Byron

GEORGE GORDON BYRON, known as Lord Byron, was a British nobleman and writer born on January 22, 1788. He died at the age of

36, due to malaria, on April 19, 1824. He is considered one of the greatest British poets of all time. His most notable poems are "Don Juan," "Childe Harold's Pilgrimage," and "She Walks in Beauty." Byron was also a politician and leading figure of the Romantic Movement. He also wrote satire. Byron lived a scandalous life. He had an illegitimate daughter with his half-sister, Augusta. The following year, he married his first wife, Annabella, and had one legitimate daughter with her. He divorced shortly thereafter and spent the summer of 1816 at Lake Geneva with the stepsister of Mary Shelley (#81), Mary Clairmont. He also had a daughter with Clairmont. Byron then traveled to Italy, where he resided for more than 6 years and had an affair with the wife of an Italian Nobleman, Teresa Guiccioli. During that time, he wrote *Don Juan*. Byron left Italy to help fight the war of independence against the Ottoman Empire with the Greek insurgents when he became ill from malaria and passed away.

"The great art of life is sensation, to feel that we exist, even in pain."
—Lord Byron

If you enjoyed this book by Julie Bawden-Davis, please leave a review on Amazon.com, or any online book or media site, including GoodReads. Your reviews make a world of difference and are greatly appreciated!

ABOUT THE CHANNELED MASTERS SERIES

The Channeled Masters Series consists of books written from various groups of individuals speaking from within the Light on specific topics. The next book in the series (#2) is *Channeled Cooking Tips from 44 Culinary Masters*. It is scheduled for release on 2/22/19.

About the Author

JULIE BAWDEN-DAVIS is a Southern California professional author, whose work has appeared in a wide variety of publications since 1985. She is also a certified medium, psychic, and healer (Reiki Master® and Karuna Reiki® II Practitioner). A Master Channeler, Julie imparts messages from Spirit/The Light, including through books, written letters, and voice.

Julie also connects people with their past lives and lends insight as to how those lives relate to this life. Guided by Spirit, Julie heals and redirects past life experiences that are holding people back in this lifetime.

Visit Julie at www.juliebawdendavis.com/spiritual-coaching
Contact Julie at Julie@JulieBawdenDavis.com

If you'd like to subscribe to Julie's weekly newsletter that features inspirational channeled messages from the Light (Weekly Inspirations/Messages from the Divine), join by signing up at: eepurl.com/doM3-X

Index

1. William Faulkner 3
2. William Shakespeare 6
3. J. D. Salinger 9
4. Leo Tolstoy 12
5. John Steinbeck 15
6. Emily Dickinson 18
7. Jules Verne 21
8. Edgar Allan Poe 24
9. Louisa May Alcott 27
10. Maeve Binchy 30
11. Mark Twain 33
12. Herman Melville 37
13. Nathaniel Hawthorne 40
14. Hans Christian Anderson 43
15. James Michener 46
16. Ayn Rand 50
17. Ralph Waldo Emerson 53
18. Gertrude Jeckyll 56
19. Somerset Maugham 59
20. Charlotte Brontë 62
21. Rudyard Kipling 65
22. Barbara Cartland 69
23. Jacqueline Susann 72
24. Daphne Du Maurier 75
25. Ernest Hemingway 78
26. Tennessee Williams 82
27. Agatha Christie 85
28. Bohumil Hrabal 88

Index

29.	Emily Brontë	91
30.	James M. Cain	94
31.	Orson Welles	97
32.	Joseph Conrad	100
33.	Anaïs Nin	103
34.	Arthur Conan Doyle	106
35.	George Elliot	109
36.	James Joyce	112
37.	Virginia Woolf	115
38.	Charles Dickens	118
39.	Gustave Flaubert	121
40.	Honoré de Balzac	124
41.	Edward Albee	127
42.	Victor Hugo	130
43.	May Sarton	133
44.	George Bernard Shaw	136
45.	Jane Austen	139
46.	Henry Thoreau	142
47.	Henry James	145
48.	Beatrix Potter	148
49.	Paul Verlaine	152
50.	Maya Angelou	155
51.	Arthur Rimbaud	158
52.	Langston Hughes	161
53.	Glenn O'Brien	164
54.	E.T.A. Hoffman	167
55.	F. Scott Fitzgerald	170
56.	Gertrude Stein	173
57.	John Dos Passos	176
58.	William Wordsworth	179
59.	Ezra Pound	182
60.	Walt Whitman	185

61.	Sherwood Anderson	188
62.	Guillaume Apollinaire	191
63.	Oscar Wilde	194
64.	Jack London	197
65.	Henry Miller	200
66.	Robert Louis Stevenson	203
67.	Lewis Carroll	206
68.	Fyodor Dostoyevsky	209
69.	George Orwell	212
70.	Edith Wharton	215
71.	Samuel Taylor Coleridge	218
72.	William Blake	221
73.	Percy Bysshe Shelley	224
74.	John Keats	227
75.	Robert Southey	230
76.	William Butler (W.B.) Yeats	233
77.	Sydney Tremayne	236
78.	Upton Sinclair	239
79.	Sinclair Lewis	242
80.	W. E. B. Du Bois (William Edward Burghardt)	245
81.	Mary Shelley	248
82.	E.B. White	251
83.	John Updike	254
84.	C.S. Lewis	257
85.	James Baldwin	260
86.	Dorothy Parker	263
87.	Gabriel García Márquez	266
88.	Theodor Seuss "Ted" Geisel	269
89.	Sylvia Plath	272
90.	Franz Kafka	275
91.	Marcel Proust	278
92.	Anton Chekhov	281

Index

93.	J. R. R. Tolkien	284
94.	Geoffrey Chaucer	287
95.	Flannery O'Connor	290
96.	Émile Zola	293
97.	Harriet Beecher Stowe	296
98.	Kurt Vonnegut	299
99.	Voltaire	302
100.	Albert Camus	305
101.	Alexandre Dumas	308
102.	Ray Bradbury	311
103.	Harper Lee	314
104.	Guy de Maupassant	317
105.	Charles Baudelaire	320
106.	Washington Irving	323
107.	Truman Capote	326
108.	L. Frank Baum	329
109.	Ken Kesey	332
110.	Doris Lessing	335
111.	Lord Byron	338

www.ingramcontent.com/pod-product-compliance
Lightning Source LLC
Chambersburg PA
CBHW022101150426
43195CB00008B/222